PERSPECTIVES IN INDUSTRIAL GEOGRAPHY

PERSPECTIVES IN INDUSTRIAL GEOGRAPHY

A Case Study of an Industrial City of Uttar Pradesh

ARUNA SAXENA

CONCEPT PUBLISHING COMPANY, NEW DELHI-110059

The Indian Council of Social Science Research (ICSSR) gave the financial support towards the publication of this work. However, the responsibility for the contents of the book - facts, opinions, conclusions etc.— are entirely that of the author and not of the ICSSR.

ISBN 81-7022-250-8

First Published 1989

Aruna **Saxena** (b. 1944 -)

Published by
Ashok Kumar Mittal
Concept Publishing Company
A/15-16, Commercial Block, Mohan Garden
NEW DELHI-110059 (India)

Lasertypeset by
Microtech Advance Printing Systems (P) Ltd.
H-13, Bali Nagar, NEW DELHI-110015

Printed in India at
Taj Press
3024, Gali Ahiran, B. Garh Road
DELHI-110006

Dedicated to my parents
Smt. Kamla Devi Saxena and
Shri Madho Prasad Saxena

Foreword

Dr. Aruna Saxena has attempted to present the industrial landscape of Ghaziabad through a geographical analysis of the dynamic processes of industrial development. In fact, the study relates to both the processes and patterns of industrial development in Ghaziabad.

This assiduous study has involved considerable field work, personal knowledge and a lucid presentation of spatial correlationships. For this purpose, the author has studied 646 industrial units, out of which 452 were in Ghaziabad City and 194 at various other centres of the district. In addition, Dr. Aruna Saxena has included 3000 others smaller industrial units for study, which share 25 per cent of the manufacturing employment and thus are quite significant in industrial development.

The entire study comprises eleven chapters; in all 247 pages of text. This account is supported by 27 figures which help to make the study vivid and clear. Out of the total of 11 chapters, four chapters have been devoted to major industries grouped as, metal-based, agro-based, chemical-based, and others. A separate chapter appraises the other manufacturing centres in the district. The theoretical and conceptual aspects have been examined in a separate chapter. The last 24 pages provide a summary of main conclusions of the study, and some viable suggestions for future industrial development and planning.

The author has thus made an in-depth study of major industries, their concentration and linkages, assessed the stage of industrial structure, and the relationship to the market, especially of the 'National Capital Region', suggested coordination between industry and agriculture, and analysed other industrial aspects, which reveals the author's highly clear perception and high degree of understanding of the analysis of processes and patterns of industrialization, and about the future perspectives.

As far as the methodology and treatment of subject matter is concerned, it is really good both conceptually and analytically. It is a highly commendable study and its publication would make a useful contribution to the literature on 'Industrial Geography of India'.

S. L. Kayastha

S. L. KAYASTHA
Banaras Hindu University, Varanasi

Preface

Ghaziabad, though until recently a small town with its inception dating back to as early as 1740, has suddenly risen into prominence as the most important industrial centre of Western Uttar Pradesh in the close vicinity of Delhi. Formation of Ghaziabad as a separate district in Nov. 1976 was motivated mainly because of extra-ordinary growth of industries at the city during post-Independence period. Although major part of intra-urban industrial locations at Ghaziabad signifies a planned industrial growth, causing little alarm for city's healthy urban life, yet there is no room for complacency if we really wish the industry to bring about economic regeneration for our masses and hence the significance of the present study. The present work, though selective in its approach, seeks to attempt an analytical study of the process of industrial development at Ghaziabad in a Geographical perspective. The findings of the present book have been based on the study of those industrial units only which are covered under Indian Factories Act. In the year 1981, there were functioning 646 such industrial units in district Ghaziabad, out of which 452 were operating at Ghaziabad city itself and remaining 194 at various other centres of the district. However, it must be recalled that the role played by smaller units which are not covered under Factories Act for the reason of employing less than 10 persons and which number about above 3000 in whole of the district, is no less significant in intensifying the general process of industrial development in the area. An appropriate reference to these small unregistered units has been duly made wherever necessary such as in the context of oil engine industry at Ghaziabad, handloom cotton textile industry at Pilkhuwa and in the case of Noida where small-scale unregistered units acquire an over-whelming significance. But as these smaller units represent only about 25% share in the total manufacturing employment of the district, they make only a feeble impact on the aggregate picture emerging from the study of industrial units covered under Factories Act. It is presumed, therefore, that the present study would prove helpful in acquiring a realistic understanding of the Geographical background of phenomenal industrial growth at Ghaziabad during post-Independence period. It would also serve to give certain important guidelines to the authorities for industrial planning at city and district level.

In the present book factory employment figures have been used as an absolute as well as relative measure of manufacturing activity while dealing with its various aspects - temporal, spatial and functional. Values of annual turnover figures could also be used for this purpose, but these were not opted mainly because of their limited relevance to a study which is mainly concerned with Geographical aspects of the industry.

Although main focus of the present study centres around Ghaziabad city, it has been aptly supplemented by a brief description of other manufacturing centres of the district as well in order to ascertain the repurcussions of Ghaziabad's phenomenal industrial growth on the general process of industrial development in the district as a whole. Besides, it was necessary also for assessing the relative positions of these centres in respect of district's total industrial set-up.

The present book is organized into 11 chapters. Part 'A' of the Chapter I of 'Introduction' deals with a brief description or the physical and cultural settings in the light of their influence on the industrial activity of the city. Part 'B' of the Chapter I concerns with the methodology adopted for accomplishing the present study. Evolution of industries and correlation between growth and dispersion of industries at Ghaziabad have been studied in Chapter II entitled 'Growth and Dispersion of Industries at Ghaziabad'. Chapter III Viz. 'Spatial Pattern of Industrial land-use at Ghaziabad' focusses on the aggregate pattern of industrial land-use and the typology of intra-urban industrial locations at Ghaziabad based on the framework of views expressed by eminent urban Geographers.

Studies of important industries at Ghaziabad have been made in Chapters IV, V, VI and VII., organized under the four major groups of Metal-based, Agro-based, Chemical-based and other manufacturing industries. Chapter VIII attempts a brief description of other manufacturing centres of the district and Chapter IX pinpoints some problems of industrial development at Ghaziabad. Chapter X deals with the theoretical and conceptual aspects of the industrial location at Ghaziabad. Chapter XI contains the conclusions arrived at regarding the salient features of industrialization at Ghaziabad and suggestions for future industrial development and planning at district and regional level.

Major part of data and information used in completing the present work has been obtained from industrial field survey. Other local offices which furnished relevant pieces of information include, Ghaziabad Development Authority. U.P. State Industrial Development Corporation, Area Development Office (Industry), U.P. Financial Corporation, U.P. Small Industries Corporation, District Industries Centre, Deputy Labour Commissioner's Office, Water Works Department and Office of the Executive Engineer, Electricity Distribution Division I. I am grateful to the concerned authorities of these offices for extending me all possible help in collecting the requisite information.

In particular I acknowledge the inspiration and guidance of Late Dr. V.S. Chauhan of Meerut college, Meerut, who gave me valuable comments and suggestions through out the period the work was in progress. I also acknowledge my debt to Dr. B. B. Singh, Principal M.M.H. College, Ghaziabad, for extending me all possible help for carrying out my research operations. My thanks are also due to Dr. N.K. Agnihotri who offered valuable suggestions regarding cartographic work of the present book. Last but not the least, I feel pleasure in acknowledging my sincerest gratitude to my father-in-law Shree B.S. Saxena, my mother-in-law Smt. Chandra Kumari Saxena, my husband Mr. S.K. Saxena and my children, Upma, Alka and Deepak whose utmost co-operation at every step gave me an unfaltering strength for coping with the problems encountered in accomplishing the present study.

ARUNA SAXENA

Contents

List of Tables

List of Figures

ONE

Introduction

The phenomenal growth of industries at Ghaziabad during last 20 years has led to the emergence of city as the second most important industrial town of U.P. after Kanpur. Tremendous increase in industrial activity here, however, owes largely to the role played by Government bodies in boosting up the cause of industrialization in the city. As part of the National Capital Region which includes the areas around Delhi for a planned and integrated development by the 'Ministry of Health, Family Planning and Urban Development', the industrial potentialities of Ghaziabad were studied by the Town and Country Planning Organization in order to relieve the increasing pressure of population and industrial growth in the capital city of Delhi and the situation was found to be the most ideal one for stepping up the tempo of industrial activity in the city which had already made considerable strides in the field of industries like oil engine and agricultural implements, hydrogenated oil, transport equipments and electrical goods.

At the instance of Government of India, a Master Plan for the city and regulated area around it was prepared for implementation through U.P. State Industrial Development Corporation and Ghaziabad Improvement Trust which was set up in 1960. In accordance with a scientific land-use plan, Master Plan set apart different areas to be developed for purposes like industry, housing, business, market, education, recreational facilities & parks etc. For the development of industries, U.P.S.I.D.C. developed seven industrial areas comprising 3435 acres where about 1500 developed industrial plots were allotted to the entrepreneurs[1]. This move on the part of Government no doubt created a big impact on the pace of industrial development in the city, but to give full credit to one single factor will be far from truth as the industry thrives only because of balanced operation of a number of factors pertaining to physical and cultural environments of a place. Some factors may exert, no doubt, more influence than others but, we cannot ignore any of the several determinants of industry altogether.

Part 'A' of the present chapter of 'INTRODUCTION' deals with a brief outline of the various physical, economic and cultural factors in the light of their effect on the industrial activity of the city. Part 'B' of the present chapter concerns with the methodology adopted in accomplishing the present work aiming at a Geographical Analysis of Industrial Landscape of Ghaziabad.

PART 'A': PHYSICAL & CULTURAL SETTINGS

1. *The Site*

Ghaziabad offers optimum conditions in respect of site requirements for all types of manufacturing activities.. The site on which the city stands consists of an almost level plain sloping gently from North to South and from East to West. River Hindon, a tributary of Jamuna, rising from Shiwalik hills, flows almost through the middle of the city's Municipal limits in North-South direction. The elevation of the city area above sea level ranges from 705′ in the East to 666′ in the West and from 695′ in the North to 667′ in the South. Maximum relative height found near village Kaila is recorded as 19′[2]. Main part of the city lies to the East of River Hindan. Area towards the West of the river contains some of the most important industrial areas of the city. Except the narrow belts of land along both the sides of River Hindan, which are susceptible to floods during rainy season, all other vacant areas of the city can be safely used for industrial establishments. Not only relief but the local geology of the city area which comprises of huge thicknesses of compact fine grained alluvium, also supports the cause of industrial activity. Manufacture of machinery and different types of metal products representing more than 60% share in the city's industrial structure, impose heavy loads upon the foundations of the building and therefore structure of the ground underneath also assumes considerable significance regarding the specific site requirements of these metal-fabricating industries.

Availability of large tracts of level land along the major highways and also along the regional level roads passing through the city, acted as a big boost in promoting the cause of industrial development in the city. Provision of general services like water supply, electric power, adequate refuse disposal facilities, efficient fire and police services, and satisfactory transport services further increased the attractions of these sites which were developed into well demarcated industrial areas with the efforts of U.P.S.I.D.C. and Ghaziabad Improvement Trust authorities. Availability of social services like education, housing, recreation and markets etc. in the town made these sites even more valuable. The price of the land which was only reasonably fixed by Government bodies also served as a decisive factor in encouraging the industrial development in the city.

2. *Situation*

No doubt, greatest resource of Ghaziabad lies in its situation at the junction of three important routes coming from Calcutta, Dehradun and Moradabad. The high degree of nodality of the town in respect of its surrounding areas is further reinforced by its proximity to the capital city of Delhi, through which it is connected with all the other parts of the country. With the municipal limits coinciding with Delhi-U.P. Border the city core of Ghaziabad stands only at a distance of 15 km. from Delhi. Stretching around 28° 39′ North of Latitude and 77° 26′ East of Longitude, the city serves as a gateway to Delhi for all parts of U.P., Bihar, West Bengal, Assam and other eastern states. It was mainly because of its extremely nodal situation coupled with its nearness to the capital, that Ghaziabad was opted by more and more entrepreneurs for establishing their firms. The temptation of its extremely favourable situation for industrial enterprise still holds good and the city continues to make even greater strides in the field of industry even today.

Apart from the high degree of modality, imparted by the meeting of important routes from different directions, another significant fact about situation of Ghaziabad is the sound economic base of the region as a whole, amidst which the city stands. Upper Ganga-Jamuna Doab constitutes not only one of the most progressive and prosperous agricultural regions of the country but also signifies one which has made considerable strides in the field of industry and urbanization. Agricultural prosperity of the region has resulted in the general well-being of the people, which in turn has facilitated the process of industrial development not only at Ghaziabad but also at many other places in the region. Quite a few of important industries at Ghaziabad such as oil engines and agricultural implements are sustained by agricultural prosperity of the area, a point which further illustrates the essence of its situation amidst one of the progressive agricultural regions of the country.

3. *Climate*

Though there are very few industries which are directly affected by prevailing climate of a place, but indirectly climate exerts a substantial influence on all types of manufacturing whatsoever. Only an equable and pleasant climate presents the optimum conditions for mental and manual work. Extremes of cold or heat and excessive dryness or humidity produce negative effects on the industrial productivity.

Ghaziabad's climate as illustrated on table No. 1.1 though not optimum, is also by no means a discouraging factor in promoting the industrial fortunes of the city. Climate is quite invigorating for about eight months from September to April, as there is seldom a severe cold spell which can bring disruption in manufacturing activities. During May and June excessively high temperatures of the day, reaching often about or above 40°C lower the rate of productivity resulting in the increased cost of production. Installation of air-conditioning equipments and cost of their operation also involve an additional expenditure, if rate of productivity is maintained with such devices. During July and August, though temperatures are a little bit lowered, humid conditions during these months considerably undermine the human efficiency which in turn affects the quality and cost of manufacturing at industrial establishments. Average annual rainfall at the city is 81.4 cm.

TABLE 1.1: **Climatic Data of Ghaziabad City***

Months	Max.Tem. (Average in °C)	Min.Tem. (Average in (°C)	Monthly Temp. (Average in °C)	Relative Humidity %	Monthly Rainfall (Average in cms.)
January	20.9	8.1	14.5	67	2.21
February	23.9	9.5	16.7	57	1.96
March	29.8	15.0	22.4	41	1.19
April	36.2	20.2	28.2	39	0.89
May	40.0	25.3	32.65	54	1.27
June	39.6	27.5	33.55	79	5.87
July	34.2	26.2	30.2	82	17.27
August	32.5	25.6	29.05	77	15.27
September	33.3	24.4	28.88	69	11.30
October	31.9	18.2	25.05	63	1.40
November	27.9	10.8	19.35	64	0.45
December	22.9	7.8	15.33	65	0.89

* *Source* : Gazetteer of India, U.P., Meerut Distt. pp. 372-374

Severe heat during summer months and excessive rains sometimes in July or August adversely affect the efficiency of transport services and this hampers the smooth and regular arrival of raw materials and lifting of manufactured products at the factory premises. Excessive rains and associated floods of River Hindan in the year 1977 disrupted the rail and road transport routes so severely that Ghaziabad remained cut-off from Delhi for about a week or so. This certainly resulted in a great loss to the industries at the city. However, such occurrences are only very rare. Normally the manufacturing operations are carried out throughout the year. Climatic conditions only seldom bring a disruption in the day-to-day life of the people.

Another effect of the climatic conditions on the manufacturing activities is reflected in the types of consumer goods manufactured here. Dominance of cotton textiles and insignificance of woollens, manufacture of hydrogenated oil, canning of fruits and vegetable products, and manufacture of cold drinks at the city do show some relevance to the prevailing climatic conditions in the city. In a way, the high reputation of the city for the manufacture of oil engines and agricultural implements also indicates the control of climatic conditions which favour the cultivation of a number of crops, thus producing a huge demand for oil engines and agricultural implements in the region.

4. *Water Supply*

Modern industry requires substantial quantities of water in its manufacturing process, a fact which makes the factor of water supply an important consideration in matters of industrial locations. However, there exist considerable variations from industry to industry in respect of total intake, level of purity required, and the type of use regarding water supply for industrial purposes.

Ghaziabad, with its vast resources of underground water and proximity to river Hindan, a tributary of Jamuna, offers good prospects for cheap and plentiful water supply for industrial and other purposes. Partly because river Hindan flows some distance apart from the main built-up areas of the city and partly because it carries relatively lower volume of water, city's water works authorities obtain major part of their water supply from subterranean sources by constructing tube-wells in different residential, industrial and commercial areas of the city. Operating costs of such water-supply are, no doubt, higher than those of surface water obtained from the river, but these are more than offset by the better quality of underground water which needs no or little prior treatment for industrial and general purposes. In the year 1981, 28 tube-wells were working in the cis-Hindan area of the city and another 6 were in the various stages under construction. At present about 46 million gallons of water are pumped daily by the tube-wells to meet the total water requirements, of which about 40% is used for various purposes by the industrial establishments of the city [3]. Daily 16 hours water supply is maintained through these tube-wells. City's water-works authorities have already undertaken a vast scheme of future expansion of water supply, taking into account the anticipated increase in water requirements as far ahead as the year 2015.

The important industries of Ghaziabad which require relatively much larger quantities of water, include manufacture of primary metal products, synthetic fibre, chemicals, paper, finishing of cotton textiles, beverages, soft drinks, food products, and drugs and medicines. It is however, to be borne in mind that only a small fraction of all water used is actually consumed. In many cases much of it can be reused for the same purpose after being given some treatment by modern techniques, though this involves considerable additional costs on the part of manufacturer and is therefore, justified only in the areas facing a shortage of water supply. If no reuse of water is made, manufacture of per ton of steel, paper and synthetic fibre requires 65000, 38000 and 2,20,000 gallons of water respectively[4]. Largest single use of water for industry is for cooling purposes, wherein purity of water is of very little consideration. However, water used for steam raising, needs to be extremely pure, otherwise it may damage the boilers by corrosion or scaling, thus causing much additional costs to the manufacturer for repairing and servicing of the equipments. Purity of process water which includes all the other types of uses other than cooling and steam raising for industrial purposes, varies greatly from industry to industry. Water used for the general purposes of washing and dyeing etc. need not be much pure but paper and textile industries require comparatively more purity of water. Industries which require very high standards of purity are those where the water actually enters the edible product such as beverages, soft drinks, drugs and medicines. In these industries specific requirements of the water purity are achieved by giving special prior treatment to water by modern techniques.

5. *Power Supply*

Modern industry, in majority of cases, can choose from amongst two or three possible sources of energy and can also use more than one source of power in the various phases of its manufacturing process. Much greater flexibility of the industry in respect of use of one form of energy or another has resulted in a considerable decline of the 'pull' of any one form of energy source in matters concerning the industrial location in modern times.

Obviously, industrial clustering at Ghaziabad does not characterize a location tied to the coal or oil producing areas of the country. Adequate and regular supply of electricity, provided by Ganga Electric Grid which connects 11 hydel power stations located on various points along Upper Ganga Canal and thermal power stations at Harduagunj, Chandausi, and Panki does exercise a favourable influence in fostering the industrial growth at the city but one should not overstress the importance of electricity, firstly because coal and oil also contribute appreciably in the total energy supplies to the city's industrial units and secondly because advantage of plentiful supplies of electricity is not confined to Ghaziabad only, but is shared by all the other towns of U.P. which are served by Ganga Electric Grid which is also connected with National Power Grid. The fact that only Ghaziabad has managed to have stolen a march over all the other towns of Western U.P. in the field of industry, itself indicates the relative insignificance of electricity in creating the industrial scenes over a place.

Another factor which lessens the role of fuel and energy supplies in influencing the industrial locations at Ghaziabad is the preponderance of those industries here which relatively consume only small quantities of industrial energy. The costs of energy supplies in the manufacture of agricultural, transport, electrical and various types of industrial machinery which constitutes about 50% share in the industrial structure of the city, represent only 2 to 3% share in the total value added by manufacturer. Other important industries of the city wherein the corresponding figures of fuel and energy costs vary from 5 to 10% include glass, chemicals and allied products, paper and paper products, structural clay products, and primary metal products. Highly power-oriented industries such as primary aluminium, cement and steel etc. wherein the corresponding costs of energy range between 10 to 25% are either totally absent or relatively much less important in the total industrial structure of the city[5].

While admitting the not so strong an impact of fuel and energy considerations in deciding the industrial locations at Ghaziabad, it becomes important to point out the relative significance of electricity, coal and oil in the total industrial energy requirements of the city. The consumption of electricity has risen to about 22 million units per month in 1982 from the corresponding figure of mere 2.5 million units in 1961. Industries consume about 4/5th the total electricity required by Ghaziabad urban agglomeration[6]. Electricity, no doubt, plays the most vital role by providing above 50% share of the total power requirements of the industry in the city, but coal and oil which together account for a little less than 50% share are no less significant, specially in view of the distant sources, from where they are obtained via rail transport. Electricity is not a self sufficient form of energy for industrial purposes. It is mainly because of inadequacies of electricity in meeting the full range of industrial energy requirements that coal and oil assume considerable significance in the total fuel and energy supplies to the city's industrial establishments. All coal required by the city's industrial units is brought from Bihar and the demand of oil is met through Indian Oil Corporation. Quite a large number of industrial units at present are using electric motors for obtaining the motive power, but the use of coal and oil in boilers and furnaces is also quite common. Electricity is preferred mainly because of its unique mobility, flexibility of operation, and no storage problem. Moreover, provisions of electricity through Grid system ensures a regular and adequate supply. But again one should be cautious not to overemphasize its importance, as it can never fully substitute coal and oil in all sorts of manufacturing.

6. *Raw Materials*

During the present times, pull of raw materials in deciding the Geographical location of the industry has been considerably reduced due to development of modern means of swift and efficient transport. Nearness of the sources of raw materials exerts an influence in the location of those industries only which use perishable or weight-losing raw materials or wherein per unit value of the raw material is lower or per unit weight of the same is comparatively heavier, e.g. manufacture of milk and fruit products, sugar and food processing industries and smelting of ores etc. Limited number of raw material oriented industries can also be attributed to the tendency, amongst large number of industries, of using more than one raw material though in varying proportions, which further lessens the pull of raw material factor in location decisions.

Industrial structure at Ghaziabad with more than 60% share of metal consuming industries in the total registered employment of the city, hardly characterizes an example wherein industrial location can be explained with reference to the raw material sources. Pig iron and the steel which are the main raw materials for metal-consuming industrial units of the city, are largely obtained from distant sources in Bihar. The only raw material obtained from local sources and from Delhi metropolitan area is scrap which is used by mini-steel making centres of the city for making special types of steel. Major part of various metals is brought from long distances. Metals specially pig iron, steel and alloy metals, do, characterize lower per unit value and higher per unit weight comparatively, but this disadvantage is more than offset by the much higher per unit value of the industrial machinery and various other types of sophisticated products made out of these. Moreover the freight charges on crude raw materials are much lower than those on finished products and the same do not increase in the same proportions as does the distance. Absence of breaks of bulk is another factor lessening the disadvantage of distant raw materials. Apart from various metals, other important raw materials which are obtained from distant sources include cotton, tobacco, apple pulp, non-metallic minerals, sand, chemicals, rubber and medicinal herbs. The only raw materials which are obtained from near by areas are oil seeds, cereals, fruits and vegetables, waste paper, and scrap. On the whole the vast and varied industrial structure of the city depicts very little relevance to the local raw materials base.

7. *Capital*

Capital, the most fundamental requirement for all types of industry, is mainly a subject of Economist but as the differentials in the availability of capital influence the Geographical location of the industry, it also needs a careful consideration in the Geographical analysis of industry at a place or a region. Capital may be classed into two groups (1) Fixed Capital consisting of equipments and goods, which is relatively immobile and therefore leads to Geographical inertia because heavy investment in it cannot be permitted to yield nothing, even when original advantages for a particular industry over an area have altogether disappeared (2) Current or money capital which is much more mobile and can be easily arranged through financial institutions and banks, if other advantages for industry are prevailing over an area. Mobility of money capital is largely confined to within national boundaries. Investment of foreign capital involves too many complexities and delicacies, and hence it is much less mobile as compared to indigenous one. However, there is no clear-cut distinction between the fixed and money capital because more often the latter is used for procuring the former.

In the context of Ghaziabad it is mainly the availability of money capital through various financial institutions and banks which has played a key role in accelerating the pace of industrial growth in the city. Offering the loans on easy terms by 'Uttar Pradesh Financial Corporation' (UPFC), 'Pradeshiya Industrial Investment Corporation of U.P.' (PICUP), 'District Industries Office, Ghaziabad', 'Industrial Development Bank of India' (IDBI) and various other nationalized and commercial banks, ensures the regular and adequate supplies of capital to entrepreneurs for establishing industries in the city. Ghaziabad would have hardly acquired the magnitude of its present industrial structure, had there been given no financial assistance to entrepreneurs by the above mentioned financial institutions and banks.

Ghaziabad also enjoys the investment of capital from big business houses like Mohans, Tata, Jaipuria, Sri Ram, Chaudharies, Jains and Rathies etc. who represent a significant share in the total industrial set-up of the city. Establishment of public sector enterprises of 'Bharat Electronics Limited', 'Central Electronics Limited' and 'Hind Cycles Limited' signifies the role of Government capital in pushing up industrial activity in the city.

Ghaziabad also managed to attract foreign capital in the form of establishment here of a number of foreign firms like M/S. Danfoss India Limited, Indo Bulgar Food Limited, and International Tobacco Company etc. However, overall share of foreign capital in the total set up is very small. At present more than 50% share of each of these foreign firms are owned by Indian Management.

8. *Population*

Availability of labour, which is of paramount importance for all sorts of manufacturing, is closely linked with the density of population over a place and its surrounding areas. Labour characterizes a mobile factor but unskilled labour is relatively much less mobile and hence a pre-existing population over an area offers a definite advantage in respect of labour supply, specially so in the case of those industries wherein proportion of labour cost to total cost of production is relatively higher. Ghaziabad with a population of 291955 in 1981 constitutes an attractive location in respect of labour supply for establishing new industrial enterprises. District's population of 18,66,778, also serves as a vast pool for supplying the necessary labour force for city's industrial establishments.

The growth of population and the industrial development in the city have kept pace with each other and this is perhaps the reason that the industrial population here which represents the major share in the total working population of the city, somehow, managed to adapt itself to an industrial environment which demands acquisition of certain basic skills of industry on the part of industrial labour force. Prevailing of relatively lower wage rate as compared to Delhi and the development of necessary basic skills of industry amongst the labour force provided considerable strength to the general process of industrial development in the city.

TABLE 1.2: **Growth of Population and Registered Industrial Employment at Ghaziabad City**

Years	Population	Total no. of persons employed in registered industrial units
1941	23,834	—
1951	43,745	2,555
1961	70,438	6,520
1971	1,20,036	22,472
1981	2,91,955	37,731

* *Source*: Population figures from Census of India, 1971 District Census Hand Book of Meerut District. Page No. 8. Population figure of 1981 obtained from paper 2 of 1981 Census of India – p. 80.
Figures of regd. industrial employment obtained from Inspector of Factories Office, Ghaziabad.

Sex ratio of the city standing at 792 in 1981, which is lower than that in Kanpur, the foremost industrial city of Uttar Pradesh, also emphasizes the preponderance of industrial population in the city. Sex ratio is lowered because of the tendency of industrial labour leaving apart their families in their native village. Female participation in city's total industrial labour force, represents an insignificant share of little more than 2% only.

While the sex ratio in the city indicates an immensely industrial character of the city's population, the age-group structure with more than 40% persons in the age group of 0-14 years speaks of the relatively lesser degree of industrial maturity, arising out of the lack of awakening amongst general public towards family planning devices. Rate of literacy existing at 52.52% in 1981, on the other hand, shows an upward trend in the direction of general well-being of city's population as a whole.

Immigration of Industrial Population

The results of a sample industrial survey of 92 registered units in the city, carried out to accomplish the present study of 'Industrial Landscape of Ghaziabad city' bring to light certain significant facts regarding the immigration of industrial labour force at Ghaziabad from different sources in the country and abroad. As shown in table No. 1.3 although major part of the industrial population has its links in the district itself, the proportion of industrial population belonging to distant sources is also not less significant. Immigrants coming from Pakistan in 1947 represent 12.1% share in the total industrial population. Other districts of Uttar Pradesh from where have come 8.6% of total industrial population, include Bulandhshahr, Aligarh, Etah, Mainpuri, Saharanpur, Gonda and Rampur. Other states of the country which have mainly supplied the skilled and unskilled persons to the city's industrial establishments, are Bihar, Delhi, Punjab, Rajasthan, Madhya Pradesh and Tamil Nadu.

TABLE 1.3: **Immigration of Industrial Population at Ghaziabad***

Source where the employee originally belonged to	No. of regd. employees in 92 industrial units chosen for sample industrial survey.	Percentage share of each source in the total industrial population of surveyed industrial units.
1. Other countries specially Pakistan	2025	12.1%
2. Other states of India	3185	18.9%
3. Other districts of Uttar Pradesh	1445	8.6%
4. Ghaziabad town & the distt.	10149	60.4%
Total	16804	100.0%

* *Source*: Based on information gathered by Industrial Field Survey.

The results of our industrial survey regarding the immigration of industrial population at Ghaziabad show a close resemblance to the views expressed by Estall and Buchanan, who believed in the relative immobility of unskilled labour and in the comparatively greater degree of mobility amongst the skilled labour force [8]. At Ghaziabad larger part of industrial immigrants is engaged in the highly technical industrial jobs which earn them fairly good salaries.

Thus, on the whole, the demographic characteristics of the city are conducive to the industrial climate prevailing in the city. The vast pool of population in the city and adjoining areas ensures an adequate supply of both skilled and unskilled labour. Prosperous agriculture in the surrounding region provides for the regular and adequate food supplies for the industrial population. Being a newly developed industrial city with an industrial history of 40 years or so only, the labour relations in the city have not yet hardened to the extent as those in other old established industrial towns of the country and this necessarily serves as an additional advantage in respect of labour supply for starting a new industry in the city.

Transportation

Transportation costs influence the location of industry through direct freight charges, cost of insurance on goods enroute, losses incurred due to damage to the products in transit, indirect capital costs arising out in the event of goods being held up and the expenditure on clerical staff who supervise the delivery and despatch of goods at the factory.

At Ghaziabad, the proportion of transportation cost in the total cost of raw materials is considerably higher because of distant sources of the latter, but the proportion of transportation cost in the total cost of production is relatively much smaller because of relative nearness of major market areas and effectiveness and efficiency of road and rail transport services available in the city. Other factors accounting for the smaller proportion of transportation cost in the total cost of production include much higher value per unit weight of the finished products and the efficient use of raw material made possible due to improved technology these days.

Ghaziabad with its vast network of roads and railways running in different directions, offers optimum conditions in respect of transportation services for industry and other purposes. The most important national highway of G.T. Road built by Sher Shah Suri in 1540-45, joining Calcutta and Peshawar via. Delhi, passes through the middle of the whole length of municipal limits in East-West direction. This route constitutes the main artery of transportation network in the city. The two state highways joining Delhi with Moradabad and Meerut merge with G.T. Road, East of River Hindan. Because of excessively high volume of traffic along G.T. Road within the city, a 250′ bye-pass road parallel to the national highway towards Sn. margin of the city has been constructed and opened for use recently joining New Delhi with the En. end of the G.T. Road inside the city area. Other important regional level roads connect the city with New Delhi and Loni. The length of Municipal roads inside the city totalled 46 Km as per District Census Handbook of Meerut 1971. Parallel to all important highways run the corresponding broad gauge railway lines connecting the city with Delhi, New Delhi, Kanpur, Meerut and Moradabad. In 1971, everyday a total of 68 trains, 183 buses, 150 taxies and 2500 trucks were running within city area on different routes connecting it with its surrounding areas in different directions.[9]

At Ghaziabad it is not the lower freight rates but the regularity, efficiency and dependability of transport services, specially road transport, which is of utmost importance in maintaining the uninterrupted supply of raw materials to the industrial units, the failure of which implies heavy losses to the manufacturer because of halting of work at the factory. While iron ore, alloy metals, coal and petroleum are mainly brought by railways, other raw materials of the industry make use of road transport mainly because of greater flexibility and on the spot delivery and despatch of the goods by the latter. Road transport competes successfully with rail even for long distances. Tobacco for Ghaziabad's M/s. International Tobacco Company and apple pulp for the manufacture of famous 'Gold Coin Apple Juice' at M/s. F.D.M. Food Products Breweries, Mohan Nagar are brought from Andhra Pradesh and Kashmir respectively by trucks. Use of road transport also facilitates a close coordination between the production and movement of goods at the factory. Existence of a number of transport agencies in the city keeps the freight charges to a reasonable minimum because of competition. Another factor enhancing the importance of road transport for industry relates to the location of major industrial areas of the city along the highways. Road transport is, no doubt, steadily gaining ground, but the importance of railways for obtaining iron ore, alloy metals, coal and petroleum from distant sources still holds as good as it did previously.

Market

In the absence of any significant pull in respect of nearness to raw material sources, industrial location at Ghaziabad vividly signifies a strong inclination to the factor of nearness of market areas. Delhi, the capital metropolis of the country, standing at a distance of just 15 Km from the city, at once provides a vast market potential at local, regional and national level, for a large variety of products. The vast size of the market itself justifies the establishment of a wide range of industries near the main market areas. While a few of Ghaziabad's main industries such as wines, glass products, fruit products and tin containers, etc. might have been guided in location decision by such factors as fragility, perishability or increase in bulk of the products, but for many other industries, market location has been chosen mainly because of a number of advantages associated with such location. Apart from the ease of marketing the products, other associated attractions of a market location include large and varied supply of labour, personal contacts with the customers which provide impulses for innovations and improvements, credit facilities by financing bodies and the social advantages of education, housing and recreation for industrial workers. Another major factor encouraging the location of industries near the market areas is the higher freight rate on finished products which require a lot of packing, careful handling and more space per unit weight to avoid damage enroute.

At Ghaziabad where largest group of industries is engaged in the manufacture of various types of agricultural, transport, and industrial machinery, market location assumes even more significance in view of the necessity of personal contacts with the customers in connection with after-sales service of these items. Another industry which gains much from personal contacts with the customer is the manufacture of ready made garments, small unregistered units of which constitute a considerable share in the cotton textiles industry of the city.

The significance of market locations at Ghaziabad is also accentuated by the fact that a number of Ghaziabad's industries themselves serve as markets for the product of a number of other industries. To quote a few examples, glass bottles, tin containers and craft paper, manufactured at the city are consumed by wine, hydrogenated oil and corrugated boxes manufacturing units respectively. Although it is a subject of linkages amongst industries, but these examples also serve to emphasize the importance of market factor in the localization of industries at the city.

Market location of Ghaziabad, not only serves as the major labour supply area, but also provides materials for a number of industries. Various machinery manufacturing Units of the city also produce huge amount of scrap as their waste products, which is used as raw material by the ministeel mills for making the special types of steel. Thus for a few industries, market location implies both a raw material-oriented and labour-oriented location at the same time. Other main industries of Ghaziabad which derive their raw material from other industries of the city, include general hardware, wires and wire-nettings, tools and gauges, and corrugated boxes.

Thus, all of Ghaziabad's industries show a market orientation towards market areas. Factors justifying the market location for different industries vary considerably, but surely there are certain common advantages which apply to all of these and it is mainly because of these associated attractions that market location is now-a-days considered the most normal location for a large variety of industries, such as those exemplified by the vast industrial structure at Ghaziabad.

PART 'B': METHODOLOGY

The present study aiming at the Geographical analysis of 'Industrial Landscape of Ghaziabad' has been accomplished on the basis of information obtained through a field survey of registered industrial units in the district with the help of a Questionnaire on a stratified sampling basis. The sequence of various stages relating to the field work and tabulation of data in the methodology adopted has been as under:

1. The present study was initiated by obtaining a list of registered industrial units (1981) of the district from the 'Inspector of Factories Office', Ghaziabad. This list contained the addresses of all registered factories along with the total number of employees therein. In the first instance registered industrial units of Ghaziabad city and the other manufacturing centres of the district were sorted out and the percentage share of each of these centres in the total registered employment of the district was calculated in order to determine the relative position of these centres in the total industrial set-up of the district,
2. Next phase of the study entailed a preliminary survey of all the registered industrial units in the district to find out the functional character of each of these units. During this preliminary survey, major part of the information about manufactured products, was obtained with the help of details given on the nameplates at the factory sites. Entry into factory premises was required only seldom. On the basis of the types of products manufactured, a general functional classification of the important industries in the district was arrived at. In Ghaziabad city, which constitutes the focal point of our study, all industries with the registered employment figure of above 300 persons have been included in the list of important industries of the city. The only industry which is important in the district as a whole but is not present at Ghaziabad city is the manufacture of sugar. Other industries which constitute amongst the important industries of the city but are relatively more important at some other manufacturing centre of the district, include cotton textile, synthetic fibre, and steel. Functional classification of the industries also established the hierarchy of 24 important industries in the city, based on the registered employment figures tabulated for each of them separately. A broader classification of industries was attempted on the basis of kind of raw materials used such as those relating to agriculture, metals, chemicals or other miscellaneous sources.
3. In order to obtain detailed information about individual industries, a sample field survey of selected registered industrial units was carried out by using a questionnaire covering queries

about all important Geographical aspects of the industry. In all 92 factories in the city and 40 at other manufacturing centres of the district were surveyed out of a total of 452 and 194 respectively. For undertaking the industrial survey at Ghaziabad city, 20% of the factories of each of the important industries were selected so as to represent all the sizes (big, medium and small) of the factories in the industry concerned and, also all the industrial areas where the industry prevailed, in the corresponding proportions. The proforma of the questionnaire used for conducting the industrial sample field survey was as under :

1. Name and address of the factory,
2. Whether proprietorship, partnership, private Ltd., public Ltd or Public undertaking concern,
3. Year when factory got registered under Factories Act,
4. Goods manufactured or the functions carried out by the factory,
5. Raw Materials used, their sources and mode of transport, percentage of cost of raw materials in the total cost of production,
6. Types of fuels and energy used, their sources and mode of transport, percentage of costs of industrial energy in the total value added by manufacturer,

7. TOTAL NUMBER OF EMPLOYEES

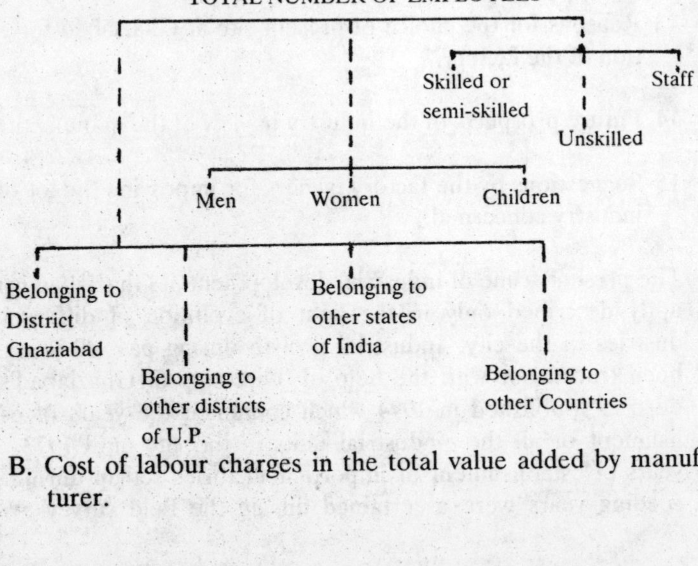

B. Cost of labour charges in the total value added by manufacturer.

8. *Market* Where the manufactured products are sent :
 i. Ghaziabad district.
 ii. Other districts of Uttar Pradesh,
 iii. Other states of India.
 iv. Other countries.

9. Facilities provided by the Government for the industry e.g. (a) Land (b) Loan (c) Technical assistance (d) Concessions in the form of tax relief (e) Any other facility.

10. Facilities provided by the employer to its employees e.g. (a) Housing accommodation (b) E.S.I. and Provident Fund benefits (c) Bonus (d) Medical facilities (e) Recreational Facilities (f) any other facility.

11. Problems relating to any of the following :
(a) Capital (b) Power (c) Labour (d) Availability of raw material (e) Taxes (f) Space (g) Market (h) Water pollution (i) Air pollution (j) Problem of disposal of liquid or solid industrial waste (k) Any other problem.

12. Reasons for the choice of Ghaziabad for establishing the factory.

13. Reasons for the choice of present site at Ghaziabad for erection of the factory.

14. Future prospects of the industry in view of the manufacturer.

15 Suggestions by the factory owners for improving the lot of the industry concerned.

4. The present scene of industrial development at Ghaziabad can be aptly described only in the light of evolution of different industries in the city. Industrial growth during past 40 years has been traced out with the help of 'Directory of Ghaziabad's Industries' published in 1974 which contained the years of establishment of all the industrial units in the city until 1973. The years of establishment of important factories set up during succeeding years were ascertained during the field survey. While

tracing out the growth of individual industries, only those factories have been taken into consideration which are functioning presently. Industrial structure during each decennial year has been portrayed by assuming the present municipal limits as the base since the very inception of industrial activity in the city.

The growth and dispersion of industries in a city occur usually simultaneously. To test this hypothesis in the case of Ghaziabad city, a correlation coefficient has been worked out between the growth and dispersion of industries in the city by applying Spearmans rank difference method. The formula used for the same is as under :

$$P = 1 - \frac{6 \Sigma D^2}{N(N^2-1)}$$

D represents difference of ranks of two variables,
N represents the number of variables.

Details of methodology for obtaining the ranks of two variables are given in the chapter concerned.

5. To understand the spatial pattern of industrial land-use in Ghaziabad city, location quotients of all important industries have been calculated in respect of different industrial areas in the city. The formula adopted for finding out the location quotient is as under [10]

$$\text{Location Ouotient} = \frac{\text{Percentage share of the industrial area in the total registered employment of a particular industry.}}{\text{Percentage share of the industrial area in the total registered industrial force of the city.}}$$

If the location quotient of an industry in an industrial area is close to unity, it implies that the area has just the right share of the industry in it. The degree of the concentration of an industry in a particular industrial area is denoted by how much the location quotient exceeds the value of unity. Spatial pattern of the various industries in the city has been analysed in the light of location quotient values calculated for different industries in respect of different industrial areas. Keeping in view the specific features of the spatial pattern of different industries, the authoress has also evolved a typology of intra-urban industrial locations in Ghaziabad city within the framework of views expressed by W. Isard, Lowerstein, Hamilton, and Pred [11].

6. A detailed description of all the important industries at Ghaziabad has been attempted on the basis of information gathered through sample industrial field survey. All the important industries have been discussed in the light of their specific locational factors, growth, functional structure, problems and future prospects in the context of Ghaziabad. Industries at other manufacturing centres of the district have been discussed separately.

7. Industrial field survey also brought to notice various specific problems related to industry & those arising out as a result of rapid industrialization which have been discussed along with the suggestions for remedying them.
The present study also led to certain derivations about the theoretical and conceptual aspects of industrial location at Ghaziabad. At the end the authoress has enlisted her conclusions regarding the salient features of industrialization at Ghaziabad and suggestions for future industrial development and planning.

REFERENCES

1. Area Development Office, Ghaziabad.
2. Topographical Sheet No. 53 H/6.
3. Information gathered from Water-works Office, Ghaziabad.
4. Estall, R.C. and Buchanan, R.O., Industrial Activity and Economic Geography, 1968, London, p.132.
5. Information gathered by field survey.
6. Information gathered from the Office of Executive Engineer, Electricity Distribution Division I, Nehru Nagar, Ghaziabad.
7. Census of India 1981. Paper 2 of 1981 - Provisional Population. Totals - Rural Urban Distribution Page No.180 & 80.
8. R.C. Estall and R.O. Buchanan - 'Industrial Activity and Economic Geography' - 1961 & 1966, London, Chapter IV, 'The influence of Factors of Production', pp.71-82.
9. Sarikwal, R.C., 'Sociology of a Growing Town' 1978, Delhi, p.109.
10. Gupta, N.S. Singh Amarjeet - 'Industrial Economy of India' 1978, Page No.43

11. W. Isard (1956) Location and space Economy 278-80 L.K. Loewenstein (1963) Location of urban land-uses 413 F.E.I. Hamilton (1967) 'Models of Industrial Location' 361-417 (London)
A.R. Pred (1964) The intra-metropolitan Location of American Manufacturing Ann.Assoc. Ani. Geogr. 54. 165-80.

Fig. 1
GHAZIABAD – PHYSIOGRAPHY

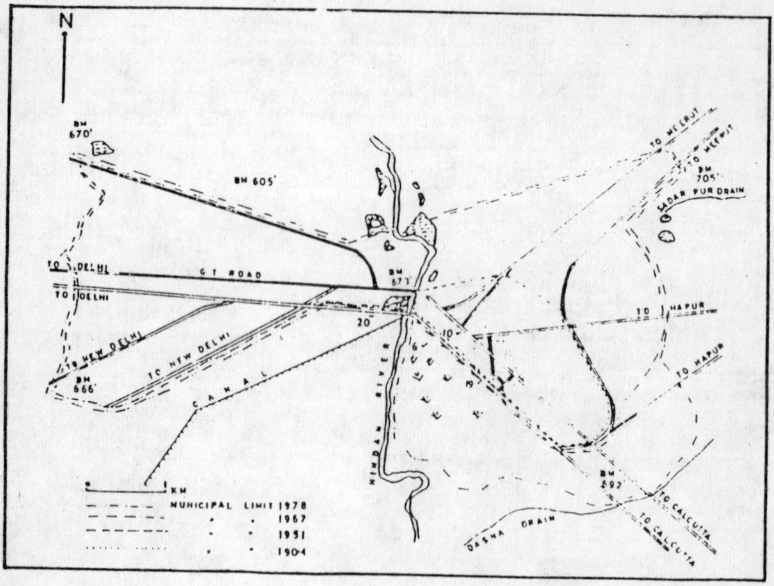

Fig 2
HOW GHAZIABAD STANDS SPATIALLY

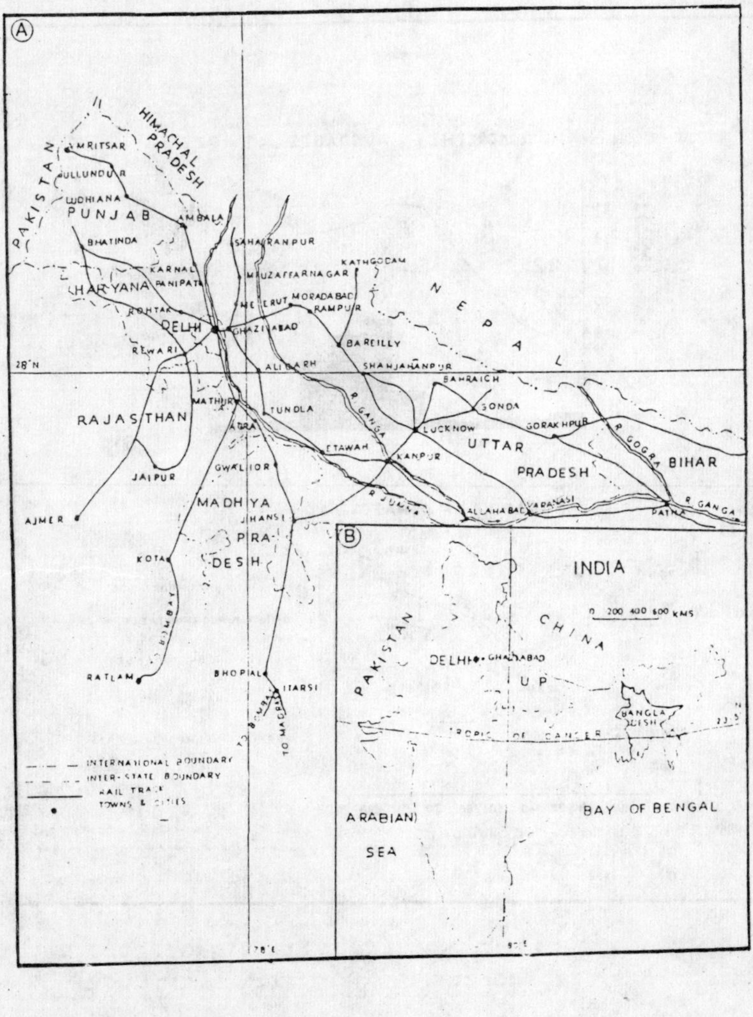

Fig 3
CLIMATIC CHARACTERISTICS

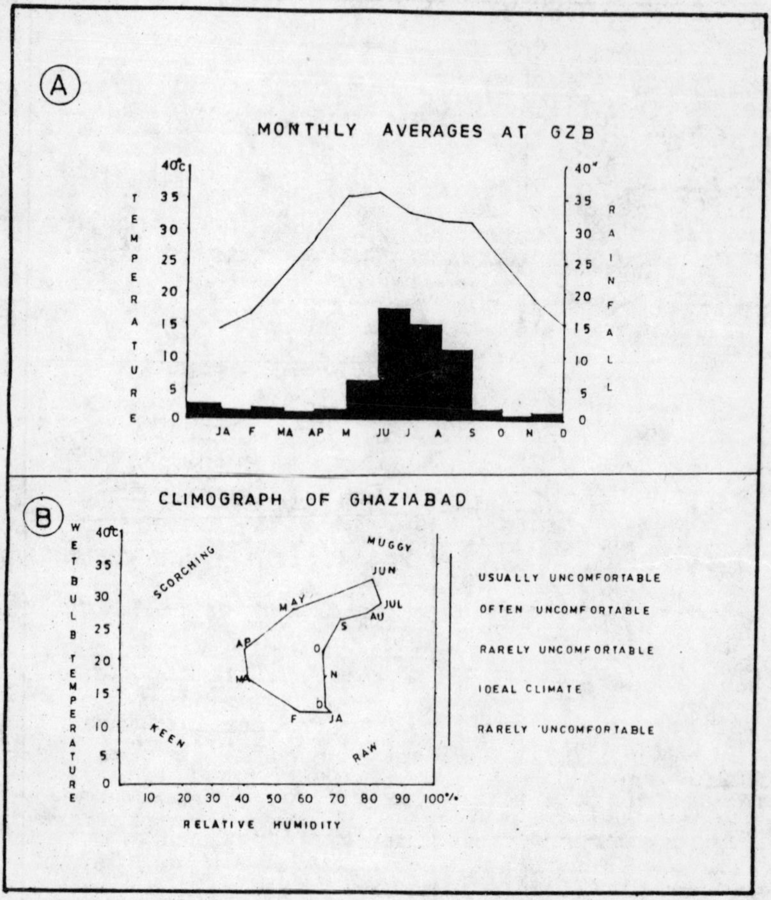

Fig 4
DEMOGRAPHIC FEATURES

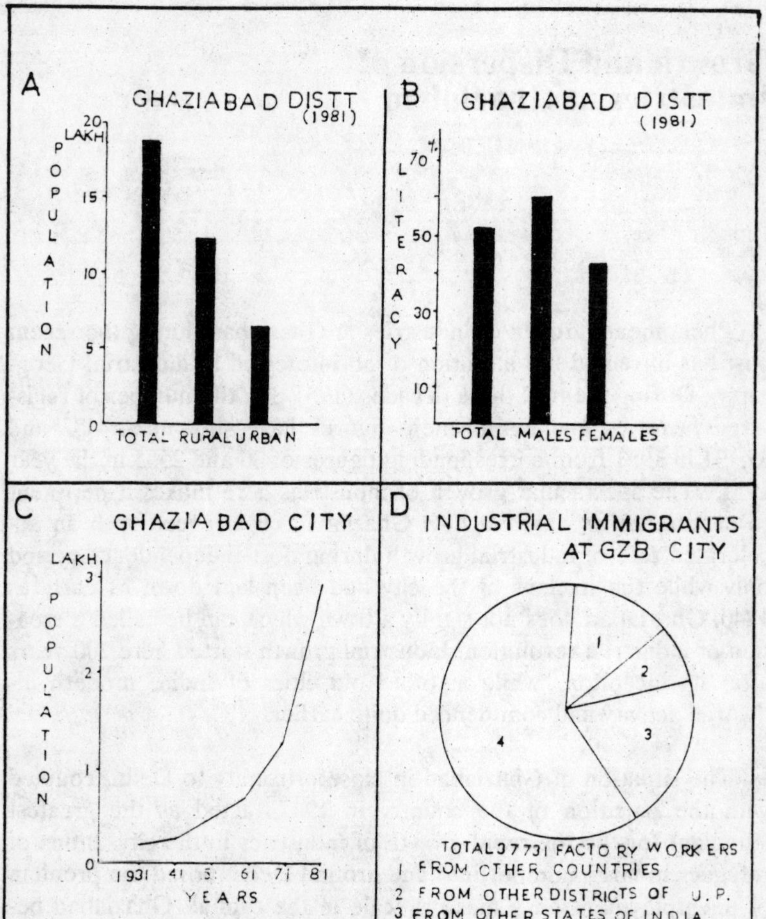

TWO

Growth and Dispersion of Industries at Ghaziabad

Phenomenal growth of industries at Ghaziabad during the recent past has attracted the attention of all interested in industrial Geography. During the past three decades (1951-81). the number of registered factories and employment figures have shot up to 452 and 37,731 in 1981 from corresponding figures of 30 and 2555 in the year 1951[1]. The spectacular growth of industries here makes it pertinent to enquire as to why and how Ghaziabad experienced such an accelerated rate of industrial growth during post-Independence period only while the nucleus of the city had been laid down as early as 1740. Ghaziabad does not signify a town which can be called a creation of industrial revolution. Industrial growth started here 200 years after its inception, while at other old cities of India, modern industrial activity had commenced quite earlier.

The situation of Ghaziabad in close proximity to Delhi, coupled with the partition of the country in 1947, acted as the greatest stimulant for the the rapid growth of industries in the city. Influx of refugees in large number into and around Delhi, posed the problem of unemployment on a massive scale in the capital. Ghaziabad because of its nearness to Delhi, started attracting the attention of private entrepreneurs coming from Pakistan and gradually a number of small and medium-sized industrial units sprang up in the city during the early post-Independence years. Setting up of 'Ghaziabad Improvement Trust' and the introduction of 'Ghaziabad Master Plan' around 1960 further paved the way for rapid industrialization.

Hitherto unplanned industrial growth of the city was given a right direction by developing a number of new industrial areas in different parts of the regulated area of Ghaziabad, specially along the major highways for accommodating further industrial expansion.

In order to properly understand the vast industrial structure of Ghaziabad, peeping into past assumes even more significance because of the great role played by inter-industry linkages in furthering the cause of industrial development in the city. How the various emerging and pre-existing industries were related to each other and how their relationships promoted the cause of industrial activity in the city, can be properly understood only if we study the different phases of industrial development at Ghaziabad. The first part of the present chapter deals with the evolution of industries at Ghaziabad during different phases. Latter part of the chapter concerns with the study of correlation between growth and dispersion of industries at Ghaziabad.

The growth of the individual industries at Ghaziabad has been traced out with the help of years of establishment of different factories given in the Directory of Industries published in the year 1974.[2] The years of establishment of the new factories were ascertained in the course of industrial field survey.

The main problem of industrial Geography is that pertaining to the measurement of industrial activity as illustrated in various studies referred to by Patni, Morrison and many others [3]. In the present study factory employment figures have been used as an absolute measure of manufacturing activities during different decades. However, as Gilmour has pointed out, temporal comparisons in respect of spatial changes often fail to portray a realistic picture because of frequent changes occurring in respect of city's municipal limits and also those pertaining to the definitions of the components of industrial activity [4]. In order to avoid practical difficulties of this nature, present municipal limits have been taken as base for all the purposes of the present study. Therefore, many such factories which are presently located within municipal limits but which fell outside the city area at the time of their inception, have also been included in the list of factories of corresponding decade.

Phases of Industrial Growth

The evolution of industries at Ghaziabad can be studied under the following four phases:

1. Earlier phase of slow industrial growth from 1940 to 1951.
2. The phase of rapid but unplanned industrial growth from 1952 to 1961.
3. The phase of very fast planned industrial growth from 1962-71.
4. The present phase of planned but moderate industrial growth commencing from the year 1972 till to-date.

1. *Earlier Phase of Slow Industrial Growth from 1940 to 1951*

Modern industrial activity at Ghaziabad owes its inception to the establishment of M/S. Amrit Vanaspati Co. Ltd. on Bulandshahr Road in the year 1940. There was no sign of modern industrial development until 1940, although the city had existed since 1740 and it got linked with the railway as early as 1865. It seems really strange as to how and why the highly nodal situation of Ghaziabad remained untapped for such a long time. The history of industrial growth in the city clearly emphasizes the role of human factor as being far more significant than that of natural advantages in harnessing the industrial potentialities of the situation. Partition of the nation in 1947 and the resultant immigration of population from Pakistan led to the realization of the industrial potentialities of Ghaziabad and it ushered into a new era of industrial development since 1947. There were hardly 8 factories in the city uptil 1947 but in the succeeding 4 years the number rose to 30 in 1951. Apart from M/S. Amrit Vanaspati Co. Ltd. other important factories of pre-independence period include M/S. Federal Chemical works, Asia Chemicals, Ghaziabad Engineering Company, Modern Industries, and Webbing and Belting Factory Pvt. Ltd.. Most of these factories were located on the Bulandshahr Road in the South-eastern part of the city. (Fig 5) Post-Independence period of industrial growth saw the emergence of two more industrial nodes along G.T. Road, one at Sahibabad and the other one at Mohan Nagar. Both of these industrial nodes fell outside the municipal limits at that time. Important factories of Sahibabad included M/S. Modern Industries, and Flowmore and those of Mohannagar were M/S. Meera Chemicals,

Peerless Foundry, and Pyare Lal & Sons. Important factories set up in Ghaziabad proper during this period included M/S. Guru Nanak Engineering Company, Punjab Oil Expeller Ltd., Azad Engineering Company, and U.P. Ceramics & Potteries Ltd. Uptil 1947 oil engines and agricultural implements industry had not assumed any special significance in the industrial structure of the city but during early post-independence years, it experienced such an accelerated rate of growth, that it became the dominant industry at Ghaziabad proper by 1951. At Sahibabad, however, manufacture of transport equipments and parts was the most important industry. Other important industries at Ghaziabad proper included hydrogenated oil, structural clay products, cotton textile and G.I. pipes. Other relatively less important industries included chemicals and gases, general hardware, and drugs and medicines.

TABLE 2.1: **Industrial Structure 1951**

Name of the Industry	No.of regd. units	No.of regd. Employment	Percentage share of the industry in the total regd. Employment of the city.
1. Oil Engines and Agricultural Implements	11	607	23.75
2. Transport Equipments and their parts.	2	674	26.37
3. Structural Clay Products	1	446	17.45
4. Electronics and Electricals	2	181	7.08
5. G.I. Pipes and Tubes	1	129	5.04
6. Cotton Textile	1	171	6.69
7. Hydrogenated oil	1	181	7.08
8. Chemical & Gases	2	72	2.81
9. General hardware	2	22	0.86
10. Drugs & Medicines	1	18	0.70
11. Other Industries	6	51	2.16
Total	30	2555	100.00%

Source: Growth of individual industries has been traced with the help of years of establishments and figures of employment of each factory. The years of establishment were known with the help of 'Directory of Ghaziabad's Industries' published in the year 1974 and field survey.

With the exception of M/S. Punjab Oil Expeller Co. which was located near the crossing of Patel Marg and Meerut Road, all the other factories in the city were located along G.T. Road. Actually the potentialities of Meerut Road industrial area were realized only after the establishment of M/S. Punjab Oil Expellers at its present site. During the sixtees Ghaziabad Improvement Trust developed this area into one of the most important industrial areas of the city.

During the earlier phase of industrial growth, industries grew almost independently of each other. The role of inter-industry and intra-industry linkages remained at its minimal. There seemed to be no obvious relationships amongst the few industries that had grown into significance by this time. Each industry had its own advantages and together they all imparted the city a sound structural base for future industrial growth.

2. *The Phase of Rapid but unplanned Industrial Growth from 1952 to 1961*

The tempo of industrial growth acquired during the post-Independence years was sustained and further geared up in the following decade. More and more factories were established which further enriched the industrial structure both functionally and spatially. Major part of industrial development during this decade took place as a result of concerted efforts made by Punjabi entrepreneurs without getting any substantial help from Govt. bodies. They possessed a good deal of experience in the field of industry and it certainly helped them a lot in establishing new factories over here. Industrial potentialities of Ghaziabad had already been proved beyond doubt by the satisfactory progress of existing factories and so more and more entrepreneurs opted for Ghaziabad to locate their new factories. Delhi had already become too much crowded and because of problem of lack of space in the metropolis, only Ghaziabad appeared to be the second best industrial location for the reason of being nearest to the capital, amongst all the ring towns. Thus despite the indifference on the part of Govt. bodies, the process of industrial expansion continued unabated. Industries chose their location themselves and by 1961 city had already assumed a predominantly industrial character. Not only did the existing industries do well during this decade, but a number of new industries also made their appearance resulting in the emergence of Ghaziabad as an important industrial centre in the close vicinity of Delhi.

As is obvious from the table No. 2.2 total industrial growth in terms of registered employment amounted to 155.18% during the decade, which undoubtedly indicated a very good progress in the field of industry. The number of registered units rose to 86 and that of registered employment to 6520 from corresponding figures of 30 and 2555 in 1951. Except structural clay products, all the other pre-existing industries have recorded growth ranging from 26.90% to 218.78%.

TABLE 2.2: **Industrial Structure 1961**

Name of the Industry	No.of regd. indl. units	No.of regd. employment	Percentage of growth in terms of employment	Percentage share of the industry in the total regd. employment of the city
1. Oil Engines &Agricultural Implements	25	928	55.88	14.23
2. Electronics & Electricals	10	577	218.78	8.84
3. Transport Equipments & their parts	6	1135	68.39	17.40
4. Primary Metal (Ferrous)	7	205	—	3.14
5. Cotton Textile	3	217	26.90	3.32
6. G.I. Pipes & Tubes	3	291	125.58	4.46
7. Machinery not classified elsewhere	2	326	—	5.00
8. General Hardware	3	40	81.81	0.61
9. Tools & Gauges, Moulds & Dies, & Jigs & fixtures, etc.	2	123	—	1.88
10. Utensils	3	85	—	1.30
11. Tin Products	1	208	—	3.20
12. Chemicals & Gases	4	112	55.55	1.72
13. Hydrogenated oil	2	463	155.80	7.10
14. Drugs & Medicines	2	30	66.66	0.46
15. Structural Clay Products	1	446	0.00	6.84
16. Breweries	1	1200	—	18.40
17. Other Industries	11	134		Remainder
Total	86	6520	155.18%	100.00%

Source: Ibid., Table No. 1.1

As regards individual industries, transport equipments and parts, and oil engines retained their positions as being the two largest groups amongst pre-existing industries with the registered employment of 1135 and 928 persons respectively. Structural clay products which stood at 3rd place in 1951 recorded no growth whatsoever and as such was superseded by electronics and electricals which exhibited the highest growth of 218.78 percent during this decade. Hydrogenated oil and G.I. pipes industries also did very well, recording 155.80 and 125.58 percent growth respectively.. The industries which grew only moderately included general hardware, drugs and medicines, chemicals and gases, and cotton textile. Apart from the good show of pre-existing industries, many new industries which acquired significance during this period included machinery other than oil engines and electrical, primary metal, tools and gauges, utensils, tin products and breweries.

Most of the new industries of this decade owed their development largely to the pre-existing industrial structure. Except M/S. Mohan Meakin Breweries, which is the famous wine-manufacturing concern of national importance, all the other new industries of the decade developed as a sequel to the pre-existing industries. Manufacture of other types of machinery thrived mainly because of the success of pre-existing oil-engine industry in the city. This already established industry of the city which dealt with the manufacture of oil engine machinery, was in a sound position to provide trained technical personnel for the manufacture of other types of machinery as well. The famous concern of M/s. Jaina Time Industries located in 1959 which manufactures export quality watches and clocks is the most important factory belonging to this group.

Because of rapid development of oil engine, and other types of machinery industries, it was quite relevant that some entrepreneurs decided to establish mini iron & steel mills, which could supply the required raw material to the machinery manufacturing units of the city. Another great temptation for starting mini iron and steel mills was the availability of scrap iron in bulk from local machinery manufacturing industrial units and also from Delhi metropolitan area, which could be used as raw material for these steel making units. Thus during this decade there were opened some small iron and steel making units which have been termed as the primary metal industries in the tables showing industrial structure of different decades. During this phase, this primary metal industry made only a steady headway but in the next decade it became one of the most important industries of the city.

Tin products industry which is mainly concerned with the manufacture of tin containers developed mainly because of large demand for tin-containers in the pre-existing vanaspati-manufacturing concerns of M/s. Amrit Vanaspati Co. Ltd., and Hindustan Lever Ltd. M/s. Hindustan Tin Works was established in the year 1958 on Bulandshahr Road just near to the above mentioned vanaspati manufacturing concerns of the city.

Other two new industries viz. tools and gauges, and utensils, belong to the group of consumer goods industries which quite naturally come up whenever an industrial nucleus expands.

As regards spatial expansion of the industries during this decade, (Fig No 6)one more new industrial area viz. Patel Marg and Mukand Nagar appeared on the industrial landscape of Ghaziabad proper. Patel Marg constitutes the westernmost road of the city which connects G.T.Road and Meerut Road. This industrial area lay quite far away from older Bulandshahr Road industrial area but it is nearer to the C.B.D. as compared to the former. Mukandnagar is an adjoining locality in the close vicinity of Patel Marg and together they form one single industrial area known as Patel Marg-Mukand Nagar industrial area. Growth of industries in this area characterizes a haphazard pattern because here residential buildings and industrial establishments are seen in close juxtaposition unlike Bulandshahr Road industrial area where we don't find any such intermingling of industrial establishments with residential areas. Haphazard growth of this industrial area owed mainly to the non-intervention of local bodies at that time in matters regarding location of the industry within city. With the establishment of famous M/s. Punjab Oil Expeller in 1948 along Patel Marg, industrial potentialities of the site had been proved and consequently during fiftees a number of oil-engine manufacturing units were located in the area. Some of the important factories opened during this decade in this area include, M/s. National Steel & General Mills, K.S. Engineering Works, Adarsh Engineering Company, Shri Ram Engineering Company and many others. All these factories are located along Patel Marg. Important factories, opened in Mukand Nagar during this decade were M/s. Jain Rolling Mills, Calcutta Engineering Company, Swastik Engineering Company, Jagat Foundry and Engineering Works and many others. Here we find a conspicuous concentration of oil engine and agricultural implements industry which accounts for more than 50% of its total registered employment in this industrial area only.

Simultaneously with the emergence of new industrial area of Patel Marg-Mukand Nagar, there occurred significant industrial expansion in the pre-existing Bulandshahr Road industrial area as well. Important factories that were located in this area during this phase included M/s. Hindustan Lever Ltd., Hindustan Tin Works, Baba Vishwakarma Engineering Works, and Saraswati Engineering Works. However during this decade, industrial expansion took place mainly in the form of roadside establishments along the national highway. It remained the major industrial area of the city, containing a wide variety of industrial activities such as hydrogenated oil, oil engines, primary metals, chemicals, cotton textiles, electronics, and tin products.

Parallel to the industrial growth in the above mentioned two industrial areas within the city, industrial nodes of Mohan Nagar and Sahibabad along G.T.Road, which lay outside municipal limits, also experienced intense industrial growth during this period. With the establishment of M/s. Mohan Meakin Breweries in Mohan Nagar, this industrial node suddenly acquired a high industrial significance because of the national character of the concern. Also this was the largest concern of that time employing about 1200 persons and is the second largest at present, the first being M/s. Bharat Electronics Ltd. a Govt. of India undertaking with the registered employment of 2850 persons.

Sahibabad, which had already become an important centre for transport equipments and parts, with the establishment of M/s. Modern Industries, also experienced rapid industrial growth. Apart from the establishment of a number of auto-parts manufacturing concerns during this period, e.g. M/s. Abilities India pvt. Ltd., and Bramic Suri Pvt. Ltd., there were also established here a number of industrial units manufacturing electricals e.g. M/s. Dass Hitachi Pvt.

Ltd., Indian Aluminium Cable Co., Shiwa Electronics, and S.K. Insulated Cable Manufacturing Company etc.

Thus evolution of industrial landscape during this period characterizes a pattern which developed exclusively of its own without any interference from the Govt. bodies. Out of the four important areas of industrial concentration, three were located on G.T. Road itself at some distances apart. The newly developed Patel Marg-Mukand Nagar industrial area which presented a haphazard growth pattern because of intermingling of industrial units with residential area, chose a location away from the national highway of G.T.Road but pointing in the direction of Meerut Road which grew into a major industrial area during the succeeding decade. There was no planning for industrial land-use during this decade. The matters relating to location of industries were decided by the entrepreneurs themselves.

3. *The phase of very fast planned industrial growth during the period from 1962 to 1971*

The decade ending in 1971 marks the peak period in the history of industrial growth of the city. During this decade there was recorded 244.66% increase in the registered employment over the preceding decade. This spectacular increase owed largely to role of Govt. activity which had been instrumental in furthering the cause of city's industrialization during this period.

By 1961 Ghaziabad had already emerged as a dominating industrial centre in the vicinity of Delhi. Uptil this time industrial growth had occurred exclusively on its own initiative. Setting up of 'Ghaziabad Improvement Trust' in the year 1960 opened a new chapter in the industrial history of the city. Being a growing industrial centre, the city required careful planning in order to avoid haphazard growth and other evils associated with rapid industrialization. The Trust adopted a 'Master plan' with a long-term planning for industrial expansion. Under the auspicies of 'Master plan' large tracts of land were developed as industrial areas in order to ensure a healthy and balanced growth of industries in the city. Major areas developed for industrial expansion were Meerut Road Industrial Area, Anand Industrial Estate, Prakash Industrial Estate, Rajendra Nagar Industrial Estate and the Loni Road Industrial Area. Provision of infrastructure facilities by the Trust and the availability of financial and other types of help from various Govt. bodies, acted as a strong stimulant for the establishment of more and more new factories here. The total number of registered units rose to 265 from 86 in 1961. All existing industries made a good progress and a number of new industries were also added in the functional structure of the city.

Except breweries, structural clay products, and hydrogenated oil. all other pre-existing industries made a good progress recording a percentage of growth between 100 to 1000. A very high percentage of growth had occurred in drugs and medicines, primary metal, cotton textiles, G.I. Pipes and tubes, tin products, tools and gauges, electronics, machinery, transport equipments and parts, and oil engines which have recorded 1060.00, 742.92, 633.17, 465.19, 458.17 380.48, 207.10, 180.36, 157.00 and 136.20 percent growth respectively during this decade. The industries which grew only moderately include general hardware, chemical and gases, and utensils which recorded 112.50, 101.78, and 118.82 percent growth respectively. Seven new industries also grew in importance, which included tobacco products, paper and board, plastic and foam products, glass and glass products, corrugated boxes, oil mills and soap, and synthetic fibre.

All industrial expansion, during this period occurred in a planned manner,thus leading to an alround welfare of the city. The city with all its industrial areas located towards the margins of city on transport arteries presents a pleasant and healthy picture of industrial growth. There was no problem posed to normal urban life by the ever-increasing number of new factories.

Another significant fact about the spectacular industrial growth of this decade was that despite a key role played by the Govt. bodies to boost up the industrialization, there was no direct intervention of Govt. in enriching city's industrial fabric. Except one factory, i.e. M/s. Hind Cycle Ltd. which is a Govt. of India undertaking, all important factories started during this period belonged to private sector.

Industrial expansion of this decade is also characterized by the establishment of a large number of large scale concerns. The famous factories established in newly developed Meerut Road Industrial Area during this decade include M/s. Jain Tube Company Ltd. (1964), Shri Ram Piston & Rings Ltd.(1963), Poysha Industrial Corporation Ltd. (1967), Danfoss India Ltd. (1968), Unichem Laboratories (1965), Mascot India Tools & Forgings Pvt. Ltd. (1969), Johnson Pumps (1970), Electric Construction & Equipment Co.(1970) and International Tobacco Co. Ltd. (1967). Along Meerut Road there is seen a heavy concentration of auto parts, G.I. pipes, tin containers, different types of industrial machinery, and drug and medicines manufacturing units. Despite being newly developed, this industrial area had assumed a vast and diversified industrial character by the end of this decade.

Apart from Meerut Road industrial area, another important addition to the industrial landscape of Ghaziabad during this period was Loni Road industrial area, (Fig 7) where were established a number of important concerns at this time, e.g. M/s. Tata Oil Mills, Ajanta Textiles, Alps Textiles, and Harsha Tractors etc. Selection of this area for industrial expansion was motivated by the growing industrial significance of Mohan Nagar after the establishment of famous M/s. Mohan Meakin Breweries in 1960. This industrial area is actually a further extension of Mohan Nagar industrial node.

Other smaller additions to the industrial landscape during this period were Anand Industrial Estate, Rajendra Nagar Industrial Estate and Prakash Industrial Estate all along G.T. Road, the former being situated in Mohan Nagar and the two at Rajendra Nagar and Sahibabad. In the area north of G.T. Road in trans-Hindan tract, Pasaunda also appeared on the industrial map of Ghaziabad though not representing an area of concentrated growth.

Not only there emerged a number of industrial areas during this period, but also there occurred a vast industrial expansion in the oldest industrial area of Bulandshahr Road of city proper. In the preceding decade, this industrial area was mainly confined to roadside establishments. During this decade, large tract of land north of G.T. Road was developed as industrial area by Ghaziabad Improvement Trust for further industrial growth. The important factories started in this industrial area during this period were M/s. Atma

Steel Pvt. Ltd., Chaudhary Steel Udyog, Chaudhary & Sons Forgings, and Sansar Foundry etc. To the south of G.T. Road in this area important factories that came up during this period were M/s. Rathi Alloys & Steel Ltd., Rathi Udyog Ltd. and Rathi Spat Ltd., Hind Cycle Ltd., and Sarin Steel Industries. During sixtees Bulandshahr Road Industrial area witnessed a phenomenal increase in the number of iron and steel making units. More than 75% of this important industry at Ghaziabad in concentrated in this industrial area only. Other industries which experienced rapid growth in this industrial area during this period were, chemicals, synthetic fibre and structural clay products.

M/s. The Swadeshi Polytex the famous polyester yarn manufacturing concern of the city was established in this area in 1970. With the establishment of this concern, this industrial area has extended upto Kavi Nagar in the area north of G.T. Road.

Thus, while concluding we must once again stress the role of Govt. activity in boosting up the cause of rapid industrialization during this period. Industrial expansion could be possible only because Ghaziabad Improvement Trust with the help of U.P.S.I.D.C. developed new industrial areas and provided infra-structure facilities to the up-coming entrepreneurs. Without Govt. efforts, Ghaziabad would have, in no case, acquired the present magnitude of industrial structure within such a short period.

4. *Present Phase of Planned but Moderate Industrial Growth commencing from the year 1972 till todate*

The present phase of industrial growth commencing from 1972 signifies a period of march towards maturity and excellence of the industrial structure, though percentage of growth (68.06%) during this decade indicates only a steady headway in terms of industrial expansion. During the decade ending in 1981, the number of registered units rose to 452 and that of registered employment to 37731 from the corresponding figures of 265 and 22472 in the preceding decade. Percentage of growth has declined considerably, but this does not mean the slackening of the process of industrial development. The unprecedented growth of the last decade was quite

TABLE 2.3: **Industrial Structure 1971**

Name of the Industry	No.of regd. indl. units	No. of regd. empl-oyment	Percentage of growth in terms of employment	Percentage share of the industry in the total regd. employ-ment in the city
1. Oil Engines & Agri-cultural implements	49	2192	136.20	9.75
2. Electronics & Electricals	20	1772	207.10	7.88
3. Transport Equipments & their parts	13	2917	157.00	12.98
4. Primary Metal (Ferrous)	18	1728	742.92	7.68
5. Cotton Textile	9	1591	633.19	6.99
6. G.I. Pipes & Tubes	8	1645	465.29	7.32
7. Machinery not classified elsewhere	9	914	180.36	4.06
8. General Hardware	4	85	112.50	0.38
9. Tools & Gauges & Moulds & Dies etc.	5	591	380.48	2.62
10. Utensils	6	186	118.82	0.83
11. Tin Products	5	1161	458.17	5.16
12. Chemical & Gases	9	226	101.98	1.01
13. Hydrogenated Oil	3	781	68.68	3.47
14 Drugs & Medicines	6	348	1060.00	1.54
15. Structural Clay Products	8	582	30.49	2.58
16. Breweries	1	1452	21.00	6.46
17. Tobacco Products	1	494	—	2.20
18. Paper Board and Paper Products	13	320	—	1.42
19. Plastic & Foam Products	8	305	—	1.35
20. Synthetic Fibre	3	790	—	3.51
21. Glass and Glass Products	3	906	—	4.03
22. Corrugated Boxes	6	301	—	1.34
23. Oil Mills & Soap	1	600	—	2.66
24. Other Industries	57	625	—	Remainder
Total	265	22472	244.66%	100.00%

Source : Ibid., Table No. 1.1.

natural in view of the initiation of great magnitude of Govt. role for exhorting industrial development. Tempo of industrial growth acquired during preceding decade has been maintained during the present phase as well, but the accelerated rate of the same cannot be maintained for ever, because city's industrial growth has already acquired substantial dimensions which hardly permit for the continuance of a very fast rate of industrial expansion in the coming years.

As illustrated in Table No. 2.4, there has occurred a great change in the relative position of various industries as depicted by their percentage share in the total set-up. Electronics have come to the top position followed by transport equipments, cotton textile, oil engines, and primary metal in order of importance. In the preceding decade first five industries in order of importance were transport equipments, oil engines, electronics, primary metal and G.I. pipes and tubes. The change has occurred due to differential rate of progress recorded by various industries. Electronics and electricals which stood at first place in 1981, recorded a very high percentage of growth of 263.82. This was due to establishment in 1973 of M/s. Bharat Electronics Ltd., and Central Electronics Ltd., both in Public sector having a strength of 2850 and 750 persons respectively. Other industries which made a good progress during the present phase are general hardware, chemical and gases, machinery, and utensils which recorded 374.11, 172.12, 115.52 and 115.05 percent growth respectively.

The rapid development of electronics industry owed partly to the role of public sector and partly to the availability of latest technology from Delhi metropolitan area, which is so vital for the existence of this industry. Apart from Govt. Undertaking of M/s. Bharat Electronics Ltd. and Central Electronics Ltd., there exist a number of important factories belonging to this group in private sector as well. There are 40 industrial units in the city manufacturing electronics and electricals and about half of these units have been started during the present phase. Some of the important concerns of this industry in the private sector include M/s. Video Electronics Pvt. Ltd., Teletube Electronics Pvt. Ltd., M.G. Electronics Pvt. Ltd., Rama Tronics Pvt. Ltd., Sansar Fan Industries, Hindustan Insulated Cable Corpn., Electric Construction and Equipment Co. Ltd., and East India Transformer & Gears Pvt. Ltd.

Rapid growth of chemical industries can be attributed to the basic nature of these industries. Chemical industries provide materials for a large number of industries and hence in a growing industrial centre, development of chemical industries is quite natural and essential. Manufacture of machinery prospered well because of the sound technical background of the city as a whole. From the very beginning, manufacture of different types of machinery such as oil engines, transport equipment, electricals etc. has been the most important industrial activity in the city.

All the other industries that have recorded growth during the present phase are those belonging to consumer goods group such as general hardware, utensils, cotton textile, tools and gauges, paper and paper board, plastic and foam products, drugs and medicines etc. These industries do not characterize stringent locational requirements and hence develop quite naturally at an established centre of industry.

The industries which recorded no progress at all during the present phase are breweries, hydrogenated oil, oil mills and soap, and glass and glass products. Of these, three belong to agro-based group of industries and hence it appears that the present phase of industrial development is not favouring the growth of agro-based industries. The relatively dismal picture of agro-based industries in the city is not because of unfavourable conditions here for the growth of these industries but rather because of stiff competition with metal-consumimg engineering industries, which are much more value-added industries as compared to the former.

The industries that grew only moderately during the present phase include tin products, synthetic fibre, G.I. pipes and tubes, corrugated boxes, and tobacco products. Only one more new industry was added to the pre-existing list of important industries. This new industry of Ayurvedic and Unani medicines owes its development to the establishment of M/s. Dabur Industries, and Hamdard Laboratories here which employ 461 and 174 persons respectively.

Other important factories opened during the present phase included M/s. Amrit Steel Pvt. Ltd., Sarveshwari Gases Pvt. Ltd., Lal Chand Anand & Sons, Kissan Steels, Disco Bright Bars, Shakti Auto Valves & Engg. Corpn., L.N. Gadodia & Sons, Metal Board Containers, Tin Manufacturing Company of India, Precision Moulds and Dies, Zenith Electricals Pvt. Ltd., and Arneja Enterprises.

TABLE 2.4: **Industrial Structure 1981**

Name of the Industry	No. of regd. units	No.of regd. employment	Percentage of growth in terms of employment	Percentage share of the industry in the total regd. employment of the city
1. Electronics & Electricals	40	6247	263.82	16.55
2. Transport Equipments & their parts	25	3871	32.70	10.25
3. Primary Metal (Ferrous)	23	2053	18.80	5.44
4. Oil Engines & Agricultural Implements	70	2595	18.38	6.87
5. Cotton Textile	15	2831	77.93	7.50
6. G.I. Pipes & Tubes	11	1692	2.85	4.48
7. Tools & Gauges, & Moulds & Dies etc.	9	886	49.91	2.35
8. General Hardware	9	403	374.11	1.06
9. Utensils	7	400	115.05	1.06
10. Tin Products	7	1268	9.21	3.45
11. Machinery not elsewhere classified	25	1969	115.52	5.21
12. Hydrogenated oil	3	781	0.00	1.84
13. Chemical & Gases	19	615	172.12	1.62
14. Drugs & Medicines	7	419	20.40	1.11
15. Plastic & Foam Products	12	428	40.32	1.13
16. Synthetic Fibre	4	812	2.78	2.15
17. Paper Products	17	526	64.37	1.39
18. Corrugated Boxes	8	301	8.63	0.79
19. Structural Clay Products	12	831	39.51	2.20
20. Glass & Glass Products	3	906	0.00	2.40
21. Breweries	1	1452	0.00	3.85
22. Tobacco Products	2	545	10.32	1.44
23. Oil Mills & Soap	1	600	0.00	1.59
24. Ayurvedic & Unani Medicines	2	635	—	1.68
25. Misc. Industries including Casting & Forging Units.	120	4655	—	Remainder
Total	452	37731	68.06%	100.00

Source : Ibid., Table No. 1.1.

Spatially the present phase of industrial development witnessed the addition of site 4 industrial area (Fig. 8) which stretches over the tract lying between the road and railway line leading to New Delhi. This newly developed industrial area falls nearest to the New Delhi and as such has attracted entrepreneurs from both New Delhi and Ghaziabad. This comprises the largest industrial area of the city - still having a vast scope for future industrial expansion. The biggest firm of Ghaziabad viz. M/s. Bharat Electronics Ltd., a Govt. of India undertaking, employing 2850 persons is located in this industrial area and forms the nucleus of this latest addition to the industrial landscape of Ghaziabad.

Thus while concluding we may say that the process of industrial growth at Ghaziabad has been a complex multifunctional phenomenon.

CORRELATION BETWEEN GROWTH & DISPERSION OF INDUSTRIES AT GHAZIABAD.

Ghaziabad as is obvious from the foregoing account, has experienced a very fast industrial growth during the last thirty years. The process of industrial expansion continued almost uninterrupted, though the rate of industrial growth varied considerably during different decades.

Normally, the process of industrial growth is almost always associated with the process of dispersion of industries. The two processes generally go simultaneously. Dispersion, i.e. moving out of the new industrial units away from the city centre, becomes inevitable because there is not always enough space in the inner part of the city to accommodate growing industrial activity. Apart from the lack of space, there are certain other factors too which are responsible for dispersion of industries at a growing industrial centre, such as high cost of land, stiff competition, rate of female participation in the labour force, and orientation of firms towards national market etc.

Whatever may be the factors behind dispersion but the fact remains that whenever there is industrial growth, dispersion of industry must follow. Amount of dispersion may not be commensurate with the amount of growth, but no rapid industrial growth is feasible with no dispersion at all. Dispersion may occur in both the directions. When the earlier industrial units are established towards the margins of city and later growth of industries moves towards the city core, dispersion shows negative correlation with growth. However negative correlation between growth and dispersion of industries occurs only very rarely. Generally there is observed a high positive correlation between these two processes. In the forthcoming paras the hypothesis of growth and dispersion of industries, as being the two highly correlated processes has been tested in the case of Ghaziabad which has undergone a spectacular industrial expansion during the recent past.

Methodology

In the present study the authoress has measured the correlation between growth and dispersion of industries at Ghaziabad during the last 20 years period from 1961 to 1981. Although the modern industrial activity of city had started since 1940, but it was only by 1961 that city had assumed an industrial character in its full form and hence the year of 1961, has been taken as the base year. For measuring the correlation Spearman's rank difference method has been adopted. The formula employed to find out the correlation is as follows:

P (rho)

$$P = 1 - \frac{6 \Sigma D^2}{N(N^2-1)}$$

D represents the difference of ranks of two variables.

N represents the number of variables.

The two variables in this study are obviously the growth and dispersion of industries. Growth has been calculated in the form of percentage increase in the registered employment of sixteen main industries during the 20 years period from 1961 to 1981. In the year 1981, the number of important industries has however risen to 24 as illustrated in the table No. 2.4 but those industries which are not included in the list of important industries of 1961, have not been taken into consideration for the reason of practical difficulties. On the basis of 20 years growth of these sixteen industries, the rankshave been assigncd, the first rank being given to that industry which recorded highest percentage of increase in registered employment during the specified period.

TABLE 2.5: **Growth of Industries at Ghaziabad During the Period 1961-81.**

Name of the Industry	Registered Employment in 1961.	Registered Employment in 1981.	Percentage of Growth	Rank Order
1. Oil Engines & Agricultural Implements	928	2595	179.63	13
2. Electronics & Electrical Goods	577	6247	982.66	3
3. Transport Equipments or parts	1135	3871	240.66	12
4. Primary Metal (Ferrous)	205	2053	901.46	5
5. Cotton Textile	217	2831	1204.60	2
6. G.I. Pipes & Tubes	291	1692	481.44	9
7. Machinery not classified elsewhere	326	1969	503.98	8
8. General Hardware	40	403	907.50	4
9. Tools, Gauges, Moulds, Dies and Jigs & Fixtures etc.	103	886	620.32	6
10. Utensils	85	400	370.58	11
11. Tin Products	208	1208	509.61	7
12. Chemical & Gases	112	615	449.10	10
13. Hydrogenated oil	463	781	68.68	15
14. Drugs & Medicines	30	419	1296.66	1
15. Structural Clay Products	446	831	86.32	14
16. Breweries	1200	1452	21.00	16

Source: Ibid., Table No. 2.1.

For establishing the rank order of another variable, i.e. of dispersion, average distances of these sixteen industries have been calculated on the basis of straight line distances of the factories from C.B.D. (Central Business District). This was done with the help of two maps showing the locations of factories in 1961 and 1981. Jawahar Gate on G.T. Road was taken as representing the C.B.D. and straight line distances of the important factories of each industry were measured on sampling basis. In the present study 25% of the factories of each industry, located in different industrial areas were selected for measuring out the distances and on the basis of these distances, average distance of each industry was found out for both the years of 1961 and 1981. The differences in the average distances of two years yielded the increase or decrease in the average distance of an industry during the past 20 years. Rank order was established by giving highest rank to the industry which recorded greatest increase in the average distance and the lowest to that which recorded highest decrease in average distance during the specified period.

After establishing the rank order of both the variables, rank difference was known and then by using the aforesaid formula, the correlation between growth and dispersion was measured which stands as .31 only in the present study.

Analysis of Results:

The positive correlation of .31 as derived by the study shows that dispersion of industries has occurred, as the industries grew in the city. But this represents a case of low positive correlation while in view of the tremendous industrial growth of the city, one might have surely anticipated a higher positive correlation. All the new industrial areas of the city, which were developed by Ghaziabad Improvement Trust after its formation in 1960, are located at 5 to 10 km of distance from C.B.D. In view of the greater distances of newly developed industrial areas, it sounds quite untoward to believe that there exists only a low correlation between the growth and dispersion of industries at Ghaziabad. But we cannot disregard the authenticity of our results because our study is based on solid quantitative facts.

As has already been made clear in the beginning of this chapter, for all the purposes of this study, present municipal limits have been taken as base. thus while, calculating the average distances of industries in 1961, all the factories located upto present municipal limits were included for the study irrespective of the fact that they fell outside the municipal limits at that time. At Ghaziabad industries did not grow around one single nucleus but instead, there grew three nodes of industrial activity simultaneously during the earlier phase of industrial growth. These three industrial nodes were represented by Ghaziabad proper, Mohan Nagar and Sahibabad. At Ghaziabad proper initially there was only one industrial area, viz. Bulandshahr Road industrial area. However, by 1961 which has been

TABLE 2.6: **Change in the Average Distance of Industries at Ghaziabad During the Period 1961-81.**

Name of the Industry	D^1 Average distance in 1961 in km.	D^2 Average distance in 1981 in km.	D^2-D^1 Change in the distance	Rank Order
1. Oil Engines & Agricultural Implements	3.4	3.6	0.2	10.5
2. Electronics & Electricals	7.7	6.8	-0.9	14
3. Transport Equipments & Parts	7.2	5.8	-1.4	15
4. Primary Metal (Ferrous)	3.6	4.7	1.1	6.5
5. Cotton Textile	2.2	5.3	3.1	2
6. G.I. Pipes & Tubes	3.0	4.6	1.6	4
7. Machinery not classified elsewhere	7.5	6.0	-1.5	16
8. General Hardware	3.0	6.3	3.3	1
9. Tools & Gauges Moulds & Dies, & Jigs & Fixtures, etc.	4.3	5.4	1.1	6.5
10. Utensils	7.2	6.4	-0.8	13
11. Tin Products	2.0	4.7	2.7	3
12. Chemical & Gases	5.2	5.4	0.2	10.5
13. Hydrogenated Oil	2.5	3.7	1.2	5
14. Drugs & Medicines	6.0	6.3	0.3	9
15. Structural Clay Products	2.5	2.9	0.4	8
16. Breweries	4.2	4.2	0	12

Source: Average distances of the industries have been measured on the basis of straight line map distance of the factories from C.B.D.

taken as base year for the present study, there had developed one more new industrial area viz. Patel Marg-Mukand Nagar Industrial Area which lay nearest to the C.B.D. Industrial nodes of Mohan Nagar and Sahibabad are located at a distance 5 to 10 km from C.B.D. While calculating the average distance of different industries in 1961, factories of all the three industrial nodes were taken into account and as a result average distances of a number of important industries in 1961 were quite as much or very little less than those in 1981. Some industries have recorded even decrease in their average distance and this is the main reason why the correlation has amounted to a low positive of .31 despite the phenomenal growth of industries recorded in this period. A case study of twin cities of Kitchener-Waterloo also revealed somewhat similar type of results.[5] Apart from studying the correlation between growth and dispersion of industries at Kitchener-Waterloo, the authoress has also strived to find out the effect of female-participation on the shift of industries from the centre of gravity.

As regards dispersion of individual industries, significant increase on the average distance has been recorded in the case of general hardware, cotton textile, tin products, G.I. pipes, hydrogenated oil, primary metal, and tools and gauges. All these industries have recorded an increase of 3.3 to 1.1 km in their average distance from C.B.D. Greater dispersion of these industries has resulted because of major part of their industrial expansion taking place during sixtees, the period which marks the emergence of a number of new industrial areas such as those of Meerut Road, Loni Road, Rajendra Nagar, Anand Industrial Estate and Prakash Industrial Estate. All these new industrial areas are located at relatively greater distance of 5 to 10 km from C.B.D. The new units of these industries were located mostly in these new areas and this is the main reason why these industries have recorded significant dispersion during the last 20 years period.

Amongst the remaining industries breweries has recorded no change in the average distance because of no addition in the number of existing unit. Industries which have moved very little from the city core include structural clay products, drugs and medicines, chemicals and gases, and oil engines and agricultural implements. These industries have moved only from .2 to .4 km, denoting a very insignificant dispersion.

The reason for only marginal increase in the average distance of structural clay products industry is relatively lesser growth of this industry during the specified period. Other industries which indicate very marginal increase in the average distance viz. drugs and

TABLE 2.7: **Correlation Between Growth & Dispersion of Industries at Ghaziabad 1961-81**

Name of the Industry	Percentage of growth (1961-81)	Change in Average distance (1961-81)	Rank I	Rank II	Rank Diff.	Rank Diff.^{2} or D^2
1. Oil Engines & Agricultural Implements	179.63	0.2 km	13	10.5	2.5	6.25
2. Electronics & Electrical Goods	982.66	-0.9	3	14	11	121
3. Transport Equipments & Parts	240.66	-1.4 "	12	15	3	9
4. Primary Metal (Ferrous)	901.46	1.1 "	5	6.5	1.5	2.25
5. Cotton Textile	1204.60	3.1 "	2	2	0	0
6. G.I. Pipes and Tubes	481.44	1.6 "	9	4	5	25
7. Machinery not classified elsewhere	503.98	-1.5 "	8	16	8	64
8. General Hardware	907.50	3.3 "	4	1	3	9
9. Tools & Gauges, Moulds & Dies & Jigs & Fixtures, etc.	620.32	1.1 "	6	6.5	.5	.25
10. Utensils	370.58	-0.8 "	11	13	2	4
11. Tin Products	509.61	2.7 "	7	3	4	16
12. Chemical & Gases	449.10	0.2 "	10	10.5	.5	.25
13. Hydrogenated Oil	68.68	1.2 "	15	5	10	100
14. Drugs & Medicines	1296.66	0.3 "	1	9	8	64
15. Structural Clay Products	86.32	0.4 "	14	8	6	36
16. Breweries	21.00	0 km	16	12	4	16
					$\sum D^2$	473

Coefficient of Correlation $= 1 - 6\sum D^2/N(N^2-1)$
$= 1 - 6 \times 473/16\,(16^2-1)$
$= 1 - 2838/16 \times 255$
$= 1 - 2838/4080 = 1 - .69 = .31$ (.31 means Low Positive Correlation.)

medicines, chemical and gases, and oil engines and agricultural implements are those which have recorded a very high percentage of growth. Despite a prodigious growth rate, they have moved very little from the C.B.D. Lesser increase in their average distance can be attributed to the marked concentration of each of these industries in any one single industrial area of the city. The industry of drugs and medicines has 84.73% of its registered employment in Meerut Road industrial area only. On the other hand more than 50% of oil engine and agricultural implements industry is concentrated in Patel Marg Mukand Nagar area. Chemicals and gases show a marked concentration in Bulandshahr Road industrial area which contains more than 40% of its total registered employment.

As the present study reveals, four of the main industries of Ghaziabad have also registered a decrease in their average distance. These industries which have come nearer to the city in the process of their growth, include other types of machinery, transport equipments and parts, electronics and electricals, and utensils. They have registered a decrease of 1.5, 1.4, .9 and .8 km respectively. The decrease in the average distance of these industries seems quite unbecoming at the first instance and more so because two out of these four, viz. electronics and electricals and transport equipments and their parts, form the first two largest groups of industries in the city which have recorded a very good progress throughout. However, a little probing into the past clears all the doubts. These are the industries which were started at the industrial node of Sahibabad during the earlier phases. Later on when these industries grew, they spread to other parts of the city as well. Because Sahibabad stands at the farthest distance from C.B.D., the average distance of these industries has decreased, despite remarkable percentage of growth maintained by them.

REFERENCES

1. Information gathered from the Inspector of Factories Office, Nehru Nagar, Ghaziabad.
2. Directory and who is who of Ghaziabad's Industries—1974, published by All Indian Manufacturers Organization, U.P. State Board, Ghaziabad.
3. Patni, R.L. (1968), A New Method for Measuring Locational Changes in a Manufacturing Industry, Economic Geography, 44, 210-217.
   Morrison, J.L. (1968), Basic Measures of Manufacturing in the United States, 1958, 'Economic Geography', 44, 296-311.
4. Gilmour, J.M. (1966), The Joint Anarchy of Confidentiality and Definitional Change, 'Canadian Geographer', 10, 40-48.
5. Baleshwar Thakur—'Intra-Urban Location of Manufacturing: A Test of the Hypothesis of Spatial Changes.' Deccan Geographer, Vol. XVII, No. 1, 1979, pp. 1 to 7.

Fig. 5
GHAZIABAD : INDUSTRIAL LANDSCAPE 1951

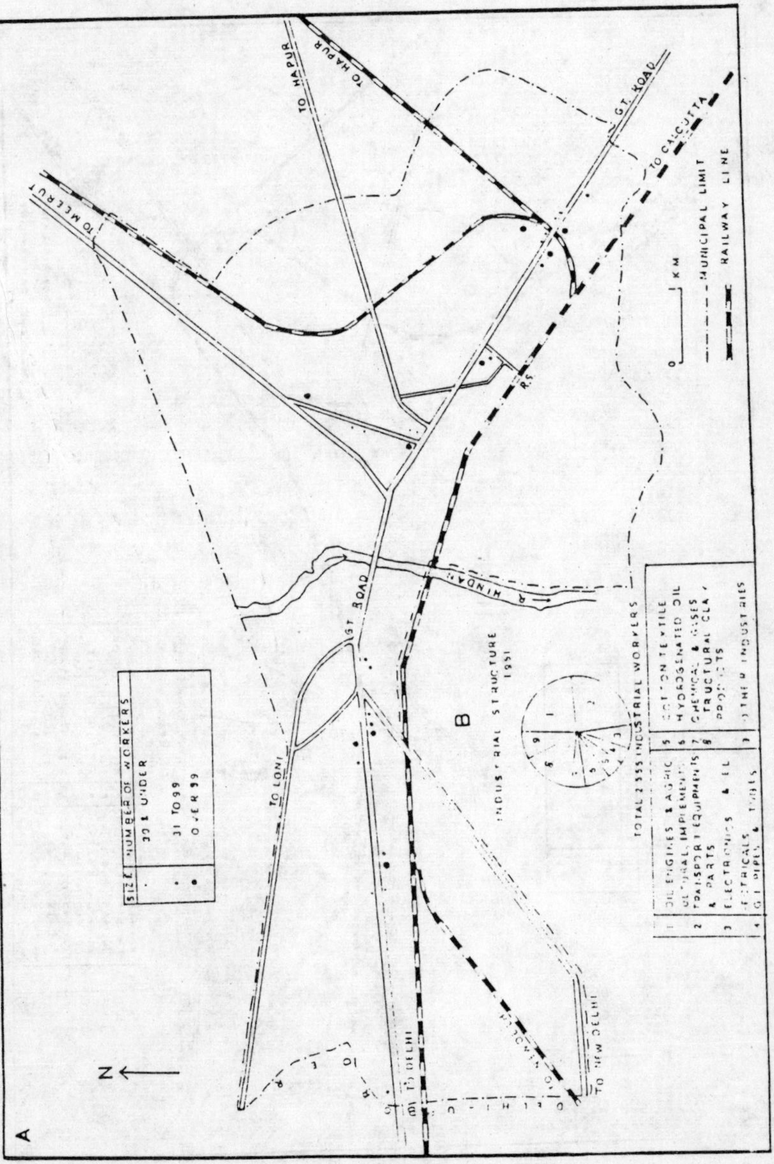

Fig. 6
GHAZIABAD : INDUSTRIAL LANDSCAPE 1961

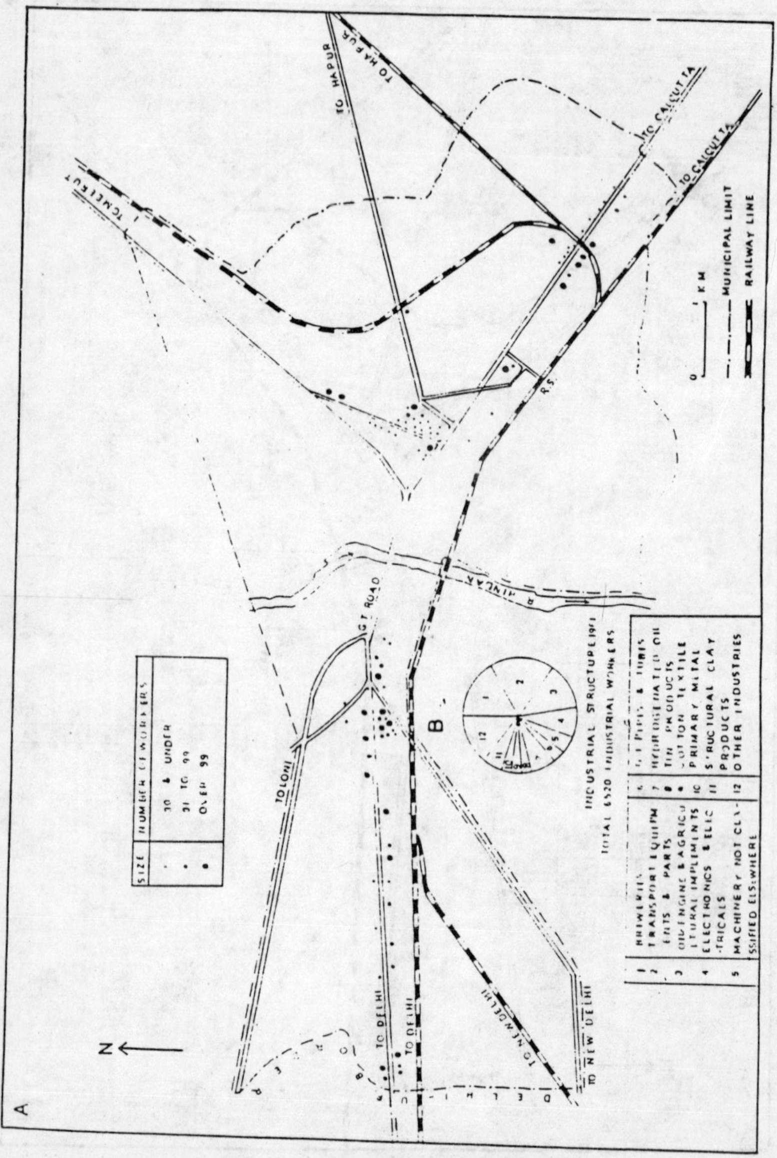

Fig. 7
GHAZIABAD : INDUSTRIAL LANDSCAPE 1971

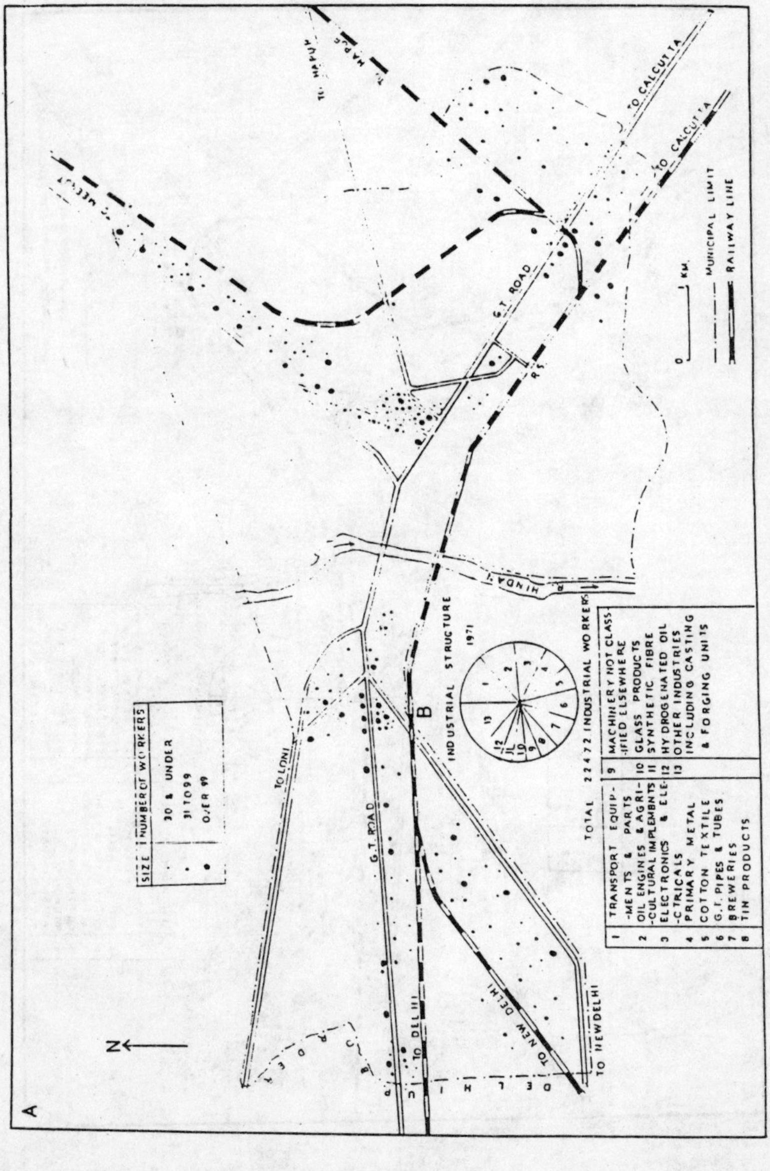

Fig. 8

GHAZIABAD : INDUSTRIAL LANDSCAPE 1981

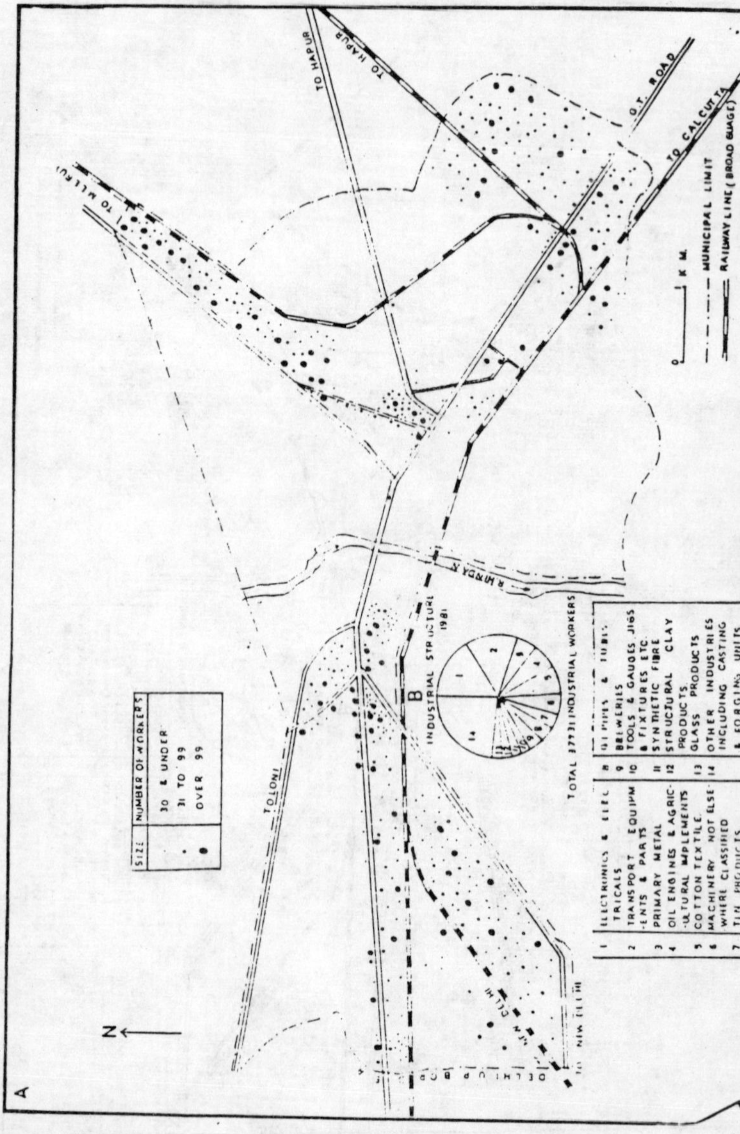

THREE

Spatial Pattern of Industrial Land-Use at Ghaziabad.

Ghaziabad, a small Tahsil town with a very limited industrial activity until 1951, today ranks amongst the dominant industrial cities of not only U.P. but whole of Northern India. Because of its growing industrial significance, Ghaziabad was carved out as a separate district in Nov. 1976 by taking territories from adjoining Meerut and Bulandshahr districts. Previously it used to be part of Meerut district.

The rapid industrial development during last three decades has brought about distinct changes in the city's industrial landscape, a fact which attracted the attention of urban geographers, city planners, and economists. Urban area given to industrial land-use has increased to 2261.17 acres of land in 1981.[1] Spectacular industrial growth has compelled the municipal authorities to extend the municipal limits thrice during the past 30 years. (fig. No. 1). In 1951 city covered an area of only 4.29 sq. kilometers while today it is spread over an area of 46.47 sq. km.[2] Largest expansion in the city area occurred in 1967 when large tract of trans-Hindan area up to Delhi-U.P. border was incorporated within Municipal limits. Because of greater size of the city, 'Ghaziabad Improvement trust' which played pivotal role in the industrial expansion of the city, has now been converted into prestigious 'Ghaziabad Development Authority' since 1979.

The tremendous industrial growth during past three decades has weighed upon heavily on city's urban requirements. In the present chapter an attempt has been made to depict and analyse an overall picture of industrial landscape in Ghaziabad. The study in this chapter is based upon the findings of industrial employment figures in different industrial areas of the city and also the employment data, of different industries in each area. These figures have been tabulated with the help of list of factories 1981 obtained from Inspector of Factories' Office, Ghaziabad. The list contained the addresses of registered factories together with the number of employees in each unit. Categorization of different types of industries was done on the basis of field survey of each industrial area.

The main purpose of the study in this chapter is to find out at Ghaziabad the areas of spatial concentration of industries and also the functional characteristics of each of these areas. On the basis of spatial arrangement of various industries within the city, the authoress has also attempted to evolve a typology of Ghaziabad's industries with respect to their intra-urban locations.

A close look at the industrial map of Ghaziabad (fig.8) indicates that the industrial activity in the city does not characterize a uniform distribution. There are distinct areas of industrial clustering with varying degree of concentration. Moreover, the industry covers a wide variety of activities ranging from breweries, cigarettes, hydrogenated oil, fruit juices and handloom textiles etc. which all belong to the group of consumer goods Agro-based industries, to oil engines, primary metal, transport equipments, different types of industrial machinery, electronics, tools and gauges, and G.I. pipes etc. which are all metal-consuming high value-added industries. Chemicals and gases, potteries, synthetic fibre, plastic and foam products, drugs and medicines, paper and paper board, tin containers, glass and glass products, and abrasives also figure amongst the important industries of Ghaziabad. So varied and vast is the manufacturing activity here, that it becomes really challenging to comprehend the whole industrial set-up over a limited space.

Not only do we find a great variety in the functional pattern of industries, but also in the pattern of industrial land-use which has emerged as a result of complex inter-play of the numerous factors of the physical and cultural environments of the city. Ghaziabad's industries as we all know have grown in a planned and systematic way during the last two decades. The first decade of industrial expansion no doubt witnessed a haphazard growth but even at that time industry did not intrude much in the inner zone of the city proper. Barring a few important concerns like Delhi Iron & Steel Company, Guru Nanak Engineering Co. and Chaudhary Hammer Works, which occupy central positions with respect to C.B.D., rest of the concerns sought locations mainly towards the margins of the city specially along the radial highways, leading to Bulandshahr, Meerut and Delhi. Later on during the planned phases of industrial development in sixtees and seventees, the industries grew in well-demarcated industrial areas located along highways. At present we can distinguish three distinct industrial zones located in three different directions along highways towards the margins of the city. Obviously except a few concerns, there is no inner zone of industry in Ghaziabad as suggested by Burgess in 1925.[3] His model of concentric zone theory of city structure containing an inner zone of heavy industry was actually meant for pre-existing towns wherein the later growth of industry took its position towards the margins or outside the city. Ghaziabad is no doubt a sufficiently old town with its inception dating back to 1740 and the introduction of railways in the year 1865 had lent the city the position of an important urban centre in the neighbourhood of Delhi but there was no sign of modern industrial activity until 1940 when was established the first important factory of Ghaziabad namely, M/s. Amrit Vanaspati Company Ltd., a famous hydrogenated oil manufacturing concern even to-date. During forties sprang up a few important concerns e.g. M/s. Ghaziabad Engineering Company, Asia Chemicals, Webbing and Belting Factory Pvt. Ltd., Guru Nanak Engineering Company and Punjab Oil Expellers etc., but most of these industrial units were established towards the margins of the city and the city core remained almost free from industrial encroachment. By the time, industrial significance of the situation of Ghaziabad was fully realized i.e. since after fifties when Delhi became overcrowded and faced the problems of lack of space and other civic amenities, the inner part of the city of Ghaziabad had already been filled up by other types of urban land uses viz. commercial, administrative, railways, educational and residential etc. and thus there was no question of industry taking position near C.B.D. in the city proper. Burgess's theory of concentric zones for describing urban land-uses seems quite out of place in the case of Ghaziabad's industrial land use pattern. His model of concentric zones theory has been rejected by urban Geographers mainly on two major grounds. Firstly his model was designed keeping in view the particular situation at a particular time in a particular country and secondly he emphasizes clear-cut boundaries which are not possible on the basis of the gradient study. He is accused of 'drawing lines that don't exist around areas that don't matter.'[4] His model remains useful only as a first approximation regarding the urban land-uses.

The pattern of industrial land-use at Ghaziabad however does reflect some conformity to Hoyt's sectoral theory of urban land-use.[5] Hoyt's main work concerned with the examination of rent areas for residential purposes in twenty five widely distributed cities in U.S.A. and on the basis of the results of his study, he formulated his famous sectoral theory of urban land-use. He suggested that different types of urban land-uses tend to conform to a pattern of sectors rather than of concentric zones. These sectors are generally extended outward along communication lines which exercise the most dominant influence on their formation. Apart from the places along communication lines, these sectors may develop also elsewhere within the city's perimeter such as high ground free from the danger of flood, open country without any physical barrier, and on areas which lie nearer to C.B.D. Some land-uses attract each other e.g. high quality residential areas and outlying business centres often form adjoining sectors while some other land uses repel other such as heavy industry and high class residential areas. They will form sectors quite apart from each other. In Hoyt's sectoral theory, it is the directional element rather than distance which exercises dominant influence on city's urban morphology and the sectors result mainly because of the operation of directional element.

Ghaziabad's industrial land-use clearly suggests a sectoral arrangement. A close look at the industrial map of the city (fig. 8) clearly gives an indication of the operation of directional force being more important than distance factor. Industries have expanded at an unprecedented rate in the trans-Hindan tract of the city in the direction towards Delhi despite the increasing distance from C.B.D. About 60% of the employment in registered industrial units is found in trans-Hindan tract or sector while remaining 40% lies in industrial zones along Bulandshahr Road and Meerut Road which are located at about half or even less than half, the distance of trans-Hindan Tract from city core.

Multiple-nuclei theory propounded by C.D. Harris and E.L. Ullman also conforms to some extent to Ghaziabad's industrial land-use pattern.[6] The present city limits include three nuclei, namely Ghaziabad proper, Mohan Nagar and Sahibabad. It was mainly because of rapidly growing industrialization around these nuclei that they have now coalesced into one big industrial city. Here it should be noted that Mohan Nagar and Sahibabad started acting as separate nuclei only after the establishment of some important industries there and hence we can say that in integrating these separate nuclei, industry alone exercised the most dominant influence.

In the foregoing pages, we have discussed the city's industrial land-scape as a whole but the study of whole cannot be complete unless we study the parts that comprise it and hence a brief description of the individual industrial zones of the city is needed.

1. *South Eastern Industrial Zone*:

Popularly known as Bulandshahr Road Industrial Area, this industrial zone constitutes the oldest and one of the two most important industrial areas of the city proper containing 106 industrial units which employ 7094 persons annually. In terms of industrial employment, this industrial zone shares 18.8% of the total registered industrial employment in the city. It covers a large area on both the sides of G.T. Road in S. En. Part of the city. In the north this area extends uptil New Kavi Nagar, in the south uptil national Bye-pass Road, in the east uptil municipal limits and in the west it merges with the commercial hub of the city which occupies quite a large stretch of G.T. Road in the En. half of Ghaziabad. This industrial zone comprises a rectangular block whose North-South extent is greater than East-West Extent.

Amongst all the industrial areas of the city, S.E. industrial Zone enjoys the special privilege of being nearest to the C.B.D. It stands at a distance of only 2 to 5 kms from the city centre, a fact which stimulated the rapid industrial growth in this area in the earlier phase. Apart from its nearness to the city centre, another great advantage of this industrial zone is the vast scope for expansion specially towards the North. It covers relatively larger area than that occupied by Meerut Road Industrial area which is spread over an elongated tract on the Eastward side of the state highway. Despite being near to the city, this industrial zone characterizes a location near the margins of the city and this has lent this industrial zone further attraction for the localization of industries here. Whole industrial set up is free from the din and noise of the city but at the same time it is so near to the city core.

TABLE 3.1: **Relative Positions of Different Industrial Zones of Ghaziabad**

Name of the Industrial zone	No. of regd. Units	No. of persons employed	Percentage share in terms of employment.
S.En. Indl. Zone	106	7094	18.8%
N.E. Central Indl. Zone	104	7018	18.6%
Trans-Hindan Indl. Zone	226	22638	60.0%
City Core or C.B.D.	16	981	2.6%
Total	452	37731	100.0%

Source: Figures tabulated from the list of Factories 1981 obtained from the Inspector of Factories' office, Nehru Nagar, Ghaziabad, which contained the addresses and number of employees of all registered industrial units at Ghaziabad.

Nucleus of this industrial zone was laid down in the year 1940 when M/s. Amrit Vanaspati Company Ltd. was located here along G.T. Road. At that time this factory stood outside the municipal limits characterizing a suburban location. Today it is one of the three leading hydrogenated oil concerns of the city. Another important concern viz. M/s. Ghaziabad Engineering Co. came about in 1944 and in the following few years this industrial zone witnessed the establishment of a chain of important industrial concerns viz. M/s. Asia Chemicals, M/s. Webbing and Belting Factory (1947), U.P. Ceramics & Potteries (1948), Hindustan Lever Ltd. (1952) and Hindustan Tin Works (1959). Almost all early industrial units of this zone except U.P. Ceramics & Potteries sought their location along G.T. Road and another characteristic feature of this area was the dominance of hydrogenated oil followed by cotton textile, potteries, agricultural implements and Tin products industries here until 1961.

After the formation of Ghaziabad Improvement Trust and the introduction of Ghaziabad Master Plan in 1960 large tracts of land on both the sides of G.T. Road were developed as industrial areas and the industries started moving Northward and Southward of the National Highway. During sixtees and seventees not only there occurred a large expansion in the industrial area, but also there was a marked change in the trend and nature of industrial expansion. During this period there sprang up a number of mini iron and steel mills and agricultural machinery manufacturing units. Being nearer to the railway station, assembling of iron and coal was comparatively easier in this industrial area and hence there occurred a heavy concentration of metal-based industries during last two decades. Area south of G.T. Road specially has greater concentration of primary metal industries, because it has the easiest access to railways. Here we find a number of important concerns manufacturing primary metal products such as M/s. Rathi Alloys Ltd., Rathi Spat, Rathi Udyog, Sachdeva Steel Casting, and Sarin Steel Industries, which are all located in the area south of G.T. Road. Apart from these primary metal products manufacturing units, there is also the famous M/s. Hind Cycles Ltd. located in the area south of G.T. Road. This is a public sector undertaking and the second biggest industrial unit of this area, the first being M/s. Rathi Alloys Ltd. With the establishment of Rathi Group of Industries, which own three concerns in this area, so conspicuous was the concentration of metal based industries here that since 1970 this area began to be appropriately called as 'Spat Nagar'.

Area North of G.T. Road which characterizes a wide variety of industrial activities viz. structural clay products, synthetic fibre, chemicals and gases, plastic and foam products, electronics, paper and paper-board etc., also depicts a distinct concentration of metal-based industries. The important metal-consuming factories of this part of S.En. Industrial Zone are M/s. Kissan Steel Pvt. Ltd., Sansar Foundry, Chaudhary & Sons Forging, Ruby Forging, and Atma Steel Pvt. Ltd. Primary metal industries form the largest group of industries in terms of registered industrial employment in S.En. Industrial Zone. Next in order are Structural Clay Products, Synthetic fibre, Transport Equipments and parts, oil engines, hydrogenated oil, Cotton textile, chemical and gases, tin products and plastic and foam products. Apart from the above mentioned 10 industrial groups, other industries of S.En. industrial zone are Electronics, machinery, G.I. pipes, general hardware, tools and gauges, corrugated boxes, paper and paper board and cold storages.

TABLE 3.2: **Relative Positions of Different Industries in South Eastern Industrial Zone**

Name of the Industrial Group	Total regd. employment in the area	Percentage share of the ind. in the area	Location quotient of the industry in the area
1. Primary Metal Industries (Ferrous)	1598	77.83	4.14
2. Structural Clay Products	803	96.63	5.14
3. Synthetic Fibre	717	88.30	4.69
4. Transport Equipments and their Parts	527	13.61	0.59
5. Oil Engines and other Agricultural Implements	471	18.15	0.97
6. Hydrogenated Oil	463	59.28	3.15
7. Cotton Textiles	271	9.57	0.51
8. Chemical & Gases	247	40.16	2.14
9. Tin Products	234	18.45	0.98
10. Electronics & Electricals	367	5.87	0.31
11. Plastic & Foam Products	48	11.21	0.59
12. Others including casting and Forging Units	1348	—	—
Total	7094	18.8%	

**SOURCE*:Figures calculated by the researcher herself with the help of the list of factories 1981 and field survey.

Amongst structural clay products, potteries and Refractories are the main industries M/s. U.P. Ceramics and Potteries Ltd. is the famous concern of potteries enjoying all India fame in this industrial zone. M/s.Lal Chand Anand & Sons is the biggest refractory of this area. Important concerns of other main groups are M/s. Swadeshi Polytex Ltd., Hind Cycles Ltd., Azad Engineering Company, Amrit Vanaspati Co. Ltd. and Hindustan lever Ltd., Webbing and Belting

Factory Pvt. Ltd., Asia Chemicals, Sarveshri Gases, Hindustan Tin Works and Kakkar Fuels Pvt. Ltd..

S.En. Industrial zone, though having a wide variety of industries, characterizes an industrial area with relatively smaller industrial units. Except M/s. Hind Cycles Ltd. which is a public sector industrial unit, all other factories represent private sector enterprises which are mostly of small to medium size. No factory in this area employs more than 500 persons. The biggest two factories are M/s. Rathi Alloys & Steel Ltd. and U.P. Ceramics & Potteries Ltd., which employ 450 to 446 persons respectively. Other big factories employing 200 to 400 persons are M/s. Hind Cycles Ltd., Hindustan Lever Ltd., Rathi Spat Ltd., Hindustan Tin Works, and Electronics Industries of India Ltd. There are only 16 factories in this area which employ above 100 persons. Quite a large number of factories in this industrial zone are those which employ less then 10 persons and hence are unregistered under Factories Act.

As regards concentration of different industries, as is evident from Table No. 3.2 (fig. No. 9) heaviest concentration occurs in the case of structural clay products synthetic fibre, primary metal, hydrogenated oil and chemicals and gases in order of priority. Location quotient in this area ranges between 2 and 6 in the case of above mentioned five industrial groups. In terms of industrial employment, however, primary metal Group holds the first place in this region but in terms of percentage share of the industry in the region, structural clay products, and synthetic fibre industries hold first and second place respectively. Registered employment of these two industries is only 50% of the primary metal Group. Location quotient denotes the concentration in view of industry's percentage share in the region irrespective of total share of that industry in the city's industrial setup. If the location quotient is more than unity, it implies that industry has greater share and hence greater concentration.

$$\text{Location Quotient} = \frac{\text{Percentage share of the industrial area in the total registered employment of a particular industry}}{\text{Percentage share of the Industrial area in the total registered industrial workforce of the city.}}$$

Other industries of the region which denote location quotient of less than unity but above .5 are tin products, oil-engines, transport equipments, plastic and foam products, and cotton textiles. These industries, though having lesser share in the area as compared to the area's share in the total industrial set-up, nevertheless constitute amongst the important industries of this zone. In the case of other industries location quotient is less than .5 and hence it follows that they are more important in the other industrial areas of the city. To this category may be mentioned electronics and electrical goods, pipes and tubes, general hardware, machinery, paper and paper board, corrugated boxes and tobacco products. Industries which are totally absent in this industrial area but are important in the city's industrial structure, are breweries, glass and glass products, drugs and medicines, and oil mills and soap.

2. *North East Central Industrial Zone*:

This zone is popularly known as Meerut Road Industrial Area. It includes industrial establishments along Meerut Road, Patel Marg and Mukand Nagar. Patel Marg and Mukand Nagar are parts of the city proper. All earlier established factories of this zone are located along Patel Marg and in Mukand Nagar. Meerut Road Industrial Area was developed during sixtees. As compared to S.En. Industrial zone Meerut Road Industrial Area is much younger but now it is in no way less significant than its S.En. counterpart. There are 104 registered industrial units in this zone employing 7018 persons representing 18.6% of the total registered industrial employment in the city.

This industrial zone occupies an elongated tract along Patel Marg and Meerut Road. Factories along Meerut Road start only after Patel Marg terminates into Meerut Road. Meerut Road industrial area is confined only to the Eastward side of the road, between state highway and corresponding railway line. The area on the other side of the road is included in the Green Belt as per Ghaziabad's Master Plan. This area was abandoned for industrial use mainly for the fear of the flood, because being a low lying area, it is liable to be flooded when River Hindan is in spate. There is very little scope for future expansion in this industrial zone. It can expand only along the Meerut side of the highway by extending the city limits further North. The biggest of three concerns of this area include M/s. Jain Tube Company, Shri Ram Piston & Rings, and Poysha Industrial Corpn., which employ 1178, 935 and 850 persons respectively. Other important concerns of this area are M/s. Unichem Laboratories, Danfoss India Ltd., Mascot (India) Tools & Forgings Pvt. Ltd., Johnson Pumps, Jain Sudh Vanaspati, International Tobacco, Hamdard Laboratories, Hindustan Monarch, Punjab Oil Expellers, Shri Guru Nanak Engineering Company, Road Master Industries of India, and S.W. Rubber Works.

In Patel Marg and Mukand Nagar localities of N.E. Central Industrial Zone, industries and residential area have intermingled with each other. This is because here the industries grew in an unplanned way during the first decade after independence while Meerut Road Industrial Area which was developed in a planned way by Ghaziabad Improvement Trust during sixtees represents an area exclusively devoted to industrial land-use. This industrial area experienced a phenomenal growth of industries during sixtees but in the preceding and current decade industrial expansion has somewhat slackened because of lack of space. Industries have already taken positions uptil municipal limits and as such no new industrial plots are being provided for entrepreneurs. However due to industrial utility of the site, new factories are still coming up over pre-existing industrial plots. A field survey of the area shows many new sufficiently large factories which are in the erection stage and therefore not included in the list of registered factories of the 1981.

As has already been said, N.E. Central Industrial Zone includes two such localities which form parts of the main city. Obviously these localities fall nearer to C.B.D., being only less than 2 kms away from it but the major part of N.E. Central Zone i.e. Meerut Road Industrial Area is quite apart from city, standing at about 4 to 8 kms away from C.B.D. Despite greater distance, industries flourished here firstly because of the infrastructure facilities provided by the Govt. Secondly location of this industrial zone along Meerut Road state highway benefitted from the easy accessibility to both Delhi and Meerut. Patel Nagar and Mukand Nagar area of N.E. Central Industrial Zone assumed an industrial character only towards late fiftees when here were established a number of oil engine manufacturing factories, e.g. M/s. Shri Guru Nanak Engineering Company, National Steel & General Mills, Shri Ram Engineering Company,

Layalpur Engineering Company, and Swastika Engineering company etc. However, the nucleus of this industrial zone was laid down as early as 1948 with the establishment of M/s. Punjab Oil Expeller Co. near Patel Marg and Meerut Road crossing. With the establishment of a number of factories in Patel Marg and Mukand Nagar, the industrial potentialities of the site were realized and eventually Meerut Road industrial area was developed with the efforts of Ghaziabad Improvement Trust to accommodate the growing industrialization in this part of the city.

A glance at the functional pattern of industries in N.E. Central Industrial Zone (fig. 10) reveals heavy concentration here of metal fabricating industries, unlike S.E. Industrial Zone which is distinguished as one with a heavy concentration of primary metal industries. In terms of registered industrial employment the major metal fabricating industries of this zone in order of importance are transport equipments and their parts, G.I. pipes and tubes, tin containers, machinery not classified elsewhere, electronics and electrical goods, and tools and gauges. The important concerns manufacturing transport equipments and their parts are M/s. Shri Ram Piston & Rings, Hindustan Monarch, and Road Master Industries of India. M/s. Shri Ram Pistons & Rings Ltd. is the second biggest factory of this area which manufactures pistons and rings for auto vehicles. The other two concerns manufacture bicycle parts. M/s. Jain Tube Company Ltd., the biggest concern of the area with 1178 employees, is the famous concern manufacturing G.I. pipes and tubes. M/s. Poysha Industrial Corporation the third biggest factory in the area with 850 employees is the famous tin-containers manufacturing unit.

Oil engines and agricultural Implements manufacturing units are located mainly along Patel Marg and Mukand Nagar viz. M/s. punjab Oil Expeller Company, Guru Nanak Engineering Company, Shri Ram Engineering Company, Layalpur Engineering Company, and Swastika Engineering Company.

Other metal fabricating industries of N.E. Central Zone include manufacturing of different types of industrial machinery, electronics and electrical goods and tools and gauges. The famous machinery manufacturing concerns are M/s. Danfoss India Ltd., Micromatic Machines, Macneill and Magor, Dewrance and Macneill Pvt. Ltd., and Pulling and Lifting Machines Pvt. Ltd. These concerns manufacture refrigerator parts, photostat machinery, cranes and several other types of machinery. M/s. Zeta Industrial Corporation Pvt. Ltd., and Electric Construction & Equipment Company Ltd., are the concerns manufacturing electrical goods and M/s. Mascot India Ltd. is the famous tools manufacturing concern in this area.

Apart from the metal fabricating industries mentioned above, other main industries of N.E. Central Zone are tobacco products, drugs and medicines, hydrogenated oil, paper and paper board, plastic and foam products, and Unani medicines. The important concerns of these industries are M/s. International Tobacco Company, Unichem Laboratories, Jain Sudh Vanaspati Ltd., Ganesh Paper Mill, B.K. Plastic Pvt. Ltd. and Hamadard Laboratories.

TABLE 3.3: **Relative Positions of Different Industries in North East Central Industrial Zone**

Name of the Industrial Group	Persons employed (registered)	Percentage share of the industry in the area.	Location Quotient of the industry in the area.
1. Transport Equipments & Parts	1457	37.64	2.02
2. G.I. pipes & Tubes	1289	76.18	4.09
3. Tin Products	865	68.22	3.67
4. Oil Engines & Agricultural Implements	801	30.87	1.67
5. Machinery not classified elsewhere	619	31.44	1.70
6. Electronics & Electrical Goods	447	7.15	0.38
7. Tools-Gauges, Moulds and Dies.	407	45.94	2.47
8. Drugs & Medicines	355	84.73	4.55
9. Hydrogenated Oil	318	40.72	2.12
10. Tobacco Products	494	90.64	5.51
11. Paper & Paper Board	209	39.73	2.14
12. Plastic & Foam Products	72	16.82	0.90
13. Ayurvedic & Unani Medicines	174	27.40	1.21
14. Utensils	78	19.50	1.05

Source: Ibid., Table No. 3.2.

Location quotients calculated for different industries in N.E. Central Zone as given in the Table No. 3.3 suggest a totally different functional set-up of industries in this area. Here tobacco products, drugs and medicines, G.I. pipes and tubes, tin products, tools and gauges, paper and board, hydrogenated oil and transport equipments have greater share in this zone and hence denote a heavy concentration each having locational quotient above 2. Other main industries of this area except electronics and electricals, and plastic and foam products, denote locational quotient of above unity but less than 2. Thus almost all the important industries in this area show a tendency toward concentration, a fact which signifies a very sound industrial base of this zone.

It is to be noted that many of the most important industries of S.En. Industrial zone viz. Structural clay products, synthetic fibre, primary metal, chemical and gases are almost totally absent or negligible in this zone. Other industries which are not present in this area are cotton textile, glass and glass products and breweries. Amongst the less important industries of this zone may be included rubber products, food industries, oil mills and soap. Functional attributes of this industrial zone simultaneously depict variation and concentration, a fact which has resulted in the emergence of this industrial zone as a vital part in the industrial landscape of Ghaziabad city.

3. *Trans-Hindan Industrial Zone*:

This is the largest industrial zone of the city representing about 50% of the total registered units and 60% of the total registered industrial employment in the city. Western half of the city where this industrial zone lies characterizes a typical landscape which is predominantly industrial with other types of urban land-uses having a very small share in the total set-up. Generally industrial development precedes urban growth but here it seems that the industrial growth has gone far too ahead of the other urban functions. Lying between Delhi on the west and Ghaziabad proper in the east, this part of the city gets its urban needs fulfilled from both the sides and this is perhaps the reason why the development of urban functions other than industrial has suffered a setback here and consequently Trans-Hindan tract of Ghaziabad has emerged as the major and most dominant industrial belt of the city. Spatially this is the largest and most extensive industrial area of the city which includes the industrial establishments along G.T. Road, New Delhi Road and Loni Road and also those located in Sahibabad Industrial Area, Mohan

Nagar and Rajendra Nagar Industrial Area. All these areas form a more or less compact zone with a very small share of land occupied by other types of urban land uses viz. commercial, residential and administrative.

Initially Trans-Hindan Industrial zone of Ghaziabad grew as a sub-urban industrial node falling outside the municipal limits. M/s. Modern Industries, Flow More, Peerless Foundry, Meera Chemicals, and Pyare Lal & Sons are some of the earliest concerns of this area. All these factories represented isolated locations and there was no sign of any industrial clustering until 1958 when was established the famous M/s. Mohan Meakins Breweries Ltd. in Mohan Nagar along G.T. Road near Loni Road crossing. Establishment of this reputed concern which is the second largest concern of Ghaziabad after M/s. Bharat Electronics Ltd. heralded a new era of industrial growth in Trans-Hindan Tract. The area around this factory which is called Mohan Nagar after the name of its founder acts as the nucleus of this Industrial Zone. It is here that the roads from New Delhi and Loni, meet G.T. Road. The three radial transport lines (New Delhi Road, G.T. Road and Loni Road) form the three major industrial belts of this area. Apart from road side establishments, industries have also taken position off side the main roads e.g. in Anand Industrial Estate, Prakash Industrial Estate, Rajendra Nagar Industrial Area, Sahibabad Industrial Area and Pasaunda. Before 1967 Ghaziabad's municipal limits extended only upto River Hindan. It was only because of growing industrialization in the trans-Hindan Tract that whole of this area uptil Delhi-U.P. Border was incorporated within Municipal limits in 1967.

The industrial growth in trans-Hindan zone has occurred in three phases. Uptil 1960, almost all industrial units chose their location along G.T. Road e.g. M/s. Mohan Meakins Breweries, Peerless Foundry, Flow More Pvt. Ltd., Pyare Lal & Sons, Jaina Time Industries all signifying roadside location along National Highway. During sixtees Loni Road, Sahibabad and Rajendra Nagar Industrial areas were developed and here were established quite a large number of important factories during this period. The important factories set up along Loni Road, during sixtees are M/s. Tata Oil Mills, Harsha Tractors, Reinz Talbros, Alps Textiles Pvt. Ltd., and Ajanta Textiles. Industrial establishment set up in Sahibabad Industrial area and along G.T. Road during sixtees are M/s. Dass Hitachi Pvt. Ltd., Harig India Pvt. Ltd., Delhi Steel Industries, John Okay Mohan Ltd., Abilities India Ltd., Dates Disc, and Victor Cables Corpn. etc.

TABLE 3.4: **Trans-Hindan Industrial Zone**

Name of the Industry	Regd. Indl. Employment	Percentage share of industry in the area	Location Quotient
1. Electronics & Electrical Goods	5407	86.56%	1.44
2. Transport Equipments & their parts	1887	48.75%	.81
3. Breweries	1452	100.00%	1.66
4. Glass & Glass Products	906	100.00%	1.66
5. Machinery not classified elsewhere	1226	62.27%	1.04
6. Oil Engines & Agricultural Implements	682	26.28%	0.44
7. Cotton Textiles	2511	88.70%	1.48
8. Oil Mills & Soap	600	100.00%	1.66
9. Ayurvedic Medicines	461	72.60%	1.21
10. Tools, Gauges, Moulds and Dies	424	47.85%	0.80
11. Chemical & Gases	352	57.24%	0.95
12. Utensils	309	77.25%	1.29
13. General Hardware	381	94.54%	1.58
14. G.I. Pipes & Tubes	306	18.09%	0.30
15. Plastic & Foam Products	308	71.97%	1.20
16. Corrugated Boxes	283	94.02%	1.57
17. Paper, Paper Products and paper Board.	282	53.61%	0.89
18. Tin Products	169	13.33%	0.22
19. Primary Metal	322	15.69%	0.26
20. Drugs & Medicines	64	15.27%	0.25
21. Others including Casting and Forging Units	4336	–	–

* *Source*: Ibid., Table No. 3.2.

Rajendra Nagar Industrial area also witnessed the establishment of some important factories such as M/s. Shiva Electronics, and Victory Engineering Company during sixtees. Thus the industrial landscape in trans-Hindan Tract expanded substantially during the decade ending 1970.

Since after 1970, industrial growth in this zone has taken place mainly over the arca lying between New Delhi Road and the corresponding railway line. This area which is known as site 4 Industrial Area is the latest addition in the industrial map of Ghaziabad. It covers a vast area and contains some of the most important factories of Ghaziabad viz. M/s. Bharat Electronics Ltd., Central Electronics Ltd., Dabur Industries, Spring India, Swadeshi Detergents Pvt. Ltd., Secure Pack, Zenith Electricals, Swik India, and Precision Moulds and Dies. Most of the present industrial growth is taking place over this site. The main factor behind the phenomenal growth of industries over this area is its relatively easier access to New Delhi both by road and rail. There is no traffic problem along this New Delhi Road as such movement of goods, both finished and unfinished is comparatively easier and less time-taking as compared to that along G.T. Road. Secondly, this area falls nearest to Delhi and hence attracted quite a good number of entrepreneurs from Delhi. Provision of infrastructure facilities by the Govt. acted as a strong stimulant for the promotion of industrial growth in this area. Here the industries are located only to the north-west side of the road because municipal limits here coincide with the other side of the road. Still there remains plenty of open tract for future industrial expansion but after a decade or so when whole area will be covered under factories, the industrial expansion in trans-Hindan tract will have to shift to the area lying north of G.T. Road. In En. part of the city i.e. in Ghaziabad proper there is not much scope for expansion for future industrial growth, unless municipal limits are extended but in trans-Hindan tract there still remains ample scope for future industrial growth despite the fact that this part of the city already accounts for half of the number of registered industrial units and 60% of total registered employment in the city.

As regards functional characteristics of this Industrial Zone, the major industries of this area in terms of registered employment are electronics and electrical goods, cotton textile, breweries, transport equipments and their parts, different types of machinery, and glass and glass products respectively (fig. no.11). The important concerns of the first group are M/s. Bharat Electronics Ltd. and Central Electronics Ltd., both of which are public sector undertakings, M/s. Ajanta Textiles, and Alps Textiles, are the major textile concerns. Mohan Meakins & Breweries is the reputed concern of breweries and M/s. Modern Industries, Bramic Suri, and Pyare Lal & Sons are the famous concerns for transport equipments and their parts. M/s. Jaina Time Industries, and Indure Pvt. Ltd. are the famous machinery manufacturing concerns and Mohan Crystal Glass Works, Universal Glass Company, and Indian Glass Agency are glass and glass products manufacturing concerns.

Other relatively less important industries of trans-Hindan Industrial Zone in terms of industrial employment include oil mills and soap, oil engines and agricultural implements, Ayurvedic medicines, tools and gauges, utensils, general hardware, chemicals, G.I. Pipes and tubes, plastic and foam products, corrugated boxes, paper and paper products, primary metal, drugs and medicines, and tin products. The industries which are almost absent or negligible in terms of industrial employment are tobacco products, structural clay products, synthetic fibre, and hydrogenated oil, out of 24 main industries of the city, 20 industries find place in the trans-Hindan industrial tract. The reason for such a wide range of industries here is comparatively much larger size of this industrial hub. Nearness to Delhi is another factor which has encouraged growth of different types of industries in this part of the city.

A look at Table No. 3.4 reveals that the highest location quotient in this area is 1.66 while in S.En. Industrial Zone and N.E. Central Industrial Zone, dominant industries showed location quotient above 5. There are many industries which have 100% share in this area e.g. breweries, glass and glass products, oil mills and soap, yet because the region's share is 60% so the highest locational factor comes to only 1.66. Hence relatively low location quotients of industries in the zone do not indicate the lesser share of the industry in the area but rather lesser degree of concentration in this zone because of its larger size. The industries having more than 50% share in this area include breweries, glass and glass products, oil mills and soap, electronics, machinery not classified elsewhere, cotton textile, Ayurvedic medicines, chemicals and gases, utensils, general hardware, plastic and foam products, corrugated boxes, and paper and paper products. All these industries indicate location quotients ranging between .89 to 1.66, a fact which denotes that despite so many industries having highest share i.e. more than 50% share in the area, the level of concentration of industries in this zone is very low in contrast to the picture presented by other two industrial areas of Ghaziabad proper. Out of the 20 main industries present in the area, percentage share of 13 industries mentioned above is above 50% while two industries i.e. transport equipments and their parts, and tools and gauges account for 48.75% and 47.85% share which though little less than 50% but are the highest in a single area. Thus there are left only five such industries which have a lower share in the area. These less important industries of this zone include drugs and medicines, primary metal, tin products, G.I. pipes, and oil engines. Percentage share of these industries varies between 13 to 26. Location quotient of these industries ranges from .22 to .44 which show least concentration of these in the area. On the basis of low location quotient values of various industries in trans-Hindan Industrial Zone, it can be safely presumed that the major part of future industrial development of the city will take place over this area, which is farthest from the city core but nearest to the capital city of Delhi. In an analysis of manufacturing industry in Uttar Pradesh, location quotient values have been used to assess the future prospects of industries in terms of dispersal and scope for new development.[7] At Ghaziabad, too, the location quotient values of different industries in respect of major industrial areas of the city, depict not only the present spatial pattern of industrial development, but also give a clear indication of future trends of changes in the industrial land-use over the city.

TYPOLOGY OF INTRA-URBAN INDUSTRIAL LOCATIONS AT GHAZIABAD

Industry is usually not confined to one single area at an industrial town but is rather spread over more than one or several areas which characterize different types of industrial combinations. There may be industries having random locations but in an industrial town there is found surely some degree of concentration in the case of a number of industries and it is here that the factors determining intra-urban locations of various industries come into play. Burgess, Hoyt, and Harris and Ullman, whose works gave a new direction in the field of urban land-use, dealt mainly with the location of industry as a whole within the city.[8] They did not elaborate as to which industries are located where within the city's structure. Walter Isard was the pioneer in throwing some light on intra-urban location of industry in the city.[9] Other great exponents on this issue were Loewenstein, Hamilton and Pred. In the following pages we shall discuss the intra-urban location of the important industries in Ghaziabad in the light of views expressed by these eminent urban geographers and while concluding an attempt has been made to evolve a typology of industrial locations in Ghaziabad on the basis of a study of various industries in the city.

Walter Isard in his book 'Location and Space Economy' states two types of industrial locations within a city depending upon the types of raw material used. He points out that industries using ubiquitous raw materials or no raw materials at all are not concentrated in any one part of the city but are found in all the industrial areas as well as anywhere within C.B.D., while the industries using localized raw materials are seen to be concentrated in specific areas.

Taking into account, Isard's points of view we find that Isard's first category of industries using ubiquitous raw materials such as, ice, bread, biscuits, dairy etc. are not much important at Ghaziabad. There are some ice factories no doubt but bread is generally brought from Delhi. However, there are quite a number of dal mills, flour mills and oil mills but majority of these units are small and hence unregistered under Factories Act. These industries are not concentrated and are found anywhere at the city as W. Isard suggests.

Isard's second category is quite evident at Ghaziabad. Here we find a number of industries which use localized raw materials and are found concentrated in one or more than one industrial areas of the city. To this category belong Ghaziabad's structural clay products, synthetic fibre, primary metal, hydrogenated oil, chemicals and gases, transport equipments, G.I. Pipes, tools and gauges, tin products, drugs and medicines, paper and paper board, breweries, tobacco, glass, electronics, oil mills and soap industries. All these industries show marked concentration in one of the industrial areas of the city as is evident from the locational quotients of these industries calculated for different industrial areas of Ghaziabad.

Lowenstein who calculated the concentration index of various types of urban land-uses including industry was of the opinion that industry is not confined to one or several parts of the city but is located throughout.[10] He recognized following four types of industrial locations:

1. *Central Locations*

Central locations are acquired by the industries requiring skilled labour and those which depend largely on urban market, because distribution from the centre is much easier. There are very few factories at Ghaziabad which characterize central locations. However, oil engine industry of the city for which Ghaziabad is famous all over India, belongs to this category. It is a industry which requires skilled labour and also enjoys the advantage of large urban market because of rich and fertile agricultural land all around. Other centrally located industries of Ghaziabad include printing presses, cold storages and ice factories which are largely dependent on urban markets.

2. *Communication Line Locations*

Ghaziabad's majority of industries belong to this category. Here industrial areas arc located.along radial transport lines giving the industrial landscape a characteristic linear appearance. However, Lowenstein included in this category only integrated industries which find assembly and distribution of items easier along main highways.

3. *Suburban Locations*

These locations indicate factories established near the suburbs outside the municipal limits. In most cases these locations are opted by industries having repellent features such as fume, noise and pollution. Amongst these groups may be listed Ghaziabad's M/s. Mohan Meakin Breweries, Modern Industries, Harsha Tractors, and Ajanta Textiles etc. These factories represented suburban locations during their initial years. Later on in the year 1967 when municipal limits were extended up to Delhi U.P. Border they were included within city's perimeters. However, except breweries, all other major industries of Trans-Hindan Zone did not have too much of repellent features. They sought locations in trans-Hindan area mainly because of its relative nearness to

Delhi.

4. *Location of big plants*

Public sector undertakings requiring very large tracts of land are generally located at some distance away from the city's municipal limits because of cheaper price of the land away from the city. However there stands no big Public sector industrial plant in the nearby suburban areas and thus this type of Lowenstein's loca tion is not applicable to the typology of intra-urban industrial locations at Ghaziabad.

Hamilton who agreed with Lowenstein's views regarding intra-urban location of manufacturing in the city, also described four types of industrial locations[11] within a city. His four types viz. (1) Central location, (2) Port location, (3) Radial or Ring Transport artery location and (4) Suburban location, are more or less the same as those described by Lowenstein. He has omitted location of big plants as suggested by Lowenstein and in its place, given a new type of 'Port location' acquired by export-oriented industries in big port cities. His 'port location' is not applicable in the case of inland cities and the remaining three types are the same as those given by Lowenstein, and these we have already discussed in the context of Ghaziabad.

Pred who based his typology of intra-urban industrial locations on Chinitz's study of industrial plants in New York metropolitan area has suggested 7 types.[12] His typology is based upon market unlike that of W. Isard who based his classification on raw materials. His seven types of intra-urban industrial locations are as under:

1 Ubiquitous industries concentrated near the C.B.D.: Pred quotes bread, cake and pie plants as belonging to this group. There are no factories of this group in the organized sector and as such Pred's this type is more or less absent in the case of Ghaziabad. Whatever cake and bread is prepared in the city, it is found only in the form of household industry.

2 Centrally located communication economy industries: These are the industries which require immediate accessibility to the purchaser prior to the process of manufacturing. Job-printing and

ready-made garments belong to this type of industries. According to Pred both these industries should occupy central locations but in the context of Ghaziabad only job printing is somewhat centrally located. Factories of ready-made garments are found mostly in Trans-Hindan Industrial Zone where relative nearness to Delhi exercises the dominant influence.

3. Local Market Industries with local raw materials: These industries characterize random locations. To this category may be included Ghaziabad's cold storages, dal mills, flour mills, oil, soap, and biscuits factories. Most of these industries represent small factories which are not registered under Factories Act. They signify random location as suggested by Pred.

4. Non Local Market industries with high value products having random location:
   Pred says that smaller units manufacturing high value products are located near the C.B.D. but the bigger units of this type may find location anywhere in the city. Ghaziabad has many such industries which manufacture high value products for national markets. To this group may be included oil engines, scientific instruments, watches and clocks, and different types of machinery. These industries do not show too much concentration in any one single area and do characterize random location as suggested by Pred.

5. Non-centrally located communication economy industries: In the words of Pred these are the industries which imperatively cluster in non-central locations to realize communication economy. These are highly technical industries which need to cluster to keep abreast of latest innovations. These are nationally oriented industries not related to C.B.D. in any way. They generally acquire transport artery location away from C.B.D. Pred has quoted electronics industries as belonging to this group. Ghaziabad's electronics industry which constitutes the biggest industry of the city in terms of registered industrial employment, is located exactly in the same way as depicted by Pred. 86.56% of the registered employment of this industry is concentrated in the site 4 area away from C.B.D. along New Delhi Road.

6. Non Local market industries on water fronts: These are industries acquiring port locations, and hence not applicable in the case of Ghaziabad which is an inland city.

7 Industries oriented towards national market: According to Pred nationally oriented industries are found in those parts of the city which have their orientation towards the national or regional markets. Pred's this category includes all such industries which produce for national markets. Industries producing high value products for national markets are included in Pred's 4th category. In this category may be included Ghaziabad's G.I. pipes, breweries, wagons, cranes, tools, potteries, synthetic fibre and many other industries which serve national markets. While Pred's 4th category belonged to random location, this category includes industries which show concentration in any one of the industrial areas of the city.

So far we have discussed Ghaziabad's intra-urban industrial locations in the light of the views of eminent urban geographers. Actually, the spatial pattern of various industries in a city does not necessarily fit into the framework suggested by different urban geographers. Ghaziabad too has its own peculiar pattern of intra-urban industrial locations. Because of its nearness to Delhi, here industry has grown almost independent of the urban requirements of the city itself. Very nominal part of the total industrial production is consumed by the local urban market. Bulk of the industrial production is diverted towards Delhi from where it moves to different other parts of the country. Some of the production is also directly sent to the regional markets, specially to different parts of U.P. and Bihar via Meerut Road, Hapur Road and Bulandshahr Road. Delhi acts as a magnetic force for determining the industrial locations in the city and hence intra-urban locations of the industry here assume a pattern which is entirely of its own and which is very much different from that obtaining in other industrial towns of the country. On the basis of study of Ghaziabad's industries, an attempt has been made to evolve the following typology of Ghaziabad's industrial locations.

1. Central locations – acquired by the industries depending largely on regional urban markets.

2. Random Locations – acquired by the industries having least tendency towards concentration.
3. Transport Artery Locations – acquired by the industries having a tendency towards concentration.
4. Suburban Locations – industries seeking locations near the suburbs of the city.

We shall discuss below each of these types in detail in the context of Ghaziabad.

1. *Central Locations*

Ghaziabad has no distinct inner zone of industries unlike other pre-existing towns. C.B.D. here accounts only for 2.6% share in the total registered industrial employment of the city. There are only sixteen factories employing between 10 to 100 employees located near the C.B.D., the most important being Guru Nanak Engineering Company, Azad Engineering Company, Delhi Iron & Steel Co., Ghaziabad Engineering Company and Chaudhary Hammer Works. All these concerns are oil engines and agricultural implements manufacturing concerns and thus we can conclude that here only oil engine and agricultural implements industry which represents 4th biggest industry of the city, signifies the central location to some extent. Other less important industries occupying central locations are cold storage, printing presses, dal mills and flour mills etc.

While talking about the centrally located industries of the city it is worthwhile to mention that all important industries of S.E. Industrial Zone namely, structural clay products, synthetic fibre, primary metal, chemical and gases and hydrogenated oil also belong to this category to some extent in view of the fact that this industrial zone, though representing a marginal location, lies only at a distance of 2 to 4 km from C.B.D., which is a much shorter distance as compared to the distant Meerut Road and Trans-Hindan Industrial Zones. Industrial units of these industries do not strictly fall within C.B.D. area but their short distance from C.B.D. does impart them the status of centrally located industries to some extent.

2 *Random Locations*:

All industries showing no tendency towards concentration in any one single area represent random locations. In this group may be included, those industries of Ghaziabad which represent very small share in the total registered industrial employment of the city. All these industries belong to miscellaneous group such as P.V.C. footwear, woollens, coated abrasives, stationery items, cosmetics, pesticides and insecticides, and fruit products etc. All these industries are present in Ghaziabad but because of small share in the total registered industrial employment, they don't seem to be concentrated in any one single area and hence signify random locations. It is to be noted that none of Ghaziabad's 24 major industries comes under this category. All these industries do show some degree of concentration in any one single area of the city.

3 *Communication Line Locations*:

Ghaziabad's all major industries belong to this category. All of Ghaziabad's three industrial areas run parallel to highways and railways and all important industries show marked concentration in any one single area out of the three industrial zones in the city. The main industries showing marked concentration along Bulandshahr Road industrial area include structural clay products, synthetic fibre, primary metal, hydrogenated oil and chemical and gases. Location quotients as calculated for these industries in this area (5.14, 4.69, 4.14, 3.15 and 2.14 respectively) show a very high degree of concentration of these industries in this area and all these industries necessarily signify communication line locational because through S.E. industrial zone pass all the three railway lines coming from Calcutta, Meerut and Moradabad and national highway of G.T. Road, along both sides of which this industrial zone is spread covering a large tracts of land.

The main industries having marked concentration in N. East, Central Industrial zone which is spread over the area lying between Meerut highway and corresponding railway line, include tobacco products, drugs and medicines, G.I. pipes and tubes, tin products, transport equipments and parts, tools and gauges, and paper and paperboard. Location quotients for these industries in this area range between 2 to 5.5 which show quite a high level of concentration of these industries in this area signifying a typically communication line location.

Major industries of the Trans-Hindan Industrial Zone also belong to the category of communication line locations because through this area, pass 3 main highways viz. G.T. Road, Loni Road and New Delhi Road and two main railway lines leading to Delhi and New Delhi. Out of 24 main industries of Ghaziabad 11 industries show a tendency of concentration in this industrial zone. However, level of concentration here is lower because of the larger share of this area in the total industrial employment. Main industries signifying communication line locations in trans-Hindan Industrial Zone include, electronics, breweries, glass and glass products, oil mills and soap, machinery, general hardware, utensils, cotton textile, corrugated boxes, Ayurvedic medicines, and plastic and foam products.

Thus we find that except oil engine which belongs to the category of centrally located industry, remaining 23 main industries belong to this 3rd category of communication line locations. Of these 23 industries 5 are important in S.En. Industrial zone, 7 in N.E. Central Zone and remaining 11 in Trans-Hindan Industrial Zone. These industries enjoy the double benefits of both highway and railways and quite a number of these use both means of communication for their movement of goods.

4 *Suburban Locations*:

Ghaziabad's present industrial structure includes very few cases of suburban industrial location. In S.En. Industrial Zone there are no factories after municipal limits end. In North-east Central Zone there is only one small paper factory viz. M/s. Aknos Paper Mill that falls outside the municipal limit. In trans-Hindan Industrial Zone municipal limits coincide with Delhi U.P. border so naturally there arises no question of suburban industrial units on this side.

Suburban industrial locations in Ghaziabad are found only along

Hapur Road which within municipal limits has attracted only a few important factories (Chaudhary Hammer Works, Everest Engineering Company, Agrico Engineering Company etc.) but has quite a number of important factories after the city limits end. Some of the important concerns characterizing sub-urban locations on Hapur Road include Ajanta Tubes, Jindal Pipes, and Hindan River Mills. Pipe industry is more prevalent here but there are found factories of other industries as well. Absence of industrial units on the city side of Hapur Road and springing up of a number of important factories along this road outside the municipal limits sounds somewhat queer at the first instance. But taking a close look at the industrial map of Ghaziabad, one is convinced with the relevance of this seemingly queer arrangement of industrial units along this highway. Lying between the two major industrial areas of the city namely Meerut Road industrial area and Bulandshahr Road industrial area, Hapur Road highway was aptly used for other types of urban land-uses such as educational, administrative and residential. There would have been too much of industrial congestion, had this highway been used for industrial purposes within the municipal limits.

The above mentioned four types of Ghaziabad's intra-urban industrial locations signify an attempt to assimilate the typology of city's industries based upon their intra-urban locations. Ghaziabad's industrial landscape can be properly understood in the light of above mentioned typology of city's intra-urban industrial locations.

REFERENCES

1&2 Town and Country Planning Office, Ghaziabad.

3. E.W. Burgess (1925): The Growth of the City: an Introduction to a Research Project'; in R.E. Park and E.W. Burgess, editors (1925): 'The City', 47 (Chicago).
4. G.H.T. Kimble (1951): "The inadequacy of the regional concept'; in D. Stamp and S.W. Wooldridge, editors (1951): London Essays in Geography' (LONDON).
5. H. Hoyt (1939): 'The structure and growth of Residential Neighbourhoods in American Cities' (Washington), 73-76.
6. C.D. Harris & E.L. Ullman (1945): 'The Nature of Cities.' Ann. Am. Acad. Pol. Sci. 242, 7.
7. S.L. Kayastha and M.B. Singh, 'A Spatial Analysis of Manufacturing in Uttar Pradesh'. Geographical Review of India. Vol. 41. No.2. 1979. p. 93-104.
8. See Reference Nos. 3, 5 and 6 of the Current Chapter.
9. W. Isard (1956) 'Location and space economy' 278-80. (New York).

10. L.K. Lowenstein (1963) 'The Location of Urban Land-uses', 'Land Economics', 39, 406-20.
11. F.E.I. Hamilton (1967) 'Models of Industrial location': Chapter 10 in R.J. Chorley and P. Hagget, editors (1967): 'Models in Geography', 361-417 (London).
12. A. R. Pred. (1964): 'The intra-metropolitan location of Manufacturing'. Ann. Assoc. Am. Geog. 54, 165-80.

Fig. 9
A SOUTH EASTERN INDUSTRIAL ZONE

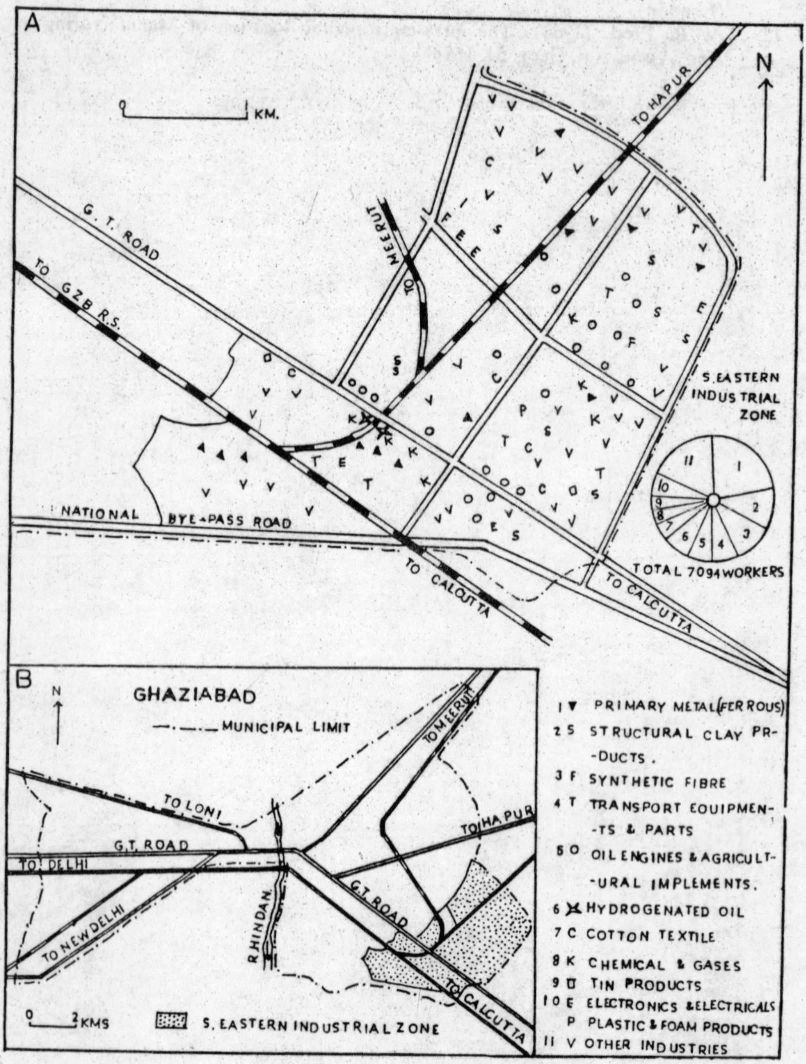

Fig. 10
N. E. CENTRAL INDUSTRIAL ZONE

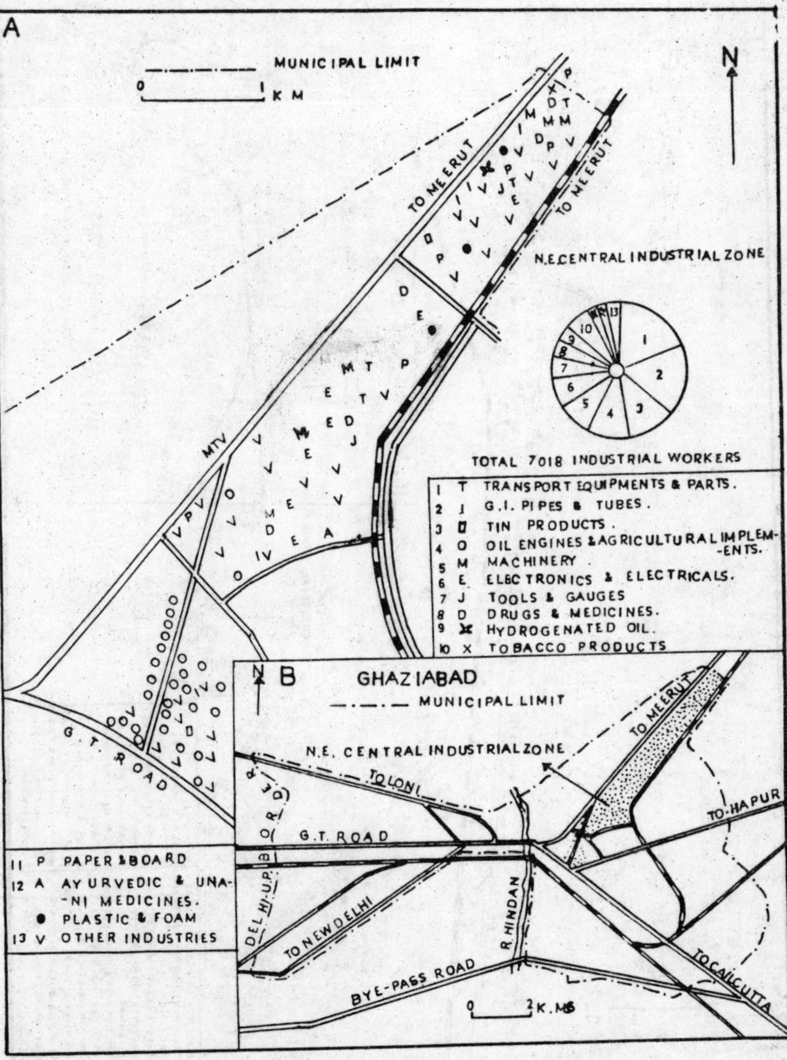

Fig. 11
TRANS–HINDAN INDUSTRIAL ZONE

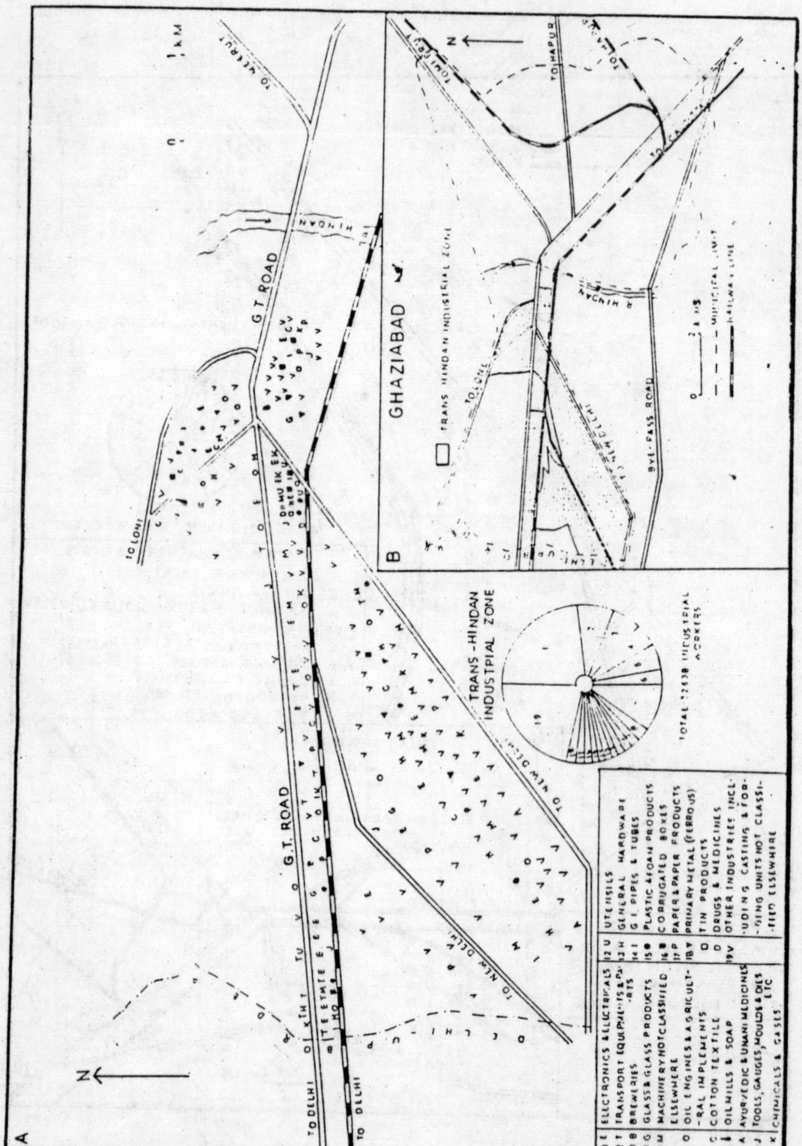

FOUR

Metal-Based Industries

Metals, specially ferrous, have become a part and parcel of our modern living. Non-ferrous metals also play a significant role in our modern industrial civilization but steel because of its strength, toughness and malleability, can be rivalled by none. Metal-based industries broadly include two major activities (1) Refining the metal and converting iron and alloys into steel which provides raw or semi finished products used as raw material by a number of other industries and (2) Manufacture of various types of machinery, tools and various other metal products with steel or other non-ferrous metals like copper, alluminium, and tin etc.

The present chapter attempts a synoptic study of metal based industries at Ghaziabad. Metal-based industries at Ghaziabad which employ 23610 persons representing 62.58% share in the total registered employment of the city, mainly belong to the second category of these industries mentioned above. Manufacture of steel from scrap is also an important industry belonging to this group, but it represents only 5.4% of the total registered employment of the city. Dominance and supremacy of metal-based industries in the city seems even more phenomenal in view of the complete absence of iron and other metals in the region as a whole. Not only in the city, but also in the district as a whole this group of industries enjoys a leading position with 48.20% share in the total registered employment of the district. Of the 48.20% share of metal-based industries in the district, 34.30% is contributed by the registered units of Ghaziabad and remaining 13.90% by other manufacturing centres of the district, notably by Muradnagar, Modinagar, and Jindal Nagar. Other relatively less important centres of these industries include Hapur, Dadri, Noida, Loni and Pilkhuwa etc.

TABLE 4.1: **Spatial Distribution of Metal-Based Industries in District Ghaziabad. (1981)**

Name of the manufacturing Centre	No. of Regd. Units	No. of Regd. employment	Percentage share in total registered employment of the district
1. Ghaziabad	276	23610	34.30
2. Modi Nagar	9	2584	3.74
3. Murad Nagar	4	4718	6.84
4. Jindal Nagar	7	824	1.20
5. Hapur	13	510	.74
6. Dadri	2	319	.46
7. Noida	14	316	.45
8. Loni	10	161	.23
9. Pilkhuwa	1	81	.12
10 Other minor Centres	2	87	.12
Total	338	33210	48.20%

* *Source*: Figures tabulated with the help of list of factories obtained from Inspector of Factories, Office, Ghaziabad and field survey.

Functional structure of metal-based industries in the district, as illustrated in Table No. 4.2 vividly emphasizes the dominance of the manufacture of machinery which includes electronics and electrical goods, oil engines and agricultural implements, transport equipments and their parts, and various other types of industrial machinery. Manufacture of defence equipments at the large establishment of Govt. Ordnance Factory at Muradnagar, employing more than 4000 persons, also holds a significant place in the functional structure of metal-based industries in the district. Other important industries of this group are those relating to the fabrication of various types of metal products e.g. pipes and tubes, various types of tools, tin containers, utensils and so on. As a single industry manufacture of steel from scrap is also an important industrial activity at Ghaziabad and Modi Nagar. However, the production of steel is far from sufficient for its enormous demand at various metal consuming units of the district. Larger part of primary steel products has to be brought from Bihar, to be used as raw material for various machinery manufacturing and metal-fabricating industrial units, more than 70% of which are located in the city of Ghaziabad. About 95% of the metal-consuming industrial units at Ghaziabad are engaged in the industries belonging to ferrous group while non-ferrous metals like alluminium, tin and copper represent only about 5% share in the total set up. Vast and prodigious development of metal-based industries at Ghaziabad and that too within such a short span of 40 years or so. makes it pertinent to probe into the underlying factors supporting their growth here. In the following pages, our discussion about these industries will mainly concern with those present in Ghaziabad city only, which constitutes the focal point of our study.

TABLE 4.2: **Functional Structure of Metal-Based Industries in District Ghaziabad* (1981)**

Name of Industry	No. of regd. Units	No. of regd. employment.	Percentage share in the total regd. employment of the district
1. Electronics & Electrical goods	48	6476	9.40
2. Transport equipments & their parts.	32	4143	6.01
3. Oil Engines and agricultural implements	77	3006	4.36
4. Primary Metal (Ferrous)	25	4023	5.84
5. Other types of Machy.	32	2347	3.41
6. Pipes & Tubes	16	2459	3.57
7. Tools & Gauges	10	923	1.34
8. Defence Equipments	2	4738	6.87
9. Tin Products	10	1349	1.96
10. Utensils	10	440	.64
11. Others	76	3306	4.80
Total	338	33210	48.20

* *Source* : Ibid, Table No. 4.1

LOCATIONAL FACTORS

Being situated in Upper Ganga Jamuna Doab, Ghaziabad lies far away from the main metal-producing areas of the country, such as Bihar, M.P. and Rajasthan. Nearness of raw materials, no doubt, serves as a definite advantage in the development of metal-based industries because of heavier and bulkier character of the metals, but relative pull of various other factors such as market, technical know-how, and capital exerts an equally significant influence in fostering these industries. Majority of Ghaziabad's metal-consuming industrial units are engaged in the manufacture of various types of machinery, which are obviously priced much higher in relation to the cost of raw materials used and this is an important factor explaining the dominance of metal based industries in the city despite the total absence of any sort of metals in the nearby areas. Higher value of manufactured products more than compensates the relatively higher costs of transportation incurred in assembling the various metals from far off sources in the country. As for various mini iron and steel mills of the city which produce special types of steel, raw material is readily available in the form of bulk supply of scrap from various machinery manufacturing units of the city and also from Delhi metropolitan area. Because of efficient rail and road transport facilities, there was seldom experienced any serious problem by the metal based industrial units of the city, with regard to supply of raw materials. Raw materials as a locational factor neither facilitated nor obstructed the growth and development of these industries in the city. However, other locational factors which have really contributed to the success of these industries in the city may be enumerated as under:

1 Country's partition in 1947, though a sad event in the political history of the country, exercised a most favourable influence for the start and growth of metal-consuming industries in the city. Because of over-crowding of Delhi by a large number of refugees, Ghaziabad, then a small tehsil town lying at the doorstep of the metropolis, naturally started attracting the attention of these displaced persons who wanted to start some industry at a place nearer to Delhi in order to earn their livelihood. Relocation of 'Guru Nanak Engineering Company' and 'Punjab Oil Expellers Ltd.' at Ghaziabad, which were previously functioning in Punjab in Pakistan, paved the way for the development of oil engines industry at the city. In the succeeding years a large number of oil engines and agricultural implements manufacturing units were established here by the Punjabi entrepreneurs and Ghaziabad became famous for its oil engines not only in the country but also abroad. Thus the pioneer industry of Ghaziabad

belonged to metal-based group of industries. Success of this industry also enhanced the prospects of other metal-based industries in the city.

2. Another major contributing factor in the development of these industries is the availability of vast near at-hand markets of Delhi metropolitan area. Advantages of an accessible expanding market ensured the continuous growth of these industries. In the absence of attraction of nearness of ores and coal, factor of nearness to markets assumed even greater significance. Moreover, transport rates on finished metal products and machinery are higher than on raw materials and this fact further enhances the significance of market as an important locational factor in the context of metal-based industries. Availability of scrap for steel is always governed by nearness to market areas. Apart from the vast metropolitan market, many of these industries are also sustained by virtue of linkages amongst themselves, which provides ready local market for many of these concerns.

3. Manufacture of machinery at Ghaziabad, which represents 65% of the total metal-based industries in the city, owes largely to the availability of highly skilled trained technical persons here not only from Delhi but from every nook and corner of the country. Because of its nearness to capital, many foreign firms also established their concerns here. However all such concerns have now more than 50% of their shares owned by indigenous companies. Existence of concerns like 'Danfoss India', 'Dewrance Mcnail', 'Mcnaill and Magor' and 'Dass Hitachi etc.' in the city clearly envisages its strong position regarding the solid technical base for the development of machinery manufacturing branches of metal-based industries here.

4. Another important prerequisite for the success of metal-based industries is the availability of relatively heavier sums of capital for the start and running of these industries. Although, majority of metal-consuming units of the city belong to small scale sector, but there also exist a number of large scale concerns e.g. M/s. Bharat Electronics, Central Electronics, Jain Tube Company, Shri Ram Pistons & Rings, Modern Industries, which employ 500 to 3000 persons. There are also many other large scale concerns

employing 100 to 500 persons. Major share of the capital requirements of all these concerns has been invested by private sector with public sector undertakings accounting only for 10% share in the total registered employment of these industries. Capital being a mobile factor, does not exert too strong an influence as a locational factor. If other requirements of an industry are met with, capital moves to any prospective location. For small scale units of these industries in the city, financial help has been provided by various Government bodies and Corporations.

5. Fuel requirements of these industries are also relatively heavier. Coal, furnace oil and electricity are required in substantial quantities at these concerns. Coal is obtained from Jharia via rail. furnace oil from Indian Oil Corporation and electricity from local supply. Because of erratic supply of electricity in the city, many of these concerns have their own generators to ensure the continuity of their manufacturing operations.

6. Excellent system of rail and road transport and the extremely nodal situation of the city, resulting from the convergence of routes here from three directions, also deserves a mention as an important conducive factor for the growth and development of these industries in the city. All metals and coal required for these industries are obtained from distant sources and hence the role of efficient transport facilities becomes even more important for the furtherance of these industries in the city.

Other factors that have contributed to the nourishment of these industries in the city are same as those availed by other industries in general. Provision of developed sites, plentiful water supply, abundant skilled and unskilled labour, and industrial peace, are also amongst the important factors for sustaining the growth of these industries in the city.

GROWTH AND DEVELOPMENT

Metal-based industries are amongst the pioneer industries of Ghaziabad. First metal-based factory to be established at Ghaziabad in the year 1944 was M/s. Ghaziabad Engineering Co. which manufactured agricultural implements and air coolers. Other important concerns manufacturing diesel engines and agricultural implements established during the earlier phase were M/s. Guru Nanak Engineering Company, Delhi Iron & Steel Company, and Punjab Oil Expeller Ltd. Success of these concerns at the city motivated many Punjabi entrepreneurs to opt for diesel and agricultural implements manufacturing units firstly because they had some previous experience in light engineering industries, and secondly they visualized a vast market potential for these items because of progressive and prosperous agricultural region all around. Consequently there sprang up a number of oil engines and agricultural implements manufacturing industrial units in the city such as M/s. Lyyalpur Engineering Corporation, Pal Engineering Co., Shri Ram Engineering Company, Swastik Engineering Company, Saraswati Engineering Company, Rana Industries, Rolex Industries, Jagat Foundry, Baba Vishwakarma Engg. Works, Azad Engineering Co., Adarsh Engineering Company, Jyoti Ltd. and many others. All theses factories were small-scale units but as a whole they contributed significantly in the total production of oil engines and agricultural implements in the country. Bigger large scale units such as M/s. Shri Guru Nanak Engineering Company, and Punjab Oil Expeller Ltd. also increased their capacities and industry grew by leaps and bounds enjoying a dominant position in the city during fiftees and early sixtees.

During late fiftees and sixtees, a number of other metal based industries also grew in significance at Ghaziabad such as manufacture of transport equipments, electrical and other types of machinery, pipes and tubes and tin products. Important concerns opened up during this period manufacturing electrical appliances and electronics components are M/s. Electronics Industries of India, Electric Construction and Equipment Company, Zeta Industrial Corporation, Johnston Pumps, Tele Tube Electronics, Eletech Service Corporation, and Garg Associates. All these concerns were established in city proper either in S. En. industrial zone or Meerut Road Industrial area. Most important concern established during this period at city proper, manufacturing transport equipments and their parts, is M/s. Shri Ram Pistons & Rings Ltd. employing 935 persons. Other important concerns of this group are M/s Hind Cycle Ltd., Hindustan Monarch Private Ltd., Road Master Industries of India, and Universal Polymer.

TABLE 4.3: **Growth of Metal-Based Industries in Ghaziabad City**

Name of the Industry	1951 No.of regd. units	1951 No.of regd. empl.	1961 No.of regd. units	1961 No.of regd. empl.	1971 No.of regd. units	1971 No.of regd. empl.	1981 No.of regd. units	1981 No.of regd. empl.
1. Electronics & Electrical goods	2	181	10	577	20	1772	40	6247
2. Transport Equipments and their parts.	2	674	6	1135	13	2917	25	3871
3. Oil engines and Agricultural Implements.	11	607	25	928	49	2192	70	2595
4. Primary Metal (Ferrous)	-	-	7	205	18	1728	23	2053
5. Other types of Machinery	-	-	2	326	9	914	25	1969
6. Pipes & Tubes	1	129	3	291	8	1645	11	1692
7. Tin Products	-	-	1	208	5	1161	7	1268
8. General Hardware	2	22	3	40	4	85	9	403
9. Tools, Gauges, Moulds & Dies	-	-	2	123	5	591	9	886
10. Utensils	-	-	3	85	6	186	7	400

* *Source* : Ibid, Table No. 4.1.

Manufacture of oil engines, transport equipments, and electrical machinery in the city also paved the way for manufacture of many other types of machinery and their parts. A number of important concerns such as M/s. Danfoss India Ltd., Macneill & Magor, Micromatic Machines, Pulling & Lifting Machines Pvt. Ltd., Dewrance & Mcneill Corpn., manufacturing different other types of machinery such as automatic solid state devices, photostate machinery and cranes etc. were also set up during the decade ending in 1971. M/s. Jain Tube Company employing 1178 persons which is India's one of the 3 most important pipe and tube manufacturing concerns, was set up in 1964 and biggest tin container manufacturing concern of the city viz. M/s. Poysha Industrial Corporation was established in 1967. Another important tin containers manufacturing unit of the city viz. Hindustan Tin Works with 208 employees was set up in 1959. Manufacture of tin container in the city developed mainly because of large demand of tins at the 3 large scale hydrogenated oil concerns of the city.

Around 1970, manufacture of special types of steel from scrap, and primary metal products like bars, rods, angles, rounds and squares etc. also made big headway because of large demand of these primary iron and steel products at the various machinery manufacturing units of the city. Important concerns belonging to this branch are M/s. Rathi Alloys and Steel Ltd., Rathi Udyog Ltd., Rathi Spat Ltd., Amrit Steel Ltd., Electro Steel Casting, Atma Steel Private Ltd., Sansar Foundry and Ambika Steel Private Ltd. All these concerns were established during the period from 1970 to 1975. Products of these concerns are utilized by the other metal-based units of the city and for building construction work. Development of this branch of metal-based industries has contributed significantly for furthering the development of other metal-based industries in the city such as manufacture of general hard-ware, tools, gauges, moulds and dies, wires and wire-nettings, structures and so on. All these industries have recorded considerable progress during the decade ending in 1981.

So far we have been discussing the growth of metal-based industries in the city proper i.e., part of the Ghaziabad lying to the East of River Hindan. In the year 1967, municipal limits of Ghaziabad were extended uptil Delhi U.P. Border thus including

Mohan Nagar and Sahibabad also within city area. During the earlier stage of industrial development at Ghaziabad, Sahibabad and Mohan Nagar also attracted a number of important metal-based industrial establishments. Below we shall discuss the growth of Metal-based industries in the trans-Hindan tract of Ghaziabad, which at present forms a part of the city area.

First industry to assume significance in this part of Ghaziabad was the manufacture of transport equipments and their parts. Establishment of famous railway wagon building concern of 'Modern Industries' in 1942 marks the beginning of industrial activity at Sahibabad. Another important concern of this industry was 'Pyarey Lal & Sons Private Ltd., established in 1951 at Mohan Nagar, which manufactures bodies for trucks and buses. Around 1960, side by side with the establishment of a number of auto parts manufacturing concerns such as M/s. Abilities India Ltd., and Bramic Suri Pvt. Ltd. etc., there also sprang up a number of concerns manufacturing electricals and electronic components. Important concerns of electronics and electrical appliances established during sixtees in this area are M/s. Dass Hitachi Private Ltd., Shiva Electronics Private Ltd., Video Electronics Pvt. Ltd., and Victor Cables Corpn. During seventies too, electronics and electrical machinery industry made the biggest strides in the trans-Hindan tract of Ghaziabad. Establishment of M/s. Bharat Electronics Ltd., and Central Electronics Ltd. during early seventees, opened a new era for the growth of electronics industries in the city, which now enjoy the dominant position in the city with the highest registered employment of 6247 persons. During the last decade, important concerns of this industry opened in private sector are M/s. Zenith Electrical Pvt. Ltd., and East India Transformers and Gears Pvt. Ltd.

Manufacture of different other types of machinery has also made a good progress in this area during the last 20 year period. Important concerns belonging to this group are famous M/s. Jaina Time Industries, Harig India Pvt. Ltd., Indure Private Ltd., Paharpur Cooling Towers, Premier Irrigation Equipments Private Ltd., and W.M.I. Cranes Ltd.

Other branches of metal-based industries that have grown into importance during last two decades in this area are the manufacture of tools, gauges, moulds and dies etc., general hardware, utensils and tin containers. Industries like oil engines and agricultural implements, primary metal products, and pipes and tubes which are important at Ghaziabad proper have made relatively little progress in trans-Hindan area.

FUNCTIONAL STRUCTURE

Metal-based industries in the city cover a wide variety of items ranging from needles for sewing machines to such huge machinery as cranes and ash handling plants. Out of city's 24 important industries 10 belong to this group only. Amongst these ten, electronics and electrical appliances, and transport equipments and their parts obtain 1st and 2nd place in the city in terms of total registered employment and oil engines and agricultural implements, primary metal products, and other types of machinery hold 4th, 5th, 6th place respectively. 3rd place is held by cotton textile belonging to the agro-based group of the industries.

A look at table no. 4.4 (Fig. 16) reveals that manufacture of machinery constitutes the most dominant industrial activity of the city. Under this head is included the manufacture of electronics and electrical equipments and various other types of industrial machinery and their parts. On the whole this branch of metal based industries in the city represents above 40% share in the total registered employment of the city and about 2/3rd share of the various metal-based industries functioning in the city. Another major activity of the metal-based industries in the city is the fabrication of various types of metal products such as pipes and tubes, structures, wires and wire nettings, tools & gauges, moulds and dies, general hardware, metal containers, utensils and others. This branch of metal-based industries represents more than 15% share in the total registered employment of the city and about 25% of the total of metal-based industries. Third important industrial activity of this group of industries is that related to the manufacture of various types of primary metal products such as steel ingots and billets, bright bars, cold rolled strips, rods and angles, etc. which are used as raw material at various metal-consuming industrial units of the city manufacturing machinery or fabricating various types of ferrous metal products. This branch represents 5.44% share in the total registered employment of the city and about 8% of the total of metal-based industries.

Relative position of various individual metal-based industries of the city as envisaged by their share in the total registered employment of the city, has been illustrated in table No. 4.4 Below we shall discuss each of the important metal-based industries of the city separately in order to have a detailed and better understanding of the various types of products turned out by the concerns of these industries at Ghaziabad.

TABLE 4.4: **Functional Structure of Metal-Based Industries at Ghaziabad**

Name of the Industry	No.of Regd. Units	No. of regd. employment	Percentage share of the industry in the total regd. employment of the city.
1. Electronics & Electricals	40	6247	16.55
2. Transport Equipments and their parts	25	3871	10.25
3. Oil Engines and Agricultural Implements	70	2595	6.87
4. Primary Metal Products (Ferrous)	23	2053	5.44
5. Other types of Machinery	25	1969	5.21
6. Pipes and Tubes	11	1692	4.48
7. Tools, Gauges, Jigs, Fixtures, Moulds & Dies	9	886	2.35
8. General Hardware	9	403	1.06
9. Wires & Wirenetting	4	188	.48
10. Steel Furniture	4	92	.24
11. Structures	5	144	.37
12. Tin Products	7	1268	3.45
13. Utensils	7	400	1.06
14. Casting & Forging not classified elsewhere	37	1802	4.77
Total	276	23610	62.58

Source : Ibid, Table No. 4.1

1. *Electronics & Electricals*

Manufacture of electronics and Electricals is the biggest industry of the city representing 16.55% share in the total registered employment of the city. There are functioning 40 registered units in the

Two biggest concerns of this industry viz. M/s. Sri Ram Piston Rings' and 'Modern Industries' émploy 935 and 636 persons respectively. Other bigger concerns employing 100 to 350 persons number 6.8 of these units are medium-sized concerns employing 40 to 90 persons and rest all are smaller concerns employing 10 to 30 persons.

'Sri Ram Piston & Rings Ltd.' the biggest concern of this industry and 4th biggest of the city, is a public limited firm established here in the year 1963 by D.C.M. Group. It is India's one of the famous concerns manufacturing piston rings and piston pins for automobiles. Another important concern manufacturing automobile pistons is 'Abilities India Pvt. Ltd.,' established in the year 1960. 'AIP' pistons are used as original parts in many motorcycles, scooters, mopeds and tempos made in the country. Other 'AIP' products include carburatter, clutch plates, sprocnets and throttle valves. Amongst other important auto parts manufacturing concerns of the city may be mentioned 'M/s. Bramic Suri Pvt. Ltd.' for brake linings,' 'BhrataJi Industries' for wind shields and wiper arms, 'Friction Materials (India) Pvt. Ltd.' for clutch facings, 'Auto Gears Ltd.' for transmission gears, and 'Shakti Auto Valves and Engg. Corpn. Private Ltd.' for automobile ancillary items such as valves, guilds and pushrods etc. Smaller units of auto parts industry include M/s. Diamond Auto Industries, Jumna Auto Industries, Uma Automobiles and Engineers Pvt. Ltd., and Usha Automobiles Ltd. Amongst the cycles and cycle parts manufacturing units, 'Hind' Cycle Ltd.,' which is a public sector undertaking employing 324 persons is the most important factory manufacturing much popular Hind Cycles enjoying a country-wide market. Important concerns manufacturing spare parts of bicycles in the city include M/s. Hindustan Monark Pvt. Ltd., Road Master Industries of India, and United Wheels Pvt. Ltd. employing 174, 170 and 386 persons respectively. Other smaller units of this branch are M/s. Furiya Brothers Cycle Pvt. Ltd., Lion Cycle Rickshaw Industries, Shiwa Wheels, Vikrant Industries, and Universal Polymor.

Last but not the least is the manufacture of railway wagons at the famous factory of 'Modern Industries' at Sahibabad. It is the oldest concern of transport equipments industry established in the year 1942. Nucleus of Sahibabad industrial area was laid down by

'Modern Industries'. Here are manufactured railway wagons and wagon components for both passenger and goods trains. This concern also specializes in the manufacture of re-rolled products and oxygen gas for industrial use. Another important concern of transport equipments industry is 'Pyarey Lal & Sons' which manufactures bodies for buses and trucks. This concern was established in 1951 at Mohan Nagar.

3. *Oil Engines and Agricultural Implements*

Foundations of Ghaziabad's present-day vast industrial edifice were originally laid down by the emergence of a number of oil engines and agricultural implements manufacturing industrial units in the city during early post-Independence years. In Ghaziabad proper i.e. part of the city lying to the East of river Hindan, this industry still retains its foremost position, although at the city as a whole it has been relegated to 4th place after electronics, transport equipments and cotton textile industries respectively, claiming only 6.8% share in the total registered employment of the city. The downward trend in its relative position does not denote any downward trend in the industry itself but has resulted because of inclusion of Sahibabad and Mohan Nagar industrial areas within municipal limits, where leading three industries of today had already acquired a strong base and where manufacture of oil engines and agricultural implements held very little significance.

Another reason for statistically not so impressive picture of this industry in the city as a whole is the marked preponderance of small-scale units in this industry which are not registered under factories Act for the reason of employing less than 10 persons. Apart from 70 registered factories employing 2595 persons in all, there exist about 300 small unregistered units in the city which manufacture oil engines, filter presses, oil expellers or their parts. Their contribution, as a whole, is of immense value in fostering the welfare of this industry in the city. Smaller size of these units has not proved a disadvantage but rather their geographical association has led to the specialization, resulting in the phenomenal growth of this industry in the city proper.

First factory manufacturing agricultural implements in the city was 'Ghaziabad Engineering Company' established in 1944. Another earlier established unit was 'Delhi Iron & Steel Company'. At present, biggest agricultural implements manufacturing unit of the city is 'Harsha Tractors' established in 1969 at Mohan Nagar. It is a public Ltd. concern of 229 persons manufacturing tractors for agricultural use. However, all the parts for these tractors are imported from Russia. The function of this concern concerns with only the assembling of different parts for manufacturing the tractors.

Pioneer concerns of the manufacture of diesel oil engines in the city are 'Punjab Oil Expellers Ltd.' and 'Sri Guru Nanak Engineering Company' established in the city in the wake of country's partition in 1947. Originally both these firms were located in Punjab in Pakistan. These are the leading oil engine manufacturing concerns of the city employing 146 and 103 persons respectively. 'Sri Guru Nanak Engineering Company' with three of its branches functioning in the city, exports its 'GNECO' brand oil engines to many African & Asian countries. It also manufactures heavy duty ammonia compressors and radial drilling machines. Its buyers are spread in countries like Iran, Iraq, Afghanistan, Nepal, Bangladesh, Kenya, Uganda and Vietnam. Total number of persons employed by all the 3 units of this concern is above 250. Biggest and oldest units is one located along G.T. Road employing 103 persons. 'Punjab Oil Expellers Ltd.' manufactures 'Popular' brand of diesel oil engines, oil expellers, filter presses, and baby boilers. The firm also undertakes jobs for all types of heavy casting and steel forgings. It specialises in the manufacture of crank shafts, connecting rods and complete rolling mills. Other assignments of this concern include manufacture of tube well tools and plants, vacuum pumps and repair work of sugar mill machinery. Third most important oil engine manufacturing concern of the city is 'Layalpur Engineering Company' which has 3 of its branches in the city each employing 30 to 50 persons. Other smaller units of the industry employing 15 to 35 persons include M/s. Adarsh Engineering Company, Sri Ram Engineering Company, Azad Engg. Co., Saraswati Engineering Company, Supreme Engineers, R.P. Industries, Jagat Foundry and Engineering Works, Calcutta Engineering Company, Rolex Industries, Swastik Engineering Company, Subhash Engineering Company and many others. All these units are located in Ghaziabad proper. In the trans-Hindan tract, where this industry has grown very little, important units manufacturing oil engines and agricultural implements apart from 'Harsha Tractors' are 'Narwar Engineering Works' & 'General Industries', employing 60 and 40 persons respectively.

4. *Primary Metal Products (Ferrous)*

Manufacture of primary metal products such as steel ingots and billets, bright bars, cold rolled strips, rods, angles, m.s. rounds and squares etc. is important industry of the city representing 5.44% share in the total registered employment at Ghaziabad. There are 23 registered units in the city, engaged in the manufacture of these various types of primary metal products which are used as raw materials at many of the machinery manufacturing and metal-fabricating units of the city and also in building construction work. Despite their utmost industrial significance, the production of these units in the city is far from being sufficient to cope with the ever increasing demand of these primary metal products at the various metal-consuming industrial units of the city. Larger part of the requirement of steel and pig iron is still brought from TISCO and Hindustan Steel Ltd. at city's various metal-consuming industrial units.

Although a few rolling mills and foundries were started in the city during earlier phase of industrial development, manufacture of steel ingots and billets, cold rolled strips and bright bars etc. started here quite late around 1970. The main attractions for starting the production of steel ingots and billets etc. lay in the bulk availability of scrap from machinery manufacturing units of the city and from Delhi metropolitan area and the ready near at-hand markets for these semi-finished products at the various metal-consuming industrial units of the city. We may also call some of these units as mini steel mills. Establishment of M/s. 'Rathi Alloys & Steel Ltd.' and 'Rathi Spat Ltd.' in 1970, proved the biggest land mark in boosting up the development of this branch of metal-based industries in the city. Former with 450 employees is the biggest unit of its kind in the city manufacturing alloy steel ingots and billets. 'Rathi Spat Ltd.' employing 136 persons manufactures steel ingots. Another unit belonging to Rathi Group viz. 'Rathi Udyog Ltd.' employing 216 persons manufactures ribbed tor steel rods and structurals. Apart from Rathi's units, other important concerns manufacturing steel ingots and billets etc. are M/s. Amrit Steel Ltd., Electro Steel Castings Ltd.

and Ambica Steel Ltd. all of which were started during early seventees.

Important concerns manufacturing cold rolled strips include M/s. Atma Steel Pvt. Ltd., Hoops & Strips India Ltd., and Sarin Steel Industries. Important bright bars manufacturing concerns of the city are M/s. Disco Bright Bars Ltd., and New India Engineering Company. Manufacture of rerolled products is important at M/s. Sachdeva Steel Rolling Mills, Mahabir Steel Rolling Mills and Jain Rolling Mills employing 38, 44 and 45 persons respectively.

5. *Manufacture of other types of Machinery*

Success of oil engines and agricultural implements, electronics and electricals, and transport equipments machinery manufacturing units in the city has stimulated the growth of a number of industrial units manufacturing different other types of machinery such as automatic control devices, ash handling plants, grinders, cranes, paper mill machinery, time pieces and clocks, scientific and surgical instruments, cutting and slothing machines, earthmoving machines, refrigerator parts, cooling tower components and various others. This branch of metal-based industries here ranks as the 6th most important industry of the city representing 5.21% share in the total registered employment of Ghaziabad. There are functioning 25 such registered units in the city with total registered employment of 1969 persons. Most important factor governing the growth of these various other types of machinery manufacturing units in the city was the availability of technical know-how, which is so vital in the case of this industry. Another conducive factor lay in the huge demand of machine tools in Delhi Metropolitan area. Various machine tool products, manufactured at Ghaziabad are also exported to countries of S.E. Asia and Middle East.

Bigger units of this branch, employing above 100 persons include M/s. Indure Private Ltd., Jaina Time Industries, Danfoss India Ltd., Dewrance Mcneill Corpn., Dwarkanath Steel Strips Ltd., and Harig India Pvt. Ltd. which employ 441, 326, 227, 129, 100 and 123 persons respectively. 'Indure Pvt. Ltd.' which has technical collaboration with world renowned Allen-Sherman-Hoff Company of U.S.A. manufactures ash handling plants for thermal power stations. 'Jaina Time Industries' manufactures famous 'JAYCO' alarm time pieces, jewelled lever clocks and battery operated clocks. It has technical collaboration with W. Germany firm. 'Danfoss India Ltd.' holds a high reputation for its thermostat automatic controls for refrigerators and other uses. Products of this concern enjoy a nationwide market. It also supplies its automatic control devices to Railways. 'Dewrance Mcneill Corpn.' is known for its steam trap valves and valvefittings. 'Dwarkanath Steel Strips Ltd.' manufactures slothing and cutting machines. 'Harig India Pvt. Ltd.' manufactures precision surface grinders and special purpose machines. It has its branches all over India.

Amongst the medium-sized concerns manufacturing various other types of machinery are important M/s. Pulling & Lifting Machines Pvt. Ltd., Mcneill and Magor Pvt. Ltd., Technochem Engineers, Khair Surgical and Allied Products Pvt Ltd., Air Tech. Pvt. Ltd, Paharpur cooling Towers, Usha Mill Associates, and Premier Irrigation Equipments Pvt. Ltd. 'Pulling & Lifting Machines Pvt. Ltd.' manufactures ratchets, hoists, cranes and dynamometers. 'Mcneill & Magor Pvt. Ltd. is a trusted name in photostat machinery. Technochem Engineers, and Khair Surgical & Allied Products Pvt. Ltd. manufacture scientific and surgical instruments respectively. Air-Tech Pvt. Ltd. manufactures spare parts for refrigerators and Paharpur Cooling Towers manufactures components for cooling towers. Both Usha Mill Associates, and Premier Irrigation Equipments Pvt. Ltd. manufacture earthmoving machinery and cutting machines.

Amongst the smaller concerns of machine tool industries are important M/s. Akantika Copiers, and Himalaya Paper Machines Pvt. Ltd. for paper mill machinery, Associated Machinery Corporation for wire-drawing machines and stranding and cable machinery, Janta Engineering Works, and Taluja Enterprises for hydraulic presses and injection moulding machines, Roshan Engineers for cylinder valves, and Allied Engineering Works for cigarettes machinery spares and other machinery parts.

6. *Manufacture of Pipes & Tubes*

Manufacture of G. I. Pipes and tubes is the 7th most important industry of the city representing 4.48% share in the total registered employment here. There exist 11 registered units of this industry in the city employing 1692 persons in all, out of which 1178 are employed by famous M/s. Jain Tube Company Ltd. which is the 3rd biggest concern of the city after 'Bharat Electronics Ltd.' and 'Mohan Meakins Breweries Ltd.' 'Jain Tube Company Ltd.' which manufactures G.I. Pipes and tubes of all sizes for sewage and other constructional work, is one of the three biggest manufacturers of its kind in whole of India, other two belonging to Tatas and Jindals. Because of rigid quality control, J.T.C. pipes and tubes are known for highest rating in quality and durability. The firm supplies its products to Bridge Corporations of various states, water-works departments and colonizers. Customers of J.T.C. tubes and pipes are also spread over Iraq and S.E. Asian countries.

Steel strips required for manufacturing G. I. Pipes and tubes are bought from TISCO and Hindustan Steel Ltd. Machinery of the plant has been imported from W. Germany. 50% of the labour employed in this firm consists of Bihari Muslims who have better resistance to the extremely high temperature of the furnaces used in the manufacturing process. Currently J.T.C. is facing a hard time because of union rivalry and also because of interruptions in the continuous supply of raw materials and electricity. But this is only a temporary phase. On the whole it holds very good future prospects because of large demand of J.T.C. tubes and pipes which are known for their superior quality not only in India but also abroad.

Other important concerns of the city manufacturing G.I. Pipes include M/s. Bharat Industrial Corpn., Super Tubes, Shekhar Tubes, Span Industries, and Vijay Industries. Important concerns manufacturing water pipes and pipe fittings are M/s. K.S. Engineering Works, Pipe Fix Industries, and Sohan Lal & Sons employing 162, 95 and 25 persons respectively.

7. *Tin Products (Containers)*

Manufacture of tin containers constitutes the 9th most important industrial activity of the city, representing 3.45% share in the total registered employment of the city. There are 7 registered industrial units in the city with a total employment of 1268 persons, manufacturing different sizes of tin containers most of which are supplied to the 3 large-scale vanaspati manufacturing units of the city. Biggest unit of this industry, viz M/s. Poysha Industrial Corporation employs 850 persons i.e. about 2/3rd of the total of this industry in the city. It was established in the city in 1967 along Meerut Road in North E. Central Industrial zone of the city. Besides supplying to the vanaspati manufacturing units of the city, it also sends its products to other industrial towns of Wn. U.P. such as Aligarh and Moradabad. Other bigger units employing above 100 persons are 'Hindustan Tin Works' and 'Tin Manufacturing Company of India' employing 208 and 112 persons respectively. Smaller units of this branch of metal-based industries in the city, include, M/s. Bhagwati Industrial Corporation, Day Drum Industries, and Bharat Tin Udyog. One of the units viz. ' Metal Board Containers' manufactures composite containers of both tin and board.

8. *Tools & Gauges, Jigs & Fixtures, Moulds and Dies etc.*

This branch of metal based industries acquires 11th place in terms of total registered employment in the city. There exist 8 industrial units in the city, engaged in the production of tools and gauges, jigs and fixtures, moulds and dies etc. Total number of persons employed by such units in the city is 886 out of which 394 persons are working in the famous concern of M/s. Mascot (India) Tools & Forgings, which manufactures drop-forged handtools and cutting tools. This firm was established in 1969 in Meerut Road Industrial Area. Products of this concern are known for their quality in whole of Northern India. Other bigger concerns of more than 100 employees include M/s. Precision Moulds and Dies, and Wadco Tools Pvt. Ltd., both of which are located in Sahibabad industrial area. Amongst the smaller and medium-sized concerns of this branch in the city may be mentioned M/s. Module Tools & Gauges Pvt. Ltd., Precision Tools and Gauges Pvt. Ltd., Precision Tools & Components, Precision Turning Corporation, Tool Forging (India) Ltd., and Kaypee Dies & Tools. Major factor motivating the growth of this branch of metal-based industries in the city is the availability of vast near-at-hand market for its products.

9. *General Hardware*

Under this head is included the manufacture of screws, nuts and bolts, nails, door springs and other plumbering fixtures. It is the most simple industry as compared to other metal-based industries of ferrous group in the city. At Ghaziabad it ranks 22nd amongst the 24 important industries of the city. There exist 9 registered units of this branch with a total employment of 403 persons, representing 1.06% share in the total registered employment of the city. Except two bigger units viz. ' Soma Plumbering Fixtures' and "Spring India Ltd.' which employ 126 and 120 persons respectively, all the other units of this industry are smaller factories of 10 to 30 persons. Both these bigger units manufacture door springs and other plumbering fixtures. Other units manufacturing plumbering fixtures in the city include M/s. Ritz Metal Works, J.B. Machine Works, Sethi Industrial Corporation, and Vijay Metal Industries. Manufacture of screws, nuts and bolts and nails is important at M/s. Four Bhai Engineering Works and 'Arneja Enterprises' employing 30 and 13 persons respectively.

10. *Utensils*

It is an important consumer goods industry of the city with 7 registered units employing 400 persons in all. This industry ranks 23rd amongst the 24 important industries of the city, representing only 1.06% share in the total registered employment of Ghaziabad.

5 out of the 7 registered units of this industry in the city manufacture various types of alluminium utensils. Alluminium for these units is brought from Hindustan Alluminium Corporation plant at Renukot in Mirzapur district of Uttar Pradesh. A few of these units bring alluminium from Assansol in W. Bengal. Biggest unit of this industry in the city, viz. M/s. Devi Dayal Alluminium Industries employs 254 persons. It manufactures Hindalium utensils which are superior in quality as compared to alluminium utensils. Next most important utensil manufacturing unit is M/s. Jain Metal Udyog employing 65 persons. Other three units are Ghaziabad Alluminium Industries, Janta Alluminium Factory and Harbans Lal Mulkraj Private Ltd., employing 14, 10, and 12 persons respectively.

Two industrial units of the industry viz. M/s. Malhotra Industries and Victory Engineering Corpn., employing 100 and 36 persons respectively, manufacture pressure cookers.

11. *Other Metal-based Industries*

Other relatively less important metal-based industries of the city include manufacture of wires and wirenettings, steel furniture, and various types of structurals which represent respectively, .48, 0.24 and .37% share in the total registered employment at Ghaziabad. Important concerns manufacturing wires and wirenettings are M/s. Arora Engineering Works, Hemkunt Steel and Wires Pvt. Ltd., Indo Wires Engineers, and Jainson Steel and Rand Pvt. Ltd. Important steel furniture manufacturing units of the city are M/s. New Era Steel industries, Glorious Steel Furniture, Pearl Steel Furniture, and Usha Udyog. Manufacture of various types of steel structurals is important at M/s. Dhiraj Enterprises, Quality Enterprises, Grover Industries, and R.S. Steel Works.

12. *Castings and Forgings not classified elsewhere*

There exist 37 such registered factories in Ghaziabad which function as casting and forging units but do not belong specially to any one of the above mentioned metal-based industries of the city. These units employing 1802 persons in all represent 4.77% share in the total registered employment of the city. Main function of these factories is concerned with undertaking the jobs in castings and forgings for manufacturing different types of parts and accessories used for various other metal-based industries of the city. Important units undertaking jobs in casting and forging include M/s. National Steel & General Mill, Panchsheel Iron Foundry and Engineering Works, Roxy Foundry and Engineering Corpn., Sadhna Foundry & Engineering Works, United Castings, Chawra Industrial Corpn., Arya Iron & Steel Industries, and many others. Some of these units also manufacture certain specific metal products such as manufacture of needles for sewing machines at M/s. Dowels and Company, mainhole covers at M/s. Northern. India Steel Industries, lanterns at 'Kohinoor General Industries' and cutter knives at 'Mayur Brothers.' A few others are functioning as repair workshops such as 'Signal Workshop Nn. Railway' and 'Track Supply Workshop' employing

630 and 108 persons respectively. As a whole this category of casting and forging units makes a substantial contribution to the functional structure of metal-based industries in the city.

DISTRIBUTION OF METAL-BASED INDUSTRIES AT GHAZIABAD CITY

Because of a wide range of products and their much larger share of 62.58% in the total registered employment of city, metal-based industries here seem to be spread over all the industrial areas of the city. There is no industrial area in the city where there is not seen predominance of atleast one or two of these industries. Apart from marked clustering of most of these industries in one or two industrial areas of the city, these industries, as a whole, too are quite unevenly distributed over several industrial areas of the city (Fig. 14). They are found everywhere but 49% of these industries is found in trans-Hindan area. Greatest share of these industries in this area is also due to its largest size containing 60% of total registered employment of the city. Important metal-based industrial units in this area include M/s. Bharat Electronics Ltd., Central Electronics Ltd., Modern Industries, Dass Hitachi Pvt. Ltd., Harig India Pvt. Ltd., Jaina Time Industries, Bramic Suri Pvt. Ltd., Abilities (India) Pvt. Ltd., Victor Cables, Zenith Electricals Private Ltd., Pyare Lal & Sons and Peerless Foundry, employing 2850, 636, 246, 123, 326, 275, 100, 196, 110, 138 and 129 persons respectively. Majority of these units belong to electronics and electricals, and transport equipments and their parts. Despite 49% share of metal-based industries being located in trans-Hindan area, this area does not characterize a heavy concentration as illustrated by location quotient of .816 of these industries as a whole here, which is less than unity.

Second largest share of these industries is upheld by N.E. Central Zone which contains 32.34% share of total registered employment of metal-based industries in the city. Despite having lesser share than trans-Hindan zone., this area depicts heaviest concentration as suggested by location quotient of 1.74 of these industries as a whole in this area which is much above unity. Highest concentration in this area has resulted because of existence of a number of big large scale concerns of these industries here such as M/s. Jain Tube Company Ltd., Sri Ram Piston & Rings Ltd., Poysha Industrial Corporation,

Punjab Oil Expellers, Danfoss (India) Ltd., Mascot (India) Tools & Forgings Pvt. Ltd., Hindustan Monarch, Road Master Industries of India, which employ 1178, 935, 850, 143, 227, 394, 170, and 174 persons respectively.

Third major area representing 16.08 share of metal-based industries is S.En. industrial zone where are located M/s. Hind Cycle Ltd., Rathi Alloys & Steel Ltd., Rathi Spat Ltd., Rathi Udyog Ltd., Electro Steel Casting. Hindustan Tin works, Sansar Foundry, & Electronic Industries of India, which employ 324, 450, 136, 210, 152, 208, 142 and 235 persons respectively. C.B.D. area of the city contains only 2.5% share of these industries. Important concerns in C.B.D. area include M/s. Shri Guru Nanak Engineering Company, Delhi Iron & Steel Company, and Chaudhary Hammer Works which employ 103, 163 and 88 persons. All these concerns belong to oil engines and agricultural implements industry, 24.70% of which is located in C.B.D. area. This is the only important industry of the city which has a number of its important units located in the city core area. Encroachment of this industry into city's core can be attributed to the predominance of this industry in the earlier phase of industrial development here, when there were not available developed sites of the industrial areas of S.En. and N.E. Central industrial Zones.

Distribution of individual metal-based industries in the city differs greatly in respect of several industrial areas of the city. Marked clustering in any one or two industrial areas of the city is characteristic feature in the case of electronics and electrical goods, primary metal products, other types of machinery, G.I. Pipes and tubes, general hardware and utensils, each of which has more than 60% of its registered employment located in one single industrial area of the city. Electronics and electrical goods, other types of machinery, general hardware and utensils have 86.56, 62.27, 94.54 and 77.25% share of their registered employment in trans-Hindan area respectively. Primary metal products industry has 77.83% share in S.En. Industrial zone and G.I. Pipes and tubes, and tin products have 76.18% and 68.22% share respectively in N.East Central Industrial Zone.

Tools and gauges, jig and fixtures etc. denote predominance in two industrial areas of the city viz. trans-Hindan tract and N. East

Central Zone where is located 47.85 and 45.94% share of its total registered employment respectively. Transport equipments and their parts also show clustering in two industrial areas with 48.75 and 37.64 per cent share of its total registered employment located in trans-Hindan and N.East Central industrial areas respectively. Oil engine and agricultural implement industry of this group is the only industry that prevails not only in C.B.D. area but is also quite uniformly distributed over other industrial areas of the city proper. More than 70% of its total registered employment is found at Ghaziabad proper.

TABLE 4.5: **Spatial Distribution of Important Metal-Based Industries at Ghaziabad.**

Name of the Industry	Percentage share of the industry in different areas			
	S.En. Industrial Zone.	North East Central Indl. Zone	C.B.D. Area	Trans-Hindan Industrial Zone.
1. Electronics and Electrical goods.	5.87	7.15	.42	86.56
2. Transport equipments and their parts	13.61	37.64	-	48.75
3. Oil Engines and Agricultural Implements	18.15	30.87	24.70	26.28
4. Primary Metal Products (Ferrous)	77.83	6.48	-	15.69
5. Manufacture of other type of machinery	6.29	31.44	-	62.27
6. Tin Products	18.45	68.22	-	13.33
7. Tools, Gauges, jigs, fixtures etc.	6.21	45.94	-	47.85
8. G.I. Pipes and Tubes	5.73	76.18	-	18.09
9. General Hardware	5.46	-	-	94.54
10. Utensils	3.25	19.50	-	77.25

Source : Ibid, Table No. 4.1

FUTURE PROSPECTS

Manufacture of high quality sophisticated machinery relating to electronics, transport equipments, oil engines and agricultural implements, scientific instruments, watches and clocks and various other types of industrial machinery is the speciality of metal-based industries at Ghaziabad. Naturally it is a branch of manufacturing which evolves after a considerable amount of experience in related fields. The industry faces a number of hardships here such as distant sources of raw materials, erratic supply of electricity, labour unrest and so on, yet machinery manufacturing branches of metal-based industries at Ghaziabad hold very good future prospects firstly because there exists a vast market potential for high quality engineering goods and secondly because there are considerable economies to be gained as a result of concentration of machinery manufacturing units in the city. These economies may be acquired in the form of availability of skilled labour in the related field, managerial skill, and specialized knowledge and equipment. Industrial maturity as manifested by a number of machinery manufacturing industrial units of the city, paves the way for further growth of these units here. The fact that about 50% of total registered employment of the city is engaged in different types of machinery manufacturing units, itself ascertains the bright future of this branch of metal-based industries in the city.

Other important metal-based industries in the city such as manufacture of pipes, wires, steel furniture and structurals etc. and mini iron and steel mills, exemplify only mediocre chances for further growth. These industries do not involve too much of specialization and hence can grow at other centres of the district also and at other district towns of the region also. However, development of machinery manufacturing units can be safely and wisely visualized only at Ghaziabad in Upper Ganga Jumna Doab region, because of city's mature position in respect of this branch of metal-based industries.

Fig. 12
METAL-BASED INDUSTRIES

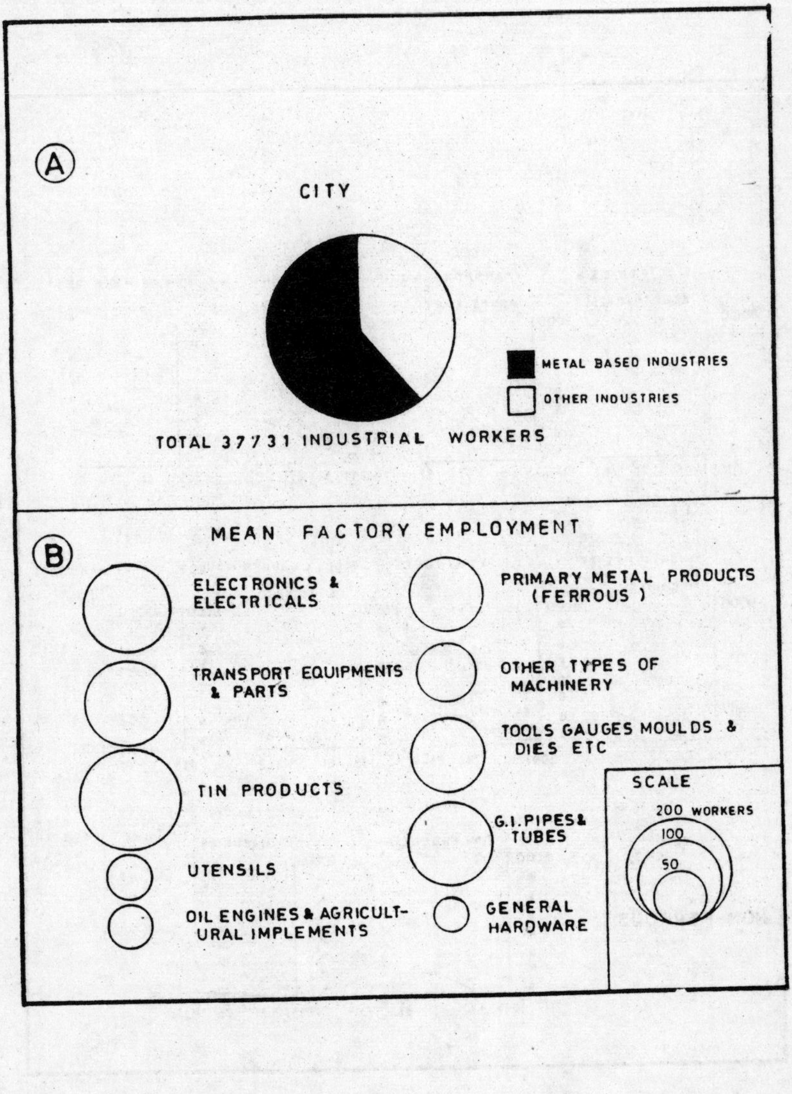

Fig. 13
METAL-BASED INDUSTRIES : GROWTH

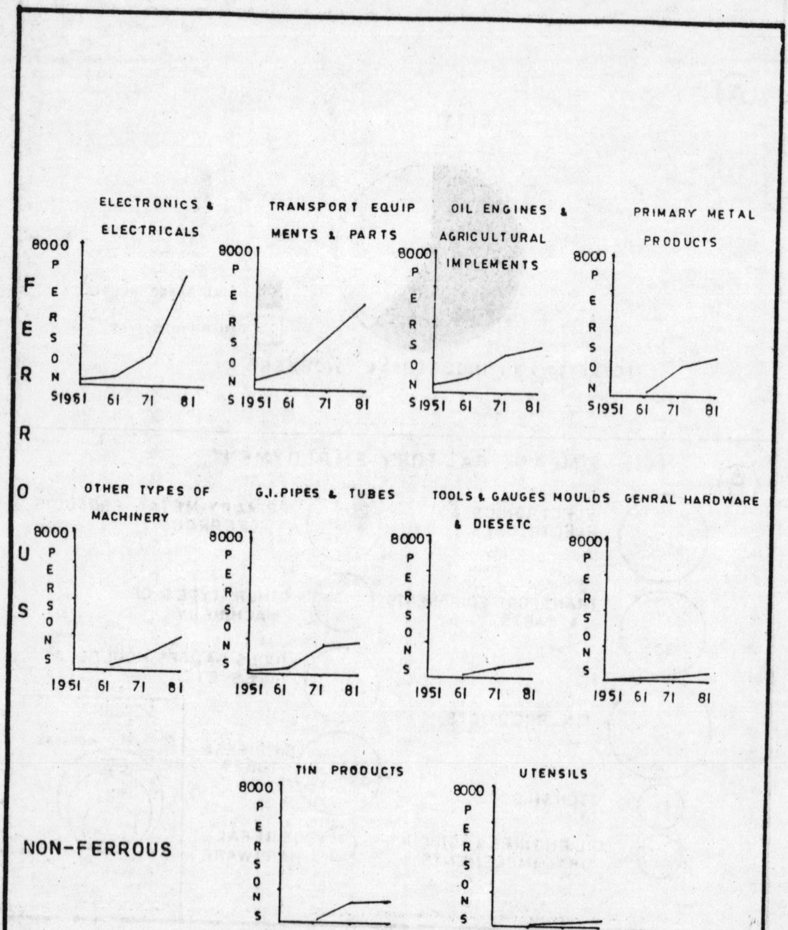

Fig. 14
SPATIAL CLUSTERING OF METAL-BASED INDUSTRIAL UNITS AT GZB.

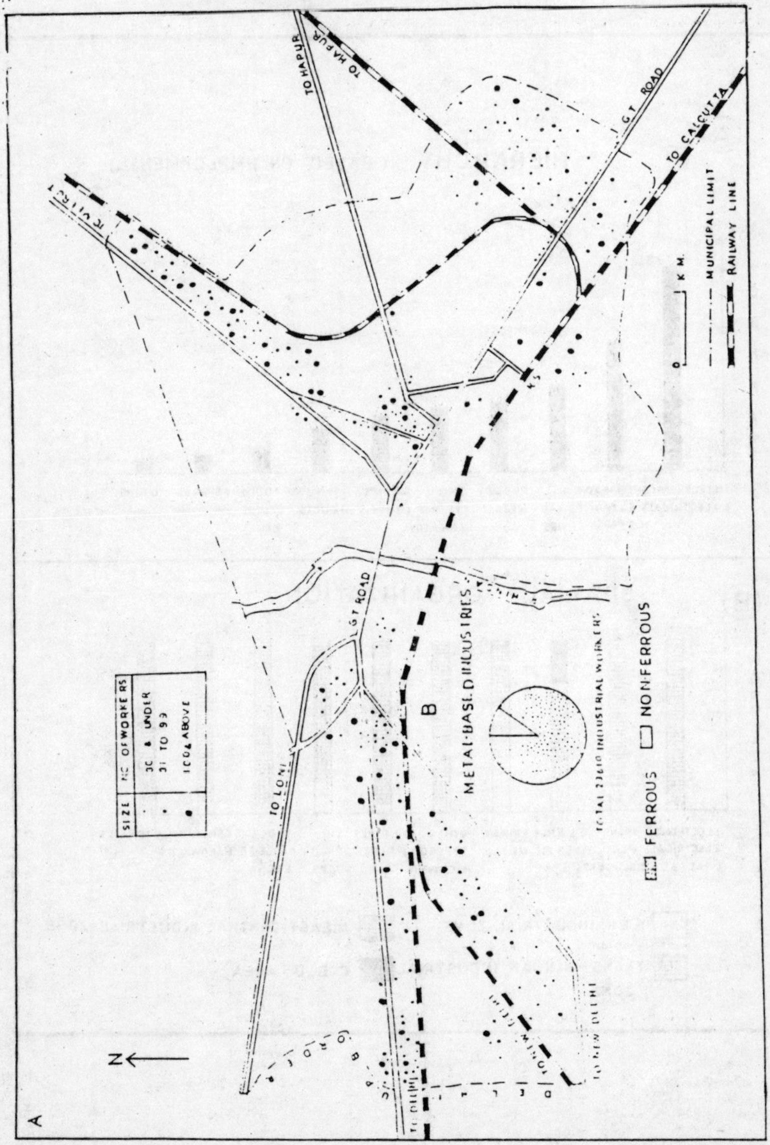

Fig 15
METAL-BASED INDUSTRIES

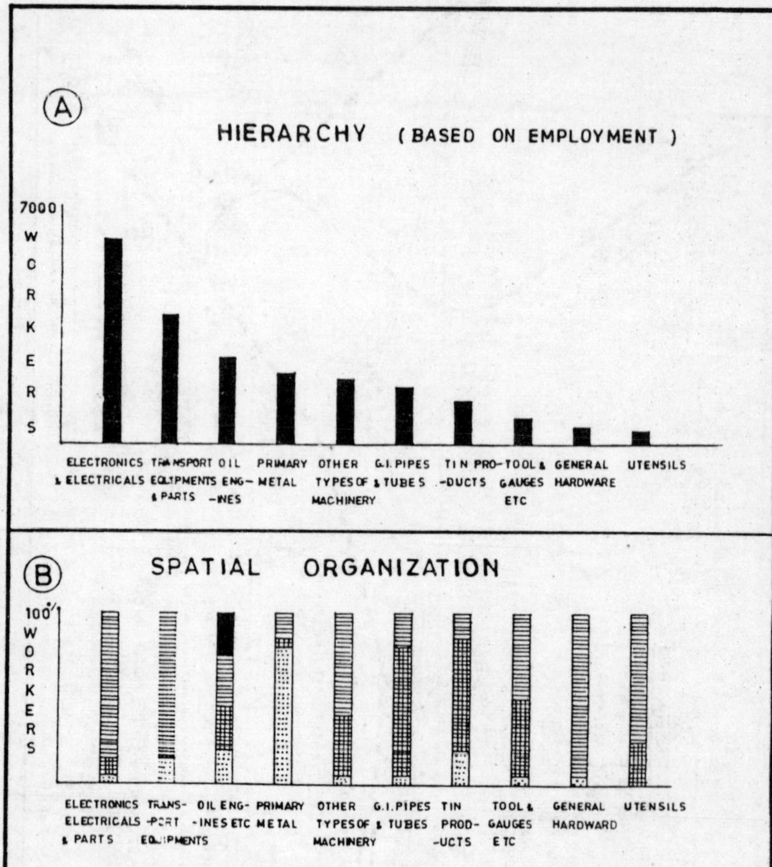

Fig. 16

GHAZIABAD: METAL-BASED INDUSTRIES (MACHINERY)

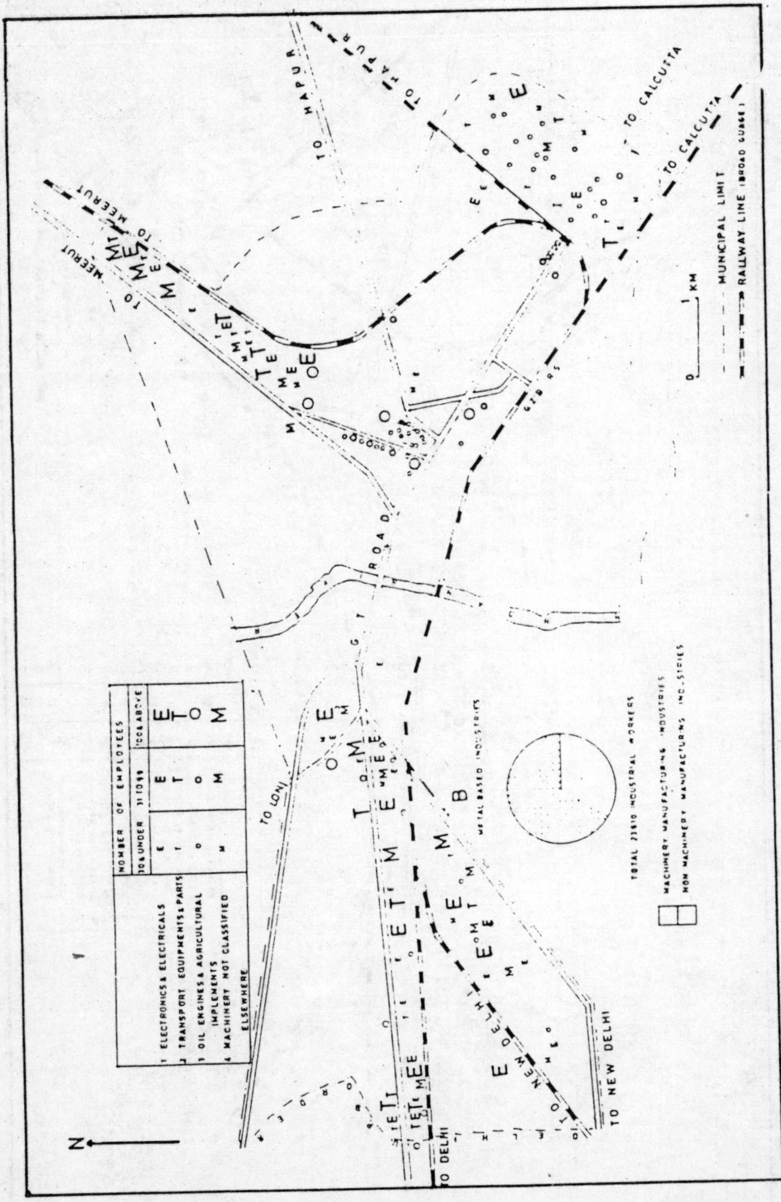

Fig. 17
GHAZIABAD: METAL-BASED INDUSTRIES (OTHER THAN MACHINERY)

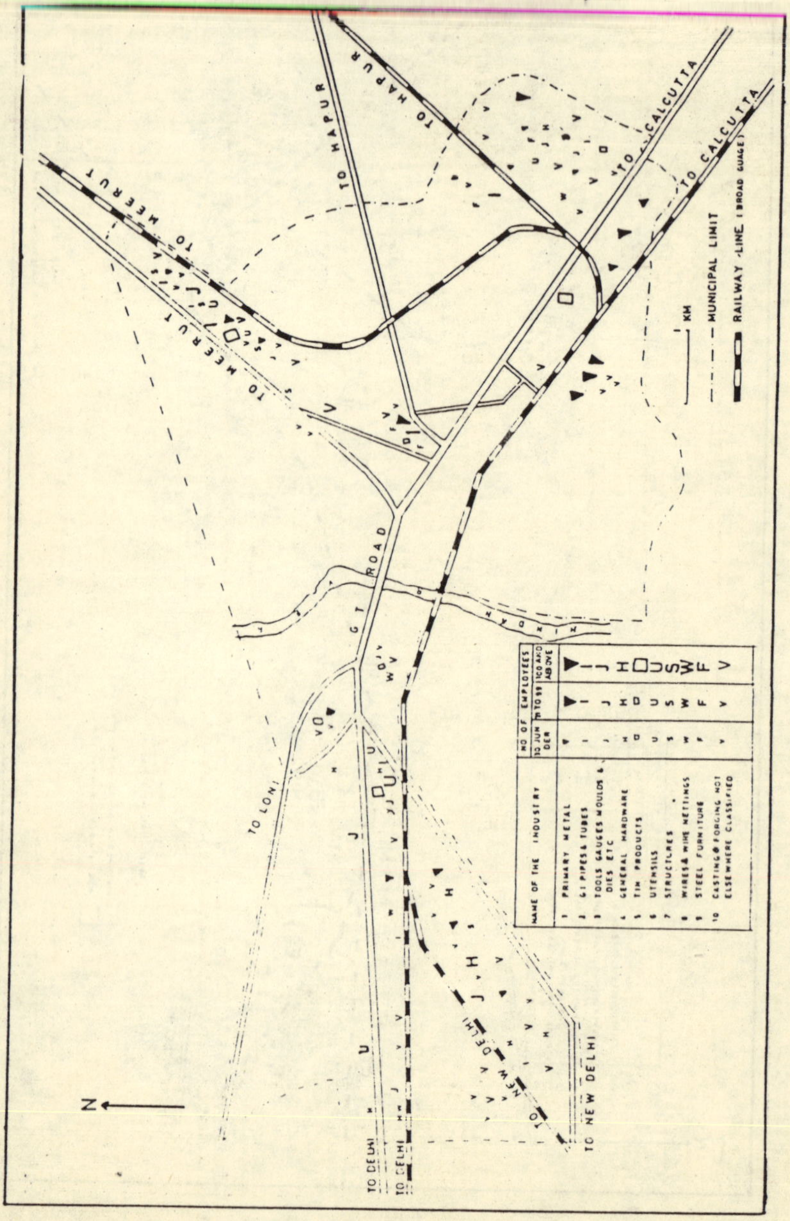

FIVE

Agro-Based Industries

Ghaziabad, the biggest industrial centre of upper Ganga Jumna Doab, which is the most prosperous and progressive agricultural region in whole of U.P., enjoys a high reputation in respect of a few of the agro-based industries such as breweries, hydrogenated oil, cigarettes, and hand-loom and powerloom textiles etc. but on the whole this group of industries represents only about 18% of the total registered employment in the city while the corresponding share of metal-based industries in the city is 62%. The overwhelming preponderance of metal-based industries and the relative insignificance of agro-based industries in the city sounds paradoxical in view of the high yields of agricultural production in the area. However, the picture is not so dismal in the district as a whole as it appears to be in the city itself. Out of the total registered employment of 68908 persons in the district, agro-based group of industries accounts for 34.16% share. This group of industries constitutes the largest single group at Modi Nagar, Pilkhuwa, Noida, Shimbhauli and Garh. The important agro-based industries as illustrated in the Table No. 5.1 are cotton-textile, sugar, breweries, hydrogenated oil, oil mills and soap and tobacco products. Cotton textile is the largest single industry of this group, which dominates the scene of industrial activity at Modi Nagar accounting for 75% of the total registered employment of this industry in the district. Next in importance is the sugar industry which is largely concentrated at Shimbhauli and Modi Nagar. Other main industries of this group such as breweries, hydrogenated oil, oil mills and soap, and tobacco products are found at Ghaziabad but the total share of agro-based industries in the city represents only 10% of the district's total as against 34% share of the district as a whole in the total registered employment of the district.

TABLE 5.1: **Functional Pattern of Agro-based Industries in District Ghaziabad.**

Name of the Industry	No.of regd. units	No.of regd. employment.	Percentage share of the Industry in the total regd. employment of the district.
1. Cotton Textile	48	15865	23.02
2. Sugar	10	2875	4.17
3. Breweries	2	1547	2.24
4. Hydrogenated oil	4	1222	1.77
5. Oil Mills & Soap	3	798	1.15
6. Tobacco Products	3	581	.84
7. Cereal Products	7	356	.53
8. Fruit Products	2	235	.35
9. Jute Products	2	65	.09
Total	81	23545	34.16%

Source: Figures tabulated with the help of the list of factories (1981) obtained from Inspector of Factories Office Ghaziabad and field survey.

Spatially the greatest concentration of agro-based industries in the district is found at Modi Nagar which accounts for about 59% share of these industries in the district. Next in importance is Ghaziabad city accounting for 28% share. Together these two centres account for more than 85% share of agro-based industries in the district. Shimbhauli, Noida and Pilkhuwa jointly account for more than 10% share and the rest is represented by Hapur, Garh and Loni.

At Ghaziabad, the main node of agro-based industries exists at Mohan Nagar and Loni Road Industrial area, which together contains about 2/3rd of the total registered employment of agro-based industries in the city. Here are located famous M/s. Mohan Meakins Breweries Ltd., Ajanta Textiles Ltd., Alps Textiles Pvt. Ltd., L.N. Gadodia and Sons Pvt. Ltd., Tata Oil Mills, Food Products (F.D.M.) Breweries, and National Cereal Products Ltd.. M/s. Mohan Meakins Breweries Ltd., Ajanta Textiles, and Tata Oil Mills which employ 1452, 920 and 600 persons respectively constitute the three biggest agro-based units at Ghaziabad. Other agro-based units in this area employ 100 to 200 persons.

TABLE 5.2: **Distribution of Agro-based Industries in District Ghaziabad***

	Name of the Industrial Centre	No. of units	No. of regd. employment.	Percentage share in the district's total regd. employment of Agro-based industries
1.	Ghaziabad City	30	6655	28.26
2.	Modi Nagar	8	13782	58.53
3.	Shimbhauli	2	1647	6.99
4.	Noida	16	744	3.16
5.	Pilkhuwa	15	331	1.42
6.	Hapur	4	172	.73
7.	Garh	2	124	.53
8.	Alipur	2	36	.15
9.	Loni	2	54	.23
	Total	81	23545	100.00

* *Source*: Ibid., Table No. 5.1.

Another area where agro-based industries hold an important place is Bulandshahr Road Industrial area where important agro-based units include M/s. Hindustan Lever Ltd., Amrit Vanaspati Co. Ltd., Webbing and Belting Factory, and Kailash Textiles. In Meerut Road Industrial area there exist two important agro-based industrial units viz. M/s. Jain Shudh Vanaspati Ltd., and International Tobacco Company which employ 318 and 494 persons respectively.

Cotton textile holds the most important place accounting for a little less than 50% of the total registered employment in agro-based industrial units at Ghaziabad. It is also one of the important industries of the city holding 3rd place after electronics, and transport equipments. Next in importance is breweries for which Ghaziabad enjoys a nationwide market. Other important industries at Ghaziabad belonging to this group, include hydrogenated oil, edible oils and soap, and tobacco products which account for 2, 1.6 and 1.5 percent share in the total registered employment at the city. Other relatively less important industries of this group are, fruit products, cereal products and jute products, all of which represent less than 1% share in the total registered employment of the city.

In order to adjudge functional and spatial importance of the different agro-based industries, each need to be studied separately.

TABLE 5.3: **Functional Pattern Agro-Based Industries at Ghaziabad***

	Name of the Industry	No. of regd. units	No. of regd. employment.	Percentage share in the total registered employment of the city
1.	Cotton Textile	15	2831	7.50
2.	Breweries	1	1452	3.85
3.	Fruit Products	2	235	.62
4.	Hydrogenated oil	3	781	2.07
5.	Tobacco Products	2	545	1.44
6.	Cereal Products	5	180	.48
7.	Oil Mills & Soap	1	600	1.59
9.	Jute Products	1	31	.08
	Total	30	6655	17.63

*Source** : Ibid., Table No. 5.1.

1. *Cotton Textile Industry*

As a single industry manufacture of cotton textile holds an important place in the industrial structure of Ghaziabad city. It is the 3rd most important industry after electronics, and transport equipments, with 7.5% share in city's total registered employment. However, the city's share in the total registered employment of this industry in the district represents only about 20% while Modi Nagar which is one of the leading textile centres of Northern India accounts for more than 75% share.

TABLE 5.4: **Distribution of Cotton Textile Units at Different Centres of District Ghaziabad.**

Name of the Centre	No. of regd. units	No. of regd. employment
Modi Nagar	3	12031
Ghaziabad	15	2831
Pilkhuwa	15	331
Noida	13	619
Loni	2	54
Total	48	15866

**Source* : Ibid., Table No. 5.1.

In the present context, discussion on cotton textile industry is mainly concerned with the development and distribution of this industry at Ghaziabad. Cotton textile industry at other centres of the district will be dealt with in Chapter Eight.

At Ghaziabad there exist 15 registered cotton textile units with an overall employment of 2831 persons. Except M/s. Ajanta Textiles Ltd., and Old Village Industries Ltd. which employ 950 and 756 persons respectively all the other textile units of the city employ below 200 persons. Some of the factories e.g. M/s. Dev Udyog, Jaini Dyeing Handloom Industries, Jai Prabha Textiles, Jawahar Niwar Factory, Kailash Textiles, and General Industries, and Rituraj Textile and General Industries Pvt. Ltd. are quite small each employing less than 50 persons. Amongst the factories employing 50 to 200 persons, M/s. Alps Textiles Pvt. Ltd., Webbing & Belting Factory Pvt. Ltd., and L.N. Gadodia & Sons Pvt. Ltd. are the reputed cotton textile manufacturing units of the city. The marked tendency towards smaller units owes much to the fact that no significant economies are gained by the large-scale production in the cotton textile industry. A small scale specialist is at a considerable advantage because he can easily adapt his manufactured products to the changing circumstances.

Another distinguishing feature of the structure of cotton textile units at Ghaziabad is the specialization in the manufacture of high quality furnishing cloth, e.g. bed sheets, curtain cloth and towels etc. Here 9 out of the 15 cotton textile units manufacture cloth used for purposes other than garments. One of the units viz. M/s. Jai Prabha Textiles manufactures gray canvass cloth for tents etc. and the another viz. M/s. Jawahar Niwar Factory manufactures 'niwar'. Bed sheets, towels and curtain cloth manufactured at M/s. Alps Textiles Pvt. Ltd., and Webbing & Belting Factory Pvt. Ltd., are exported to the countries of Middle East and S. East Asia.

Of the total 15 textile units only two viz M/s. Ajanta Textiles Ltd., and Basant Spinners manufacture yarn. Four of these units are engaged in the finishing branches related to dyeing and printing etc.

The first cotton textile factory at Ghaziabad viz. 'Webbing & Belting Factory Pvt. Ltd.' was established in the year 1947 along G.T. Road in S.En. Industrial Zone. Despite an early start, there was no significant progress made by this industry until 1960. The greatest development of cotton textile occurred in the decade ending in 1971 as is evident from Table No. 5.5. The astounding progress of cotton textile industry in this period was only a part of the vast industrial expansion made possible because of the development of a number of new industrial areas under the auspices of Ghaziabad Master Plan. The vast complex of cotton textile units along Loni Road (M/s. Ajanta Textiles Ltd., Alps Textiles Pvt. Ltd. and L.N. Gadodia and Sons Pvt. Ltd.) is the outcome of industrial expansion signifying this period. The textile units located at site 4 industrial area e.g. M/s. Old Village Industries Ltd., and Enter Craft Pvt. Ltd. were established during the decade ending in 1981. Except during sixtees, the cotton textile industry of the city has witnessed only a moderate growth throughout. The relatively slower rate of growth of this industry can be attributed partly to the intense competition with the metal consuming units of the city and partly to the external competition with the large scale textile mills of Delhi and Modi Nagar. The industry has averted its decline only by adapting its textile manufacture to the specific needs of the area.

TABLE 5.5: **Growth of Cotton Textile Industry at Ghaziabad***

Years	No. of regd. units	No. of regd. employment	Percentage Increase in terms of regd. employment.	Percentage share in the total regd. employment of the city.
1951	1	171	-	6.69
1969	3	217	26.90	3.32
1971	9	1591	633.17	6.99
1981	15	2831	77.93	7.50

**Source* : Ibid., Table No. 5.1.

Some may argue that the relatively lesser importance of cotton textile manufacture in the city may be well due to the absence of favourable physical and economic factors for the location of this industry. But the point is invalidated in view of the fact that the industries which have made a startling progress throughout, have done so in the face of no lesser disadvantages as those encountered by cotton textile. The only handicap for cotton textile units in the city is that of distant raw material, but this is the case with many of the fast-growing industries belonging to metal-based group as well. Other physical and economic factors such as those of availability of soft water, fuel, wide-spread market, plentiful supply of both skilled and unskilled labour, efficient transport facilities, and easy access to capital are just the same as in the case of other industries. Therefore, any approach seeking to explain the relatively slower progress of cotton textile industry on the aforesaid grounds seems quite unrealistic.

In fact it is very rarely that a given geographical area has suitable conditions for the development of only one single industry. Almost any potential industrial area offers opportunities for a wide range of manufacturing processes and it is only after a period of trial and error that the most efficient use of the opportunities present in the area is discovered. Hence it can be inferred that relatively lesser significance of the cotton textile industry in the city is not due to unsuitable physical or economic conditions but because of the interplay of the factor of comparative costs. An industry can develop and successfully maintain itself only if it has clear-cut advantage over other competing industries.

TABLE 5.6: **Spatial Distribution of Cotton Textile Units at Ghaziabad**

Name of the Area	No. of regd. units	No. of regd. employment	Percentage share in the total regd. employment of Cotton Textile Industry at Ghaziabad
1. S. En. Industrial Zone	5	271	9.57
2. N. East Central Industrial Zone'	1	49	1.73
3. C.B.D. Area	-	-	-
4. Trans-Hindon Industrial Zone	9	2511	88.70
Total	15	2831	100.00

A look at Table No. 5.6 (Figure No. 19) indicates that cotton textile units of the city are uniformly distributed over the different industrial areas. There is seen a marked concentration of this industry in Trans-Hindan Industrial Zone which represents 88.7% share of the total employment in the industry. Such a heavy clustering of textile units in an industrial area which lies nearest to Delhi clearly reveals the pull of market factor in respect of the establishment of textile units many of which are engaged in the weaving and finishing branches of the industry. Except M/s. Webbing and Belting Factory Pvt. Ltd. all the other important textile units have found locations in the trans-Hindan area, a fact which further emphasizes the nearness of large urban market as being vital for the success of this industry. M/s. Alps Textiles Pvt. Ltd., L.N.Gadodia & Sons, Ajanta Textiles Ltd., Enter Craft Pvt. Ltd. and Old Village Industries Ltd. are some of the reputed cotton textile units. Not only does the proximity to Delhi ensures large urban market for the specialized cotton textile manufacture of the city, but it also facilitates attending to the various formalities required in connection with the export of the furnishing fabrics produced at Ghaziabad's factories viz. M/s. Webbing & Belting Factory Pvt. Ltd., and Alps Textiles Pvt. Ltd.

Another area where textile unites appear somewhat important is the S.En. Industrial Zone which represents 9.57% share in the total registered employment of the industry. Except M/s. Webbing & Belting Factory Pvt. Ltd. which employs 199 persons, all the other four textile units of the area are small-scale factories employing less than 50 persons. One of these four smaller factories viz. M/s. Jai Prabha Textiles Pvt. Ltd. manufactures canvass cloth and the remaining three produce various types of furnishing fabrics.

There is found no textile unit in the C.B.D. area and there is located only one factory viz. M/s. Ritu Raj Textile and General Industries Pvt. Ltd. in Mukand Nagar which comprises a part of N.E. Central industrial zone. It is really striking that there is located not even a single factory of cotton textile in Meerut Road Industrial Area which is one of the two major industrial areas of the city proper. As far as physical and economic advantages of the area are concerned, they are almost the same as in S. Eastern Industrial Zone which represents 9.57% share in the cotton textile manufacture while there is not found even a small textile unit in the former. The only answer to this some-what strange situation lies in the orientation of Meerut Road Industrial Area towards the direction of Modi Nagar, the biggest cotton textile centre of the district, which has discouraged the emergence of new textile units in its umland that certainly stretches far too long along the transport arteries radiating from it.

Thus while concluding our discussion on the cotton textile industry of the city, we shall once again emphasize that this industry has not been going through an easy period right from its beginning in 1947. It signifies an industry which has struggled hard to grow and to maintain itself. The adaptation of this industry to the specific needs of the area, has been the major motivating factor for its sustenance. It has grown from within and sets a living example of a dynamic industry in the growing industrial structure of the city.

2. *Brewery and Distillary*

This constitutes the second most important agro-based industry in the city after cotton textile, with a total registered employment of 1452 persons. Whole of this industry at Ghaziabad is represented by the single firm of 'Mohan Meakins Breweries Ltd.' which is the second largest factory of the city. 'Mohan Meakings Breweries' is one of the reputed concerns of India, manufacturing English liquors. It has also three sister concerns located at Solan, Lucknow and Kasauli. The only other liquor manufacturing unit of the district is that of 'Modi Distillary' at Modi Nagar, which is relatively a smaller concern employing 95 persons in all.

The establishment of M/s. Mohan Meakins Breweries Ltd. at Mohan Nagar in the year 1961 marks an important event for the promotion and welfare of agro-based industries at Ghaziabad. The choice for present site was inspired for the reason of its nearness to Delhi and the availability of cheap land, and efficient transport facilities. This industry has not only imparted a distinctive attribute to the city's industrial structure but has also helped in the development of a new industrial node of Mohan Nagar, around which rapid industrial expansion took place in the following decade.

M/s. Mohan Meakins Breweries Ltd. at present are manufacturing more than 20 brands of whisky, brandy, bear and rum etc. The 'Black Knight' and the 'Diplomat' brands of whisky manufactured here are known for their superior quality all over India. Other important brands of liquor are 'Colonel' and 'Old Monk'. The firm also specializes in the manufacture of beer. Mohan Meakin's 'Golden Eagle' beer is supposed to be one of the best in the country.

'Mohan Meakins Breweries Ltd.' enjoys a nation-wide market and a small proportion of the production is also exported specially to the countries of Middle East where there exists a great craze for its products. However, heavy excise duty on the products does create some problems related to the malpractices in the marketing operations. Differential rates of excise duty in states make the problem even worse because this leads to indulgence in too much of black marketing of their products. Auction system adopted by the Govt. for giving out the contracts also proves detrimental to the interests and welfare of the industry. Because of superior quality, the cost of production at this firm is relatively higher and often there is very little margin of profit in the wake of auctions organized by the Government.

The raw materials required by the firm include barley, molasses, sugar, hobs flower, spirit and water. Barley which is used for preparing beer is obtained from Haryana. Sugar and molasses are brought from the sugar factories located at other centres of the district Ghaziabad. Hobs flower which constitutes a very essential item in preparing the liquors is obtained from Kashmir where it grows in abundance. Barley is processed into malt. CO^2 gas emitted by boilers used for processing the barley malt is used in the distillary for preparing the liquors. Whisky is prepared with the molasses. Whole manufacturing process is quite a complex one, requiring a highly developed technology.

Both coal and electricity are used as fuel for the manufacturing process. Coal is mainly used in the furnaces and rest of the manufacturing process is carried out with the help of electricity. Coal is brought from Jharia by railways and electricity is obtained locally. The firm also owns its own generator, because city's electric supply is quite erratic.

M/s. Mohan Meakins Breweries Ltd. are supposed to be one of the best employers of the city. Besides providing the benefits of E.S.I., provident fund and bonus etc., the management also provides a number of recreational facilities to its employees. A full-fledged club, an auditorium, a swimming pool, and spacious play-grounds are the characteristic features inside the factory campus. Various cultural programmes are arranged at the auditorium and the management sponsors its own teams for cricket and basket ball etc. There seems to be a constant striving on the part of management towards an alround welfare of its employees, which is a very rare phenomenon. The management also owns its own hospital where medical facilities of highly qualified doctors are available for all.

No doubt M/s. Mohan Meakins Breweries Ltd. at Ghaziabad enjoys considerable advantages with regard to efficient transport system, vast market and skilled labour etc., yet it is not a smooth sailing in all its aspects. Apart from being a victim to heavy excise duty, another problem concerning this industry is that of the disposal of its liquid effluent which spreads all round in the nearby areas out side factory precincts. Not only does this cause an abnoxious smell in the area but also poses a serious threat of the problem of water pollution. Erection of a plant for the treatment of the liquid effluent within the factory premises is under consideration but because of heavy investment required for it, nothing has been done so far in this respect.

3. *Hydrogenated Oil*

Manufacturing of hydrogenated oil is the third most important agro-based industry at Ghaziabad after cotton textile and breweries. Ghaziabad is one of the important vanaspati manufacturing centres of the country. Here are located three large scale public Ltd. vanaspati-manufacturing concerns with a total registered employment of 781 persons which represents about 2% share in the total industrial structure of the city. All these three concerns manufacture popular brands of vanaspati which are known for their superior quality in Indian markets all over the country.

Most famous vanaspati manufacturing factory of the city is M/s. Hindustan Lever Ltd. located along Bulandshahr Road with a registered employment of 282 persons. This company owns several other factories too in different parts of the country. At its Ghaziabad unit, it is engaged in the large scale production of 'Dalda' and 'Dalda Pure Refined oil'. Apart from these, the famous detergent of 'Vim' and popular toilet soaps of 'Lux', 'Rexona' and 'Pears' are also manufactured here. The company holds a high reputation for all of its products all over the country. It is also supposed to be the best employer in the city for the reason of paying very attractive salaries to its employees.

Other two concerns producing hydrogenated oil at Ghaziabad are M/s. Amrit Vanasapati Co. Ltd., and Jain Shudh Vanaspati Ltd. with the registered employment of 181 and 318 persons respectively. M/s. Amrit Vanaspati Company Ltd. which was established as early as 1940, produces 'Golden Arrow' brand of vanaspati. It also produces acids and soap for washing purposes. This concern is located just near to M/s. Hindustan Levers Ltd. along Bulandshahr Road in S.En. Industrial Zone of the city.

M/s. Jain Shudh Vanaspati Ltd. was started in 1971. It is the biggest vanaspati manufacturing unit of the city. Here is produced the popular 'Ajanta' brand of vanaspati and J.S.V. soap. It is located along Meerut Road.

Apart from the three large scale concerns at Ghaziabad, there is also functioning one large-scale vanaspati-manufacturing unit at Modi Nagar, viz. M/s. Modi Vanaspati Manufacturing Corpn., which employs 441 persons and produces the famous 'Ruchi' vanaspati.

Hydrogenated oil or vanaspati industry of the city marks an early entry in the industrial history of Ghaziabad, yet the progress of this industry has not been very satisfactory. The major handicap suffered by this industry is the inadequate supply of raw materials, a fact, which has compelled the factories to produce much below their installed capacity. These factories require large quantities of edible oils such as those of groundnuts, cottonseeds and soyabeans etc. which are generally in the short supply and consequently factories are not able to produce to their maximum capacity. In respect of other requirements, the industry is well placed and holds good prospects, if the supply of raw materials increases considerably.

4. *Oil Mills and Soap*

This is an important domestic industry in the rural areas of the district. It is also important at other urban centres of the district where it is carried out by small unregistered oil mills. However, at Ghaziabad, this industry is represented by the single concern of the M/s. Tata Oil Mills Co. Ltd. established in 1964 along Loni Road in Mohan Nagar industrial area. This is a large scale public Ltd. concern with a total registered employment of 600 persons which represents 1.6% share in the city's total industrial structure. Unlike small oil mills which use different types of oil seeds for extracting edible oils, this factory is engaged in the production of coconut oil. Raw oil is obtained from Bombay and Cochin via road transport. The main manufacturing process at the factory consists of refining the oil and then packing it into sealed tins.

Apart from the packed coconut oil tins, the factory also manufactures different varieties of toilet soaps, which are known for their superior quality all over the country. 'Jai', 'Moti', 'Hamam', 'O.K.' and 'Golden Mist' are the popular brands of toilet soaps manufactured at M/s. Tata Oil Mills Co. Ltd. Actually at its Ghaziabad unit, manufacture of toilet soaps has assumed greater importance than coconut oil. The factory also manufactures cattle and poultry feed which is prepared with the by-products at the mills. It enjoys a nation-wide market for all its products and thus adds considerably to the industrial prestige of the city.

5. *Tobacco Products*

This is the fifth most important agro-based industry of city with a total registered employment of 544 persons which represents 1.44% share in the city's total. M/s.International Tobacco Company Ltd. is the major concern belonging to this group at Ghaziabad. It is a large scale concern of 494 persons, set up in collaboration with the foreign firm of M/s. Phillips and Morris which has its cigarette manufacturing concerns all over the world. In India there are three factories having links with this famous company, one each at Bombay. Sikkim and Ghaziabad.

At its Ghaziabad units of M/s. International Tobacco Co. Ltd., the largest shares are now owned by Modis who have an important say in all managerial matters. The headquarter of the company which was previously located at Bombay has now been shifted to New Delhi.

M/s. International Tobacco Company Ltd. at Ghaziabad was started in 1967 along Meerut Road. It is engaged in the large scale production of cigarettes. The famous brands of cigarettes manufactured here are 'Cavanders' and 'Red and White' both of which enjoy a nation-wide market. There exists an enormous demand for 'Cavanders' in Northern India. Whole of the manufacturing process including packing is accomplished inside the factory premises. The factory is known for its efficient management and is supposed to be one of the best employers in the city.

Main raw material required by this industry is, of course, the raw tobacco which is obtained from Guntur in Andhra Pradesh via road transport. Another important raw material required for the industry is special varieties of paper required for manufacturing the cigarettes and for packing cases. Paper and all the other items which are required only in small quantities are obtained from Delhi. Except for distant sources of tobacco, the factory is well-placed in respect of all the other physical and economic factors, essential for the fortunes of this industry. Despite very heavy excise duty and other taxes, the company earns a good profit every year. Vast expansions are taking place and very shortly the production of the cigarettes at the factory is likely to be more than double

Apart from this major cigarette manufacturing concern of the city, there is also one small-scale unit in the city viz. M/s. Jagannath & Dalip Singh Pvt. Ltd. which produces tobacco products other than cigarettes. This is a small factory of 51 persons located in Bulandshahr Road Industrial Area. Other urban centres of the district have no such unit except one at Noida viz. M/s. Dharampal Satya pal Pvt. Ltd. This is also a small factory of 36 persons engaged in the manufacture of various types of tobacco products.

6. *Fruit Products*

At Ghaziabad there exist only two factories viz. M/s. Food Products F.D.M. Breweries Ltd., and Indo Bulgar Foods Pvt. Ltd., which manufacture different types of fruit products. Other centres of the district have no such factories. The industry is present in the city only, with a registered employment of 235 persons representing only 0.62% share in city's total.

Of these two units, the former i.e. M/s. Food Products F.D.M. Breweries Ltd., which employs 199 persons, is under the same management as that of M/s. Mohan Meakins Breweries Ltd. and is located within the same premises. This factory was set up in the year 1963 as a public limited concern. It is India's one of the famous fruit-products manufacturing concerns. Here are manufactured different varieties of Jams, canned fruit juices of mango, guava and pine-apple, bottled apple juice and vinegar. The concern is known for the superior quality of its mango nectar and 'Gold Coin Apple Juice', which are also sent to the countries of Middle East.

Another fruit products manufacturing concern viz. M/s. Indo Bulgar Foods Pvt. Ltd. is a smaller factory of 36 persons which was established in 1969 along Meerut Road in collaboration with some Bulgarian firm. Apart from fruit juices, this concern also produces packed dehydrated vegetables such as green peas, potatoes, onions and cabbage etc.

Main raw material required by this industry is obviously the various types of fruits and vegetables which are easily procured from nearby areas. Apples, however, are obtained from Kashmir through contractors. These contractors supply apple pulp which is used for extracting juice to prepare famous 'Gold Coin Apple Juice' at M/s. Food Products F.D.M. Breweries Ltd. Besides fruits and vegetables, sugar, carbon-dioxide gas and some acids are also needed in the manufacturing process. All these items are locally available. Industry, on the whole , faces no major problem, but still there is a sort of stagnation in the industry which may be attributed to the relatively lower margin of profit in it. Cost of raw materials is sufficiently high and therefore there is very little scope of profit as compared to that at the liquor manufacturing unit. Relatively little margin of profit has compelled the management to introduce some new lines of manufacturing and for the last three years the concern has also started manufacturing cold drinks of 'Merri' and 'Pick Up'. The plant for manufacturing the cold drinks has been purchased from the makers of Coca-Cola. The production capacity of the plant is much above the actual production, which could not be increased mainly because of relatively lower demand of these new brands.

7. *Cereal Products*

Dal Mills, rice mills, flour mills and bakeries come under the purview of this group of industries. Processing of foodgrains can be most economically carried out in the producing areas and this is perhaps the reason why this industry is not so important in the city's industrial structure. The total registered employment under this group is only 180 persons in the city. Of the 5 registered units only one viz. M/s. National Cereal Products Ltd. with a strength of 124 persons is a public limited concern. Rest of the units are in the form of smaller factories employing 10 to 25 persons.

At M/s. National Cereal Products Ltd. which is an ancillary unit of 'Mohan Meakins Breweries Ltd.' inside the same premises, the manufacturing process is concerned mainly with the converting of barley into malt which is used to prepare beer at M/s. Mohan Meakins Breweries Ltd. Other units are mainly flour mills. One of the three flour mills of the city, also processes rice. All these flour mills are located in Bulandshahr Road Industrial Area. The fourth unit which is located in Meerut Road Industrial area, manufactures biscuits and allied products.

Lack of foodgrain processing units at Ghaziabad seems quite reasonable and one to be expected but what seems perhaps more surprising is the relative insignificance of these units at other centres of the district as well, which happens to be a part of the agriculturally most prosperous region of Upper Ganga-Jumna Doab. There are only two such units functioning at Shimbhauli and Noida with a total strength of 176 persons. Both these units manufacture biscuits and allied products. The reason why the food processing industry has not assumed greater significance at district level, may be explained only in the light of the factor of comparative costs. Other agro-based industries such as cotton textile and sugar have better prospects from the profit point of view and hence the cereal products industry has lagged behind in the district. But as the district has a considerable surplus of agricultural produce, there can be no denying of the importance of food-processing activity at the district level. As a matter of fact, major part of this industry in the district is carried out by small industrial units which are not covered under Factories Act and hence unregistered. Bigger units of the industry could not develop mainly because of competition with other agro-based industries in the district.

8. *Jute Products*

At Ghaziabad, this industry is represented by a single small factory viz. Hanuman Jute Factory employing 31 persons which manufactures ropes or sutli required for packing purposes. The main allurement for the setting up of this unit at Ghaziabad was the large local demand of sutli at this growing industrial centre for packing purposes.

The other unit of this industry in the district is that of Bharat Textiles Pvt. Ltd. located at Modi Nagar, which is also engaged in the manufacture of sutli to meet the local demand.

Future Prospects

Limited share of agro-based industries in the industrial structure at Ghaziabad does not denote an unusual phenomenon but rather signifies a healthy and balanced industrial growth by allowing ample scope for these industries to be developed at various other urban centres of the district which are either devoid of any industry or have very little of it. There is no relevance either in promoting these industries at Ghaziabad which specialises in the manufacture of high value-added products of various types of machinery. Being simple in nature agro-based industries can be most conveniently developed in the producing areas and therefore it is quite logical not to plead their case in the context of Ghaziabad city, where these have to face a stiff competition with various metal-based industries. Industries related to the manufacture of sugar, oil, cereal products and cotton textile etc. have a vast scope to grow at centres like Garh, Hapur, Pilkhuwa, Murad Nagar, Loni and Dadri. Moreover, relative insignificance of these industries at Ghaziabad would create a favourable impact on the growth of these industries at these centres. Thus it can be concluded that although agro-based industries stand very little chance of future expansion in the context of Ghaziabad city, these hold fairly good future prospects at other urban centres of the district in view of the sound agricultural base of the area as a whole.

Fig. 18

AGRO-BASED INDUSTRIES

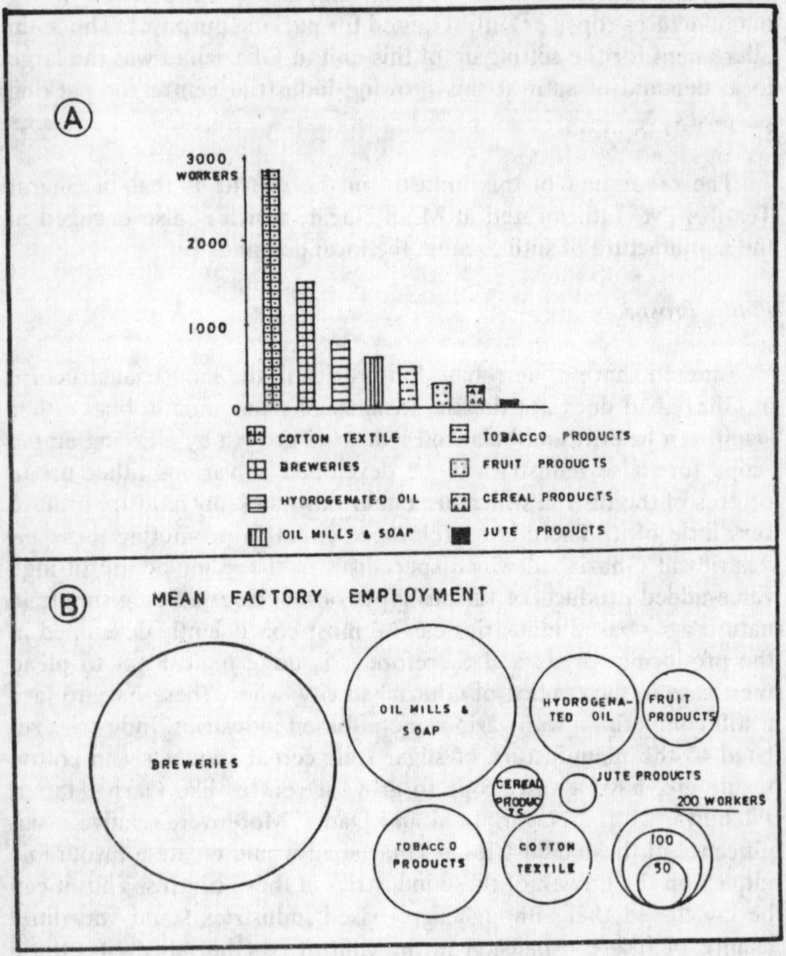

Fig. 19
AGRO-BASED INDUSTRIES AT GHAZIABAD

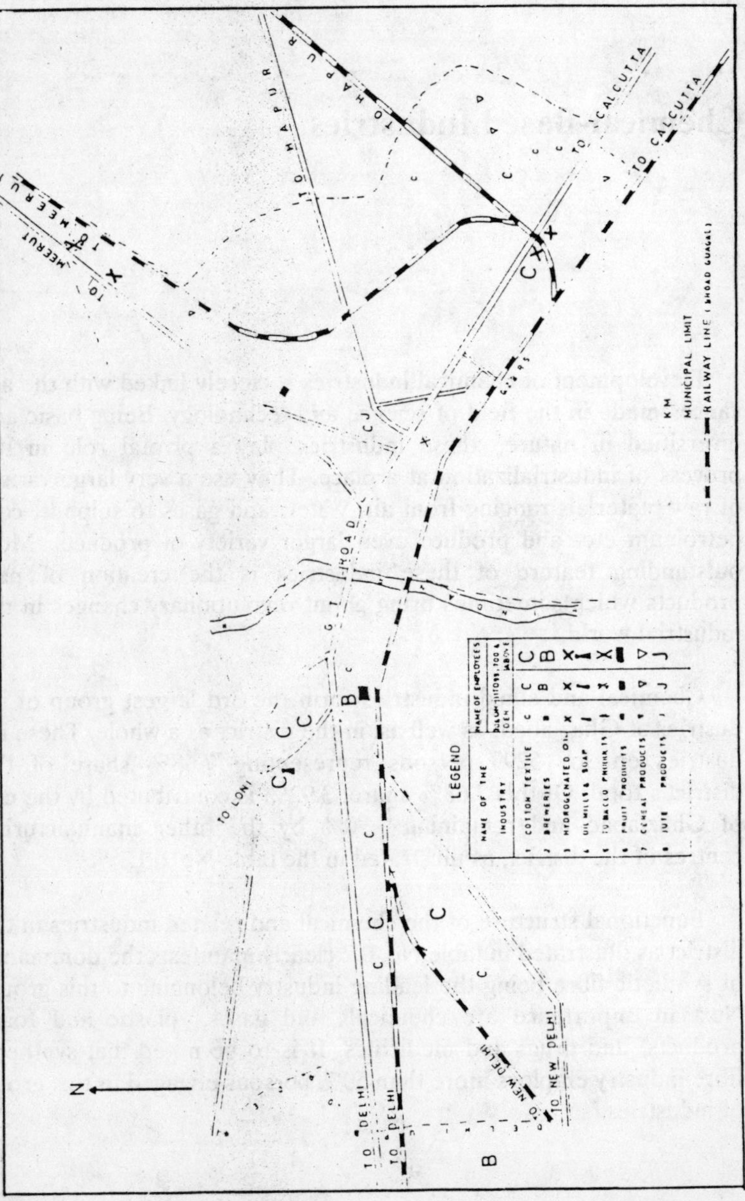

SIX

Chemical-Based Industries

Development of chemical industries is closely linked with the advances made in the field of science and technology. Being basic and diversified in nature, these industries play a pivotal role in the process of industrialization at a place. They use a very large variety of raw materials ranging from air, water, and gases to sulphur, coal petroleum etc. and produce even larger variety of products. Most outstanding feature of these industries is the creation of new products which sometimes bring about revolutionary changes in the industrial world.

Chemical and allied industries form the 3rd largest group of industries at Ghaziabad, as well as, in the district as a whole. These industries employ 5299 persons representing 7.68% share of the district's total. Of this 7.68% share, 3.92% is contributed by the city of Ghaziabad and remaining 3.70% by the other manufacturing centres of the district, as illustrated in the table No. 6.1.

Functional structure of the chemical and related industries in the district as illustrated in table No. 6.2 clearly manifests the dominance of synthetic fibre being the leading industry belonging to this group. Next in importance are chemicals and gases, plastic and foam products, and drugs and medicines. It is to be noted that synthetic fibre industry employs more than 50% persons engaged in this group of industries.

TABLE 6.1: **Distribution of Chemical-Based Industrial Units in District Ghaziabad.**

Manufacturing Centres	No. of Regd. Units	No. of Regd. employment	Percentage of total regd. employment of chemical-based industries in the district.
1. Ghaziabad	50	2707	51.09%
2. Modi Nagar	3	1815	34.25%
3. Dasna	1	494	9.32%
4. Hapur	6	116	2.20%
5. Noida	4	84	1.58%
6. Loni	4	69	1.30%
7. Murad Nagar	1	13	0.26%
Total	69	5299	100.00%

Source: Figures tabulated with the help of list of factories (1981), obtained from the Inspector of Factories office Ghaziabad.

TABLE 6.2: **Functional Structure of Chemical-Based Industries in District Ghaziabad.**

Name of the Industry	No. of regd. Units	No. of regd. employment	Percentage share in the district's total regd. employment.
1. Synthetic Fibre	6	2906	4.22
2. Chemicals & Gases	24	867	1.25
3. Plastic & Fibre Products	17	606	0.88
4. Drugs & Medicines	8	429	0.62
5. Others	14	490	0.71
Total	69	5298	7.68%

Source: Figures tabulated with the help of list of factories 1981 and field survey.

In the present chapter, the description of chemical-based industries will mainly centre around those present in Ghaziabad city. Description of chemical-based industries at other manufacturing centres will be dealt with in chapter Eight entitled 'Other Manufacturing Centres of District Ghaziabad.'

Locational Factors

Chemical and allied industries at Ghaziabad include production of basic heavy chemicals, paints, varnishes and lacquers, dye stuffs and dyes, synthetic resin and plastics, synthetic fibre, drugs and pharmaceuticals, soaps and detergents, glue and gelatine and many others. Obviously, the various chemical substances required for the manufacture of such a vast variety of products are derived from different types of sources ranging from air and water which are so ubiquitous and inexpensive to such items as petroleum, sulphur and natural gas which are in short supply in the country. Many chemicals are made from different raw materials and the same chemical can be made from a single raw material by a number of processes. Thus these industries are free from rigidity as far as raw materials are concerned. Almost all locations are suitable for at least some sorts of chemical industries, because many of these industries use air, water and electric current as their raw materials. However, other locational requirements of these industries are quite specific and stringent. The essential requirements of these industries may be listed as below:

1. Chemical industries involve the most complicated and intricate processes, as such they require highly skilled and trained employees for operating the machinery of the plant. There is no margin for error in the various chemical processes required for manufacturing the different chemical products. At Ghaziabad, availability of skilled trained persons for the industry is no problem because of its nearness to Delhi metropolitan area.
2. Another most important requirement for the successful chemical industry is the investment on research and development work in the related field. Research forms the foundation and backbone of these industries. Delhi, the capital metropolis of India, is an important centre of research in chemicals and related fields. Ghaziabad being near to it, is at a considerable advantage because the chemical-based industrial units here can easily keep themselves abreast with the latest developments going on in the field of chemical industries.
3. Capital investment required for the setting up of the chemical and related industries are considerably heavy as compared with those in other groups of industries. Majority of the factories of these industries at Ghaziabad are small-scale industrial units employing around 50 persons. There are only two large scale public Ltd. concerns at Ghaziabad, belonging to this group, viz. Swadeshi Polytex Ltd. and Unichem Laboratories Ltd. which employ 705 and 235 persons respectively. Capital investment per

employee is the highest in chemical industries amongst all the other industries. The bigger units of these industries can be set up only if huge sums of capital are available.

4. Another important condition for successful chemical industry is that related to geographical association. Majority of the products of these industries are used by related chemical factories. Cases of vertical linkage are commonly found with respect to these industries and hence it becomes necessary and convenient also for various linked units to be located near to each other in order to avoid long distance hauls of products from one factory to another. Chemical-based industrial units at Ghaziabad characterize a marked concentration in certain specific areas of the city and therefore hold good future prospects if other requirements are satisfactorily met with.
5. Nearness to market is also an important factor for the development of chemical-based industries. In most of the chemical industries, cost of raw materials is secondary and hence there is observed a marked orientation towards the market in the location of these industries. Chemical-based industrial units at Ghaziabad benefit not only from the large demand of chemical products at various other industrial units of the city but also from the large market available in Delhi Metropolitan area.

Growth and Development of Chemical-based Industries at Ghaziabad.

Although chemical industries were started in the city as early as 1946, these played only a meagre role in the industrial structure of the city uptil 1961. There were present only two chemical industries in the city uptil 1961, manufacture of chemicals and gases, and drugs and medicines. Of these two, only chemicals and gases assumed considerable significance from the point of view of registered employment. Manufacture of drugs and medicines was quite unimportant because it employed only 30 persons at two small factories in 1961. Real progress in the manufacture of drugs and medicines occurred during sixtees when were set-up M/s. Unichem Laboratories Ltd., G.D. Pharmaceutical Products, and Emson & Company. During seventies too, this industry progressed well and is continuing so even at present also.

The decade ending in 1971 not only registered a phenomenal

progress in the pre-existing industries of chemicals and gases, and drugs and medicines, but also witnessed the introduction of two new chemical industries in the city, viz. synthetic fibre and plastic and foam products. At present both these industries acquire 1st and 3rd place amongst the chemical industries of the city in terms of registered employment. Synthetic fibre industry got a big spurt with the establishment of M/s. Swadeshi Polytex Ltd. in 1970, a large scale concern of 705 persons manufacturing staple polyester fibre.

Manufacture of plastic and foam products also started during sixtees, but because of smaller size of the industrial units, this industry has maintained only a steady progress all through. It is still faring well, while synthetic fibre industry which picked up suddenly in 1971 because of establishment of M/s. Swadeshi Polytex Ltd., is facing a sort of stagnation. Future prospects of this industry also are much dismal as compared to those of plastic and foam products.

TABLE 6.3: **Growth of Chemical Industries in Ghaziabad City***

Name of the Industry		1951	1961	1971	1981
Synthetic Fibre	No. of regd. units	-	-	3	4
	No. of regd. employment	-	-	790	812
	Percentage share in City's total regd. employment	-	-	3.51	2.15
Chemicals and Gases	No. of regd. units	2	4	9	19
	No. of regd. employment	72	112	226	615
	Percentage share in City's total regd. employment	2.81	1.72	1.01	1.62
Plastic and foam Products	No. of Regd. units	-	-	8	12
	No. of regd. employment	-	-	305	428
	Percentage share in city's total regd. employment	-	-	1.35	1.13
Drugs and Medicines	No. of regd. units	1	2	6	7
	No. of regd. employment	18	30	348	419
	Percentage share in city's total regd. employment	.70	.46	1.54	1.11

*SOURCE: Ibid, Table No. 6.2.

Manufacture of chemicals and gases which is one of the earliest established industries of the city, recorded only a steady progress until 1961. During sixtees industry gained some momentum which further picked up in the following decade.

Functional Structure of Chemical-based Industries at Ghaziabad.

Functional structure of chemical based industries in the city follows the same pattern as that the district as a whole. Synthetic fibre remains the leading industry with 2.15% of total registered employment in the city. Next in importance is the manufacture of chemicals and gases followed by plastic and foam products and drugs and medicines. All these three industries represent 1.63%, 1.40%, and 1.11% share in the city's total respectively.. Other less important industries belonging to this group in the city are manufacture of cosmetics, pesticides and insecticides, and glue and gelatine. Some of the concerns do not produce any items, but perform certain chemical functions such as enamelling, japaning and polishing of metal products, and bleaching of yarn. the important chemical-based industries of the city can be discussed separately as under:

TABLE 6.4: **Functional Structure of Chemical-based Industries at Ghaziabad.**

Name of the Industry	No. of Regd. units	No. of regd. employ.	Percentage share in the city's total regd. employ.
1. Synthetic Fibre and allied products	4	812	2.15%
2. Chemicals and Gases	19	615	1.63%
3. Plastic and Foam Products	12	528	1.40%
4. Drugs and Medicines	7	419	1.11%
5. Others	8	333	0.88%
Total	50	2707	7.17%

Source: Ibid, Table No. 6.2.

1. *Synthetic Fibre & Allied products*

Synthetic fibres are the non-cellulosic fibres such as nylon, orlon, dacron, acrilon and others which are exclusively made from chemical substances. The chemicals used in the manufacture of synthetic fibre are derived from coal, petroleum, natural gas, other chemicals, water and air.

Ghaziabad ranks as the second most important synthetic fibre manufacturing centre in the district, after Modi Nagar where the famous 'Modi Pon' factory with a strength of 1600 employees, ranks as one of the most important synthetic fibre manufacturing concern of the country.

At Ghaziabad there are 4 registered units of synthetic fibre and allied industries. The total number of persons employed by these 4 units is 812 out of which 705 persons work in the single large scale concern of M/s. Swadeshi Polytex Ltd. which is located in the S.En. industrial zone of the city. This is a public limited concern started in the year 1970. It is a most modern automatic, computer-controlled factory which is engaged in the bulk production of 'Jailene' Polyester staple fibre. Manufacture of synthetic fibre at this concern involves complicated and highly controlled chemical processes. The requirements of highly skilled and trained personnel for this concern are easily met with from Delhi Metropolitan area as well as from other parts of the country.

Manufacture of synthetic fibre requires expensive machinery and more capital as compared to other chemical-based industries. M/s. Swadeshi Polytex Ltd. is the largest concern of chemical-based industries in the city. The major share of the huge capital required for its establishment has been invested by Jaipurias who are one of the famous industrial magnets in the country. Other advantages enjoyed by this famous concern are adequate supply of water for steaming purposes, spacious site in the newly developed Kavi Nagar industrial area, adequate availability of electricity and the efficient transport facilities for assembling the necessary chemicals.

However, the greatest stimulant for the establishment of 'Swadeshi Polytex Ltd.' at Ghaziabad lay in the fact that the city had already acquired reasonably good progress in cotton textile and other chemical industries. Synthetic fibre industry has close affinities with both of these industries.

The development of substantial quantum of chemical industries in the city provided the concern with established channels for assembling the chemical substances required for the industry. On the other hand, the cotton textile units in the capital provided near-at-hand markets for the finished products of the factory. Synthetic fibre blends well with cotton and therefore the cotton textile units are its biggest consumers. Instead of pure polyester cloth, there is more liking these days for polyester mixed cotton cloth. All synthetic fibres are moth-resistant, non-allergenic, washable, quick-drying and shrink-resistant. It is mainly because of their versatility, that they are being increasingly used for manufacturing different types of cloth. The location of the synthetic fibre manufacturing plant is near the cotton textile units. Establishment of M/s. Swadeshi Polytex Ltd. at Ghaziabad clearly elucidates this point in question. It is the only concern which manufactures synthetic fibre in the city. The remaining 3 units viz. M/s. The Housing and General Finance Pvt. Ltd., Pawa Engineering Company and Krishna Woollens Pvt. Ltd. are only small-scale units employing 75, 20 and 12 persons respectively. First two of these three factories manufacture high density polythene woven sacks which are so much in demand these days as a substitute for jute sacks. The third one manufactures synthetic woollens. None of these three factories have the characteristic features associated with the synthetic fibre manufacturing plant.

2. *Chemicals and Gases*

Manufacture of chemicals and gases is considered as the most important branch of chemical industry. At Ghaziabad, this branch of chemical industries ranks second after synthetic fibre. There are 19 such units in the city with a total registered employment of 615 persons which represent 1.63% share in the city's total. All of these units are small-scale factories engaged in the production of basic heavy chemicals, paints, varnish and lacquers, gases, and dyestuffs and dyes. 9 of these factories produce basic heavy chemicals both organic and inorganic. Majority of the factories manufacture organic chemicals which are synthesized from coal, petroleum, natural gas, wood, cotton and other plants. Some of the important organic chemicals include benzene, acetylene, ascetic acid, alcohol and ethyl acetate. Most of these chemicals are lighter and costlier than inorganic ones which are bulky and cheap. At Ghaziabad some of the factories do produce inorganic chemicals but because of smaller units, output is quite insignificant in view of the huge demand of these chemicals. At Ghaziabad the important units producing organic and inorganic chemicals include, M/s. A.K. Chemical Works, Air Reduction Company Ltd., Cryogenics India Ltd., Naval Chemical Industries, Pravin Chemical Industries, Manu Chemicals, and Malviya Chemicals .

Side by side with the production of chemicals, production of industrial gases is also an important chemical activity in the city. There are three gas manufacturing units viz. M/s. Industrial Oxygen Ltd., Sarveshri Gases Pvt. Ltd., and Kamal Industrial Gases and Allied Products. Of these former two produce pure oxygen and third one produces different other types of industrial gases.

Paints, varnish and lacquers are also manufactured in substantial quantity at the city. Important concerns manufacturing these chemicals are M/s. Asia Chemicals, Meera Chemicals, and Bansi Lal & Sons Pvt. Ltd. Of these three M/s. Bansi Lal & Sons is the oldest concern employing 35 persons. It was established in 1942 at Sahibabad. Asia Chemicals, and Meera Chemicals were established in 1946 and 1948 respectively.

Two of the chemical factories manufacture dyestuffs and dyes. These are M/s. Pristolite Chemicals, and N.K. Dyeing. One concern viz. 'Ganges Printing Ink' manufactures Ink.

Apart from 19 chemical units in Ghaziabad city, there are also 5 such units functioning at other manufacturing centres of the district with a total registered employment of 252 persons. Of these 5 units one located at Modi Nagar, viz. M/s. Modi Paints and Varnish Company is a large-scale public Ltd. concern employing 182 persons. All the other four units located one each at Loni, Noida, Murad Nagar and Hapur, are small scale factories producing various types of organic and inorganic chemicals.

As is clear from foregoing account, there is no large scale chemical-manufacturing unit in the city, a fact which pinpoints the gloomy side of the chemical industry in the city. Because of comparatively heavier requirements of capital, private entrepreneurs can hardly think of setting up a large-scale chemical plant. This is possible only if some big industrial magnet comes forward or if some public sector establishment is envisaged for boosting up the chemical manufacturing in the city on a bigger scale.

3. *Plastic and Foam Products*

Manufacture of plastic and foam products is the 3rd most important chemical-based industry in the city, after synthetic fibre, and chemicals and gases. Plastics have a wide range of application. It is widely used in electrical and communication equipments and household appliances.

There are two main phases of the manufacture of plastic and foam products. 1. the manufacture of plastic chemicals. 2. fabrication of various types of plastic products with plastic chemicals.

At Ghaziabad this industry is mainly concerned with the fabrication of various types of plastic products ranging from household items to those used for defence purposes. Plastic chemicals required for fabricating different types of plastic and foam products are obtained from Bombay which is the major centre of the production of various plastic chemicals in the country. Plastic chemicals are also manufactured at various petro-chemical plants set up near oil refineries at Koyali, Barauni and Madras.

There are 12 registered factories at Ghaziabad engaged in the fabrication of various types of plastic and foam products. Total number of persons employed in these factories is 528 which represents 1.4% share in the total registered employment of the city. Except two units viz. 'Leatherite Industries Pvt. Ltd.', and Wavin India Pvt. Ltd., which employ 126 and 93 persons respectively, all the other factories of this industry in the city are smaller units employing 20 to 50 persons. As far as manufacture of plastic and foam products is concerned, smaller factories are at no disadvantage. This is the main reason why, despite a late start, this industry has assumed considerable importance in the industrial structure of the city.

Majority of Ghaziabad's plastic units manufacture household and industrial items. Buckets, jar, combs, button, fruit containers, plastic crockery, trays, and bed cushions etc. are the main household items produced here. Important factories producing household and industrial items include M/s. B.K. Plastics Pvt. Ltd., Expanded Plastics, Bengal Plastic Industries, Shila Foam Products Pvt. Ltd. and Black Diamond Industries. Packaging items such as plastic containers and foam sheets are produced in substantial quantities at many of these factories, because of the large demand of these items at various factories of the city. M/s. Leatherite Industries Pvt. Ltd. which is the biggest concern of this industry in the city with 126 employees, manufactures acrylic plastic sheets. M/s. Wavin India Pvt. Ltd. is the famous concern manufacturing plastic items used for electrical goods. M/s. Plastic Fabricators manufactures plastic products meant for defence services.

Partly because of the versatility of plastic and partly because of suitability of the smaller size of the factory in this industry, manufacture of plastic and foam products holds good future prospects in the city. It is a market-oriented industry and Ghaziabad, because of its nearness to Delhi, offers the best possible opportunities in this respect. This industry was started in the city during sixtees and within a period of less than two decades, it has grown into one of the important industries of the city.

Manufacture of plastic products is also important at Hapur and Noida. There are three such units at Hapur and two at Noida, with a total registered employment of 78 persons. At all these factories, household items are fabricated for local requirements.

4. *Drugs and Medicines*

Manufacture of drugs and medicines is an important industrial activity associated with chemical industry. Drugs and pharmaceuticals manufacturing has assumed considerable significance at Ghaziabad during last two decades. Although the first drugs and pharmaceuticals industrial unit viz. 'Federal Chemical Works' was started much earlier but the real progress of industry has occurred during last 20 years.

Equipments required for the manufacture of drugs and medicines may be medium to high cost but the more specific requirement for this industry is that of highly skilled labour because of accuracy and perfection needed for the processing of various drugs and medicines. This industry also needs relatively higher investment on research which is the keynote for its success. 'The Indian Drugs and Pharmaceutical Ltd.' was established in the year 1961 with the main objective of promoting the growth of drugs and pharmaceutical manufacturing in the country. Institutions like WHO and UNICEF have also contributed a lot in fostering this industry in the country. Ghaziabad being near to Delhi is in a better position to keep in touch with the latest development taking place in the field of medicine at various research institutions in Delhi.

Raw materials required for this industry are relatively high-priced but as most of these are required only in small quantities, it is not difficult to assemble them even from distant sources.

Geographical association is the characteristic feature of the manufacture of drugs and pharmaceuticals. These concerns gain much by being near to each other not because of too much of linkage but because of technical delicacies involved. Newer concerns tend to locate near other drug and pharmaceutical units in order to take advantage of the established channels for assembling of materials and distributing of products. Ghaziabad's 70% drug manufacturing units are located in a single industrial area, a fact which clearly emphasizes the importance of geographical association for the success of this industry.

There are seven registered units at Ghaziabad, engaged in the manufacture of various types of drugs and medicines. Total registered employment in these seven units is 419 which represents over 1% share in the city's total. M/s. Unichem Laboratories which employs 235 persons, is the only large-scale public limited concern of this industry. Apart from various patent and proprietory drugs, this concern also manufactures high protein biscuits.

All the other units of this industry are small-scale units. Except 'M.M. Laboratories' which employs 71 persons, all the other concerns employ 10 to 45 persons.

M/s. Piya Pharmaceuticals is engaged in capsuling and tableting the basic raw materials. M/s. Emson and Company are the approved suppliers of D.G.S. & D. Other main concerns are M/s. G.D. Pharmaceutical Products, Omega Pharmaceuticals, and Federal Chemical Works. The much common anti-septic cream of 'Boroline' is manufactured at M/s. G.D. Pharmaceuticals Products.

Manufacture of drugs and medicines is not at all important at other manufacturing centres in the district. There is only one registered unit of this industry outside Ghaziabad city. This is a small factory of 10 person located at Hapur, which manufactures biological medicines.

5. *Other Chemical Industries*

Amongst the other chemical-based industries present in Ghaziabad city, a mention may be made of manufacture of cosmetics, pesticides and insecticides, glue and gelatine, and enamelling, japaning and polishing of metal products. There are 8 units with a registered employment of 333 persons, which fabricate these different other types of chemical products. M/s. Swadeshi Detergents, which is a bigger concern of 178 persons manufactures cosmetics like shampoos, lipstick and nail polishes etc. Four of these units viz. M/s. Saluja Udyog, Sulekha Works, Sundeo Chemical Industries. and Everest Plastics, manufacture glue and gelatine. 2 of these units viz. M/s. Bright Star Industries, and Mittal Engineering Works are engaged in enamelling, japaning and polishing of metal products. Pesticides and insecticides are manufactured at M/s. Industrial Chemicals and Mineral Private Limited.

At other manufacturing centres of the district, there are 6 such units with the total registered employment of 157 persons, which perform these different other types of chemical activity. Of these 6 units, 2 manufacturing rubber chemical and pesticides are located at Loni, two producing bone powder, and glue and gelatine are at Hapur, one at Noida, manufacturing mixed fertilizer and one at Modi Nagar which is engaged in enamelling, japaning and polishing of metal products.

Distribution of Chemical-based Industries at Ghaziabad

A glance at the table No. 6.5 (fig. No. 21) clearly reveals the marked concentration of different chemical industries in specific industrial areas of the city. Synthetic fibre and drugs and medicines depict the highest concentration. In both these cases more than 80% of the total registered employment of the industry is located in one single industrial area. S. En. industrial zone contains 88% share of synthetic fibre industry and Meerut Road industrial area, which constitutes the major part of N.E. Central Zone, contains 85% share of the manufacture of drugs and medicines. Concentration in the manufacture of drugs and medicines has resulted from the geographical association of 5 out of 7 concerns in one single industrial area of Meerut Road. Synthetic fibre industry appears to be concentrated in S.En. zone because of establishment in this area, of the large scale concern of M/s. Swadeshi Polytex Ltd. which employ 705 persons out of the total 812 engaged in this industry.

TABLE 6.5: **Distribution of Chemical-based Industries at Ghaziabad***

Name of the Industry		S. En. zone	North East Central Zone	C.B.D. Area	Trans-Hindan Zone
Synthetic Fibre	No. of regd. units	2	-	-	2
	No. of regd. employment	717	-	-	95
	Percentage share in the area	88.30%	-	-	11.70%
Chemicals & Gases	No. of regd. units	7	1	-	11
	No. of regd. employment	247	16	-	352
	Percentage share in the area	40.16%	2.60%	-	57.24%
Plastic & Foam Products	No. of regd.Units	1	3	-	8
	No. of regd. employment	48	72	-	308
	Percentage share in the area	11.21%	16.82%	-	71.97%
Drugs & Medicines	No. of regd. Units	-	5	-	2
	No. of regd. employment	-	355	-	64
	Percentage share in the area	-	84.73%	-	15.27%

**Source*: Ibid, Table No. 6.2.

Other two important chemical industries of the city, namely chemicals and gases, and plastic and foam products, also characterize concentration though to a lesser degree. About 72% of registered employment in plastic and foam products industry is found in

Trans-Hindan Industrial Area which falls nearest to the vast market potential of Delhi metropolitan area. Manufacture of chemicals and gases exhibits concentration in two distinct industrial areas. Trans-Hindan and S. En. Industrial zones contain about 57 and 40 percent share respectively of the total registered employment in the manufacture of chemicals and gases. The factories of chemicals and gases in S.En. industrial zone catered to the needs of various industrial units within the city area while those in Trans-Hindan zone served the numerous industrial units of Mohan Nagar and Sahibabad.

Though different chemical industries of the city show marked concentration in specific industrial areas of the city, the distribution of chemical industries as a whole shows highest concentration in S.En. industrial zone. This zone alone contains more than 50% share of the total registered employment in chemical industries. Synthetic fibre, and chemicals and gases are the two most important chemical industries here. Next important area is Trans-Hindan industrial zone followed by N.E. Central zone. There is no such factory in the C.B.D. area, notwithstanding the early start of these industries in the industrial history of Ghaziabad.

Future Prospects

At the end, we would stress that it is very difficult to make a prophecy regarding the future of chemical industries in the city. Apart from the difficulty of huge sums of capital required for the establishment of these industries, the products of these industries also suffer from intense competition not only amongst themselves but also with natural products like rubber, cotton, leather and wood. Rapid development of new products outdates the pre-existing ones and thus many of the factories which are not able to adapt themselves to new developments, have to suffer serious financial losses. Involvement of stake factor is too great as compared to many other industries, a fact that considerably dampens the future prospects of these industries at Ghaziabad. However, in view of the proximity of Mathura Oil Refinery. development of petro-chemical industries may hold a good future in the city but how will future unfold itself in respect of chemical industries at Ghaziabad, will be best ascertained only by the coming years ahead.

Fig. 20
CHEMICAL–BASED INDUSTRIES

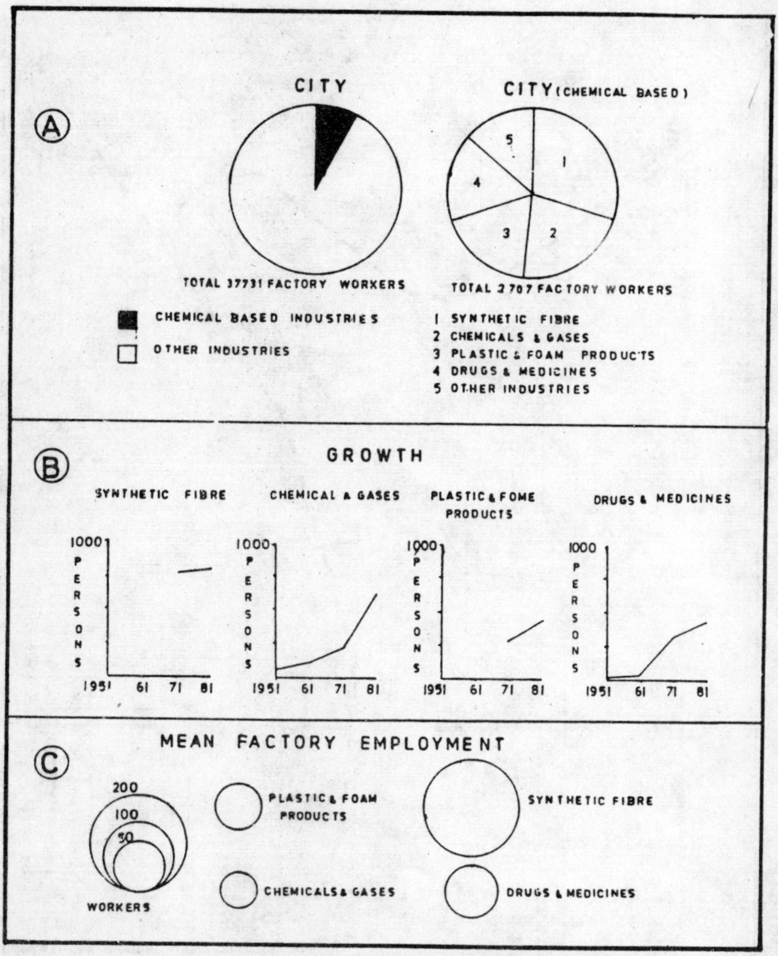

Fig. 21
CHEMICAL-BASED INDUSTRIES AT GHAZIABAD

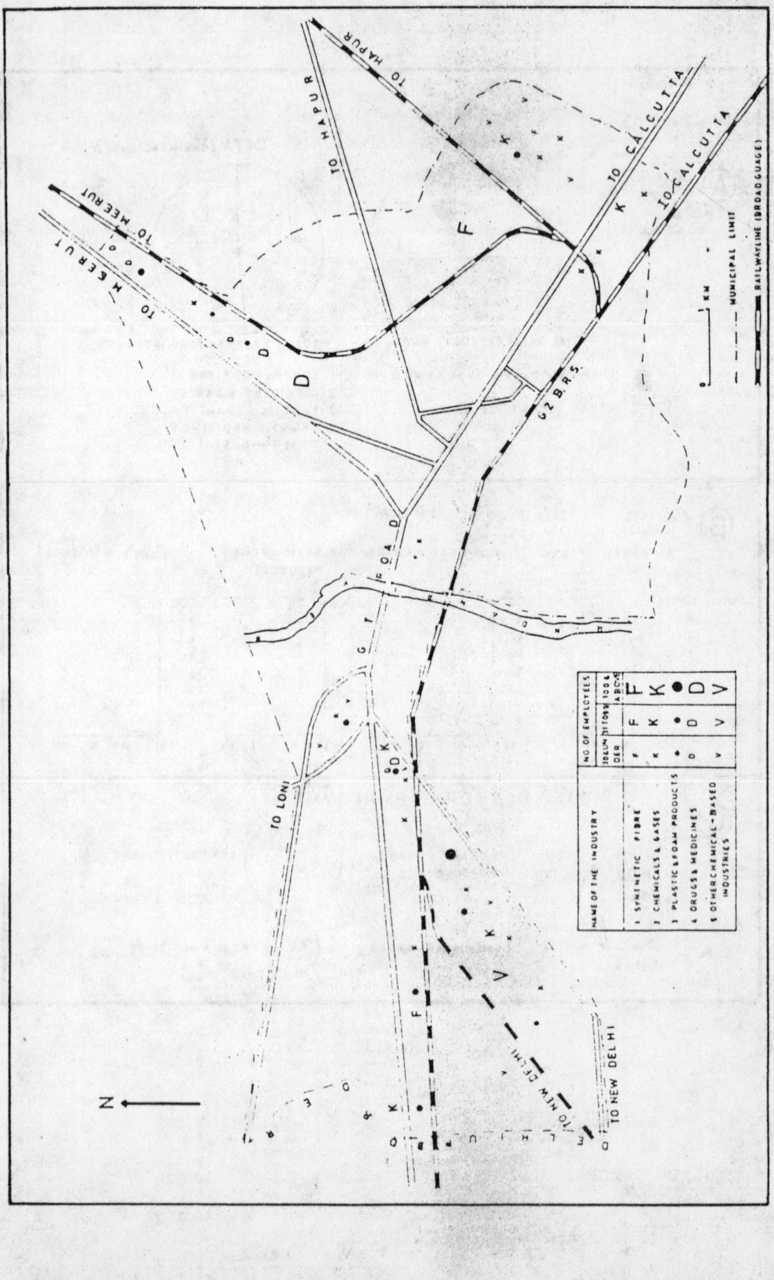

SEVEN

Other Manufacturing Industries

Ghaziabad's vast industrial structure also includes a number of other manufacturing industries which do not belong to any of the three groups discussed in the preceding chapters. There are 96 registered factories in the city which are engaged in various other types of manufacturing activities, e.g. paper and paper products, glassware, structural clay products, Ayurvedic and Unani medicines, coated abrasives, printing presses, cold storages, foot-wear, woollens and so on. Total number of persons engaged in the registered factories of these industries is about 4000, which represents more than 10% share in the total registered employment of the city. Some of these industries like glassware, structural clay products, paper and paper products, corrugated boxes, Ayurvedic and Unani medicines, are amongst the important industries of the city in terms of total registered employment.

These miscellaneous industries are also important at other manufacturing centres of the district. Total number of such registered units at these centres is 62 employing 2096 persons which represents 6.72% share in the total registered employment of these other manufacturing centres in the district of Ghaziabad. The present chapter, however, is concerned mainly with a brief description of these miscellaneous industries in the city of Ghaziabad.

1. *Glass and Glass Products*

Manufacture of glass and glass products is the 10th most

important industrial activity of the city, employing 903 persons at 3 large scale concerns, which represent 2.40% share in the total registered employment of the city.

The origin and development of this industry owes mainly to the large demand of bottleware at Mohan Meakins Breweries Ltd., the famous wine manufacturing concern of the city. Manufacture of drugs and medicines in the city also acted as a stimulant for the growth of this industry. First factory of this industry viz. 'Mohan Crystal Glass Works' with 630 employees which is the largest public Ltd. concern of this industry in the city, was established in the year 1965. It supplies whole of its production to M/s. Mohan Meakins Breweries Ltd., and to F.D.M. Food Products Breweries Ltd. Other concerns viz. 'Indian Glass Agency' and 'Universal Glass Ltd.' were established a few years later. M/s. Indian Glass Agency with 103 employees is a partnership concern and Universal Glass Ltd. with 170 employees is a public limited unit. Throughout since its inception in 1965, industry has grown steadily. There was no sudden spurt ever, because of the need-based character of this industry in the city.

Partly because of late start and partly because of nearness of its major customer, M/s. Mohan Meakins Breweries Ltd., all the three glass and glass products manufacturing concerns of the city, have been located in the trans-Hindan industrial zone.

Availability of raw materials, trained and skilled labour, huge capital and nearness to market are amongst the main factors responsible for the development of the glass and glass products industry at Ghaziabad. Main raw materials required for glass manufacturing are cycleasid sand and dolomite powder, which are both obtained from Rajasthan via road transport. Cost of assembling the raw material is relatively higher in relation to the cost of raw material itself, but because of brittle nature of the glass, nearness to market is more important factor in this industry than the nearness to the sources of raw material. Because of efficient transport facilities, it is not at all difficult to arrange the supply of raw material at glass and glass products manufacturing concerns. Apart from cycleasid sand and dolomite powder, broken glass which is obtained in fairly big quantity from Delhi, is also used as a raw material for manufacturing glass and glass products in the city. However it supplies only a small proportion of the total requirements of raw material. Larger part of the production is obtained from cycleasid sand and dolomite powder brought from Rajasthan.

Apart from the raw materials of sand and dolomite or broken glass, glass manufacturing also requires certain chemicals such as sodium carbide and boreux which are easily obtained from Delhi. In respect of skilled labour and near at-hand market, Gaziabad's glass and glass products manufacturing concerns are at considerable advantage. Major part of the production is utilized by local concerns and only a small proportion is sent to Delhi and other nearby areas. Because of nearness to Delhi, trained and skilled labour for the industry is easily available. Many of the technical persons working at these concerns belong to far off places in the country.

Power requirements of this industry are relatively heavier. Both coal and oil are used as a source of fuel. Oil is obtained from Indian Oil Corporation and coal from Jharia. Electricity is used for other general purposes.

Characteristic feature of the functional structure of glass industry at Ghaziabad is the mass production of bottleware for wines and other uses. Other branches of the industry, e.g. manufacture of sheet glass and scientific glassware have not made any headway mainly because of the huge demand of bottleware at other industrial establishments of the city. Existing units of the industry suffice only for meeting the bottleware requirements of the city. Other branches of glass manufacturing may be introduced, only if newer units are set up in the city.

Glass factories at Ghaziabad have acquired specialization in the manufacture of bottleware. Bottles manufactured for wines at 'Mohan Crystal Glass Works' are superb in their shape, design, and finishing. Mere appearance of these wine bottles yields a sense of art and ecstasy. Other two concerns manufacture bottles for the various drugs and medicines manufacturing units of the city. A small proportion of the production is also sent to Nepal and Bhutan where are located sister concerns of 'Mohan Meakins Breweries Ltd.'

Need-based character of the glass and glass products industry at Ghaziabad may well indicate a prospective future in view of the growing industrial activity at the city. Industry has made only a steady progress since its inception in 1965 and the same may be maintained in future also. There is not much hope for any big spurt because of the various difficulties confronted by this industry in the city.

Apart from distant raw material, another problem faced by the industry is that of importing the furnace bricks from Japan or Germany, after every five years or so, for replacing the old ones at the factory. 'Mohan Crystal Glass Works' imports furnace bricks worth Rs. 15 lacs after every five years to replace the old ones at the factory. This is not only a costly affair but also entails a lot of difficulties in arranging the imports.

Another difficulty faced by the industry is regarding the licence policy of the Govt. Concerns are forced to produce much below their installed capacity for the reason of not having the licence to produce more. 'Mohan Crystal Glass Works' which has a installed capacity of 21 thousand tons of production, have been provided the licence only for the production of 7000 tons of glass and glass products. This is really a gloomy aspect of the industry.

Despite all these handicaps, there is every likelihood that this industry may expand further in future. Glass is gradually replacing metals for various industrial purposes, including pipes in many of the chemical factories and also many other types of industrial items. New branches of glass manufacturing may be introduced depending upon the requirements of these new products at the various industrial units of the city. However, increasing use of plastic bottles for different purposes leaves little hope for any substantial expansion of glass bottleware industry at Ghaziabad.

2. *Structural Clay Products*

Manufacture of structural clay products constitutes the 12th most important industrial activity in the city with 12 registered units employing 831 persons which represent 2.20% share in the total registered employment of the city. Structural clay products cover a wide variety of manufactured items. At Ghaziabad, this industry includes manufacture of ceramics and pottery, cement and marble products, refractories and mineral products consisting of various types of powders like graphite powder, steam coal powder and clay powder etc. This industry, as a whole , plays an important role in the industrial structure of the city. However, at other manufacturing centres of the district, it is quite insignificant with a total registered employment of only 65 persons in 3 registered units. These three units are located one each at Dasna, Jindal Nagar and Noida, employing 18, 10 and 37 persons respectively. In the following pages, we will discuss this industry only in the context of Ghaziabad city, where it assumes considerable significance in the total industrial structure of the city.

This industry took its inception in the city with the establishment of famous 'U.P. Ceramics & Pottery Ltd: in the year 1948. It is a large scale public limited concern employing more than 400 persons. Despite an early and big start, the industry did not fare well, as no new unit was set up until 1961 either of pottery or of any other related branch. However, other branches of this industry viz. refractories, cement and concrete products, and mineral products have been progressing well during the last 20 years. 'U.P. Ceramics and Pottery Ltd.' is the only public limited concern. All the other units of structural clay products industry are small factories employing less than 50 persons except one viz. 'Lal Chand Anand & Sons' which is a partnership concern of refractory with 150 employees.

Spatial distribution of structural clay products industry reveals a very high degree of concentration in S.En. industrial zone.

TABLE 7.1 **Growth of Structural Clay Products Industry at Ghaziabad**

Years	No. of regd. units	No. of regd. employment	Percentage share in the city's total employment
1951	1	446	17.45
1961	1	446	6.84
1971	8	582	2.58
1981	12	831	2.20

Source: Ibid Table No. 6.2.

Here are located 10 out of the total 12 industrial units representing 96.63% share in terms of total registered employment of the industry in the city. Factories located in S.En. Industrial Zone include M/s. U.P. Ceramics & Pottery Ltd., Supreme Ceramics Pvt. Ltd., Lal Chand Anand & Sons Pvt. Ltd., Janta Refractories Pvt. Ltd., Indoseisin Refractories Pvt. Ltd., Marbelene India, Ghaziabad Minerals, Diamond Mineral Industries, Neelam Graphites and Minerals, and U.P. Ceramics & Pottery Ltd. Unit No. 2. Two registered factories located outside this industrial zone are 'Reliance Refractories' in Meerut Road Industrial area and 'Cement Pipe Corporation' in Rajendra Nagar Industrial Estate. Too much of concentration in this industry owes largely to requirements of trained and skilled persons which are easy to procure at an established area of concerned manufacturing activity.

TABLE 7.2: Spatial Distribution of Structural Clay Products Industry at Ghaziabad.

Name of the Area	No. of regd. units	No. of regd. employment	Percentage share of the industry in terms of regd. employment.
1. S.En. Industrial Zone	10	803	96.63
2. N. Central Industrial Zone	1	18	2.17
3. C.B.D. Area	-	-	1.20
4. Trans-Hindan Industrial Zone	1	10	1.20
Total	12	831	100.00%

Source : Ibid Table No. 6.2

Main raw material required for most of these industries is the various special varieties of clay. Depending upon its specific properties, clay may vary a lot in its price range. There is no problem, however, in obtaining these special varieties of clay from nearby areas by trucks. Apart from the clay which is used in the manufacture of ceramics and in refractories, mineral industries require certain specific minerals which are obtained from far off places in Bihar and M.P. Another requirement of these industries is certain specific chemicals which are easily available locally or from Delhi.

Structural clay products industries place comparatively greater emphasis on trained and skilled persons, specially in the case of ceramics and refractories. Manufacture of ceramics depends much on the traditionally skilled labour, which is in short supply in the city, a fact which has resulted in the relegation of this branch of industry into insignificance as compared to other main industries in the city.

In respect of other requirements, this industry enjoys the same advantages as those availed by other industries.

More than 70% of the total employees engaged in structural clay products industries are working in the two units of U.P. Ceramics & Pottery Ltd., which employ 446 and 90 persons respectively. Both these concerns are large scale units. Smaller unit is engaged in the manufacture of bone china, i.e., clay obtained by crushing the bones of animals, which is mixed with the ordinary clay to fabricate ceramic products. Bigger unit manufacture china tea sets, dinner sets, bowls, mugs, cups, saucers and plates under the trade mark of 'Hitkari Pottery'. Pottery manufactured by this famous concern enjoys a good reputation and is also sent to other states in Nn. India. Apart from the two large-scale units of U.P. Ceramic & Pottery Ltd., there is also one small factory viz. M/s. Supreme Ceramics Pvt. Ltd. of 24 persons engaged in the manufacture of ordinary china products.

Second most important structural clay products industry is the manufacture of furnace bricks at the four refractories located in the city. M/s. Lal Chand Anand & Sons Pvt. Ltd. is the biggest refractory of the city with 150 employees out of the total 207 engaged in this branch of industry. Here are manufactured high alumina bricks, and insulation and acid free bricks used in various types of furnaces. Other three refractories are M/s. Janta Refractory, Indoseisin Refractory, and Reliance Refractory. Of these four, 3 refractories are located in S.En. Industrial zone and one in Meerut Road Industrial Area.

Another important activity of structural clay products industry is the manufacture of graphite powder, bentonite powder, steam coal powder and clay powder, which is carried out at 3 registered units of M/s. Ghaziabad Minerals, Neelam Graphites & Minerals, and

Diamond Mineral Industries, all of which are located in S.En. industrial zone.

Amongst other concerns, M/s. Cement Pipe Corporation at Rajendra Nagar industrial estate manufactures R.C.C. pipes and 'Marbelene India' at S.En. industrial zone produces marble and concrete tiles, cement jalis and blocks.

Except cement products and ceramics, products of all the other branches of this industry cater to the needs of various industrial establishments of the city. Major part of the furnace bricks produced at Ghaziabad's refractories, is consumed by local industrial units which use furnaces in their manufacturing process. Similarly larger part of the various types of mineral products like graphite powder, bentonite powder, clay powder etc. is utilized by various other concerns of the city. Most of the cement products manufactured here are used in the building construction work of the city. Thus it can be safely presumed that refractories, mineral industries, and manufacture of cement products hold good future prospects in view of the rapidly growing industrialization and urbanization taking place in the city.

However, manufacture of ceramics and pottery suffers from certain inherent disadvantages which have caused a sort of stagnation in this branch of industry since after the establishment of M/s. U.P. Ceramics & Pottery Ltd. in 1948. This branch of industry had to face stiff competition with the ceramic products manufactured at Khurja which is a traditional centre of handicraft ceramics and potteries. Products of Khurja Pottery are much cheaper firstly because the particular clay required for the manufacture of pottery is found in abundance at Khurja itself, and secondly there is available cheap and plentiful labour having a traditional skill in this branch of industry. Ghaziabad is at a disadvantage in both these respects and hence manufacture of ceramics and pottery could not thrive here despite an early and good beginning. Further prospects for the further expansion of ceramics and pottery in the city are quite dismal, as compared to other branches of structural clay products industry at Ghaziabad.

3. *Ayurvedic & Unani Medicines*

At Ghaziabad not only is the manufacture of allopathic drugs and medicines an important industrial activity, but even more important than the former is the manufacture of Ayurvedic and Unani medicines which represents 1.68% share in the industrial structure of the city as against 1.11% of that of the former.

There exist only two big large scale units of this industry in the city viz. M/s. Dabur Industries Ltd. and Hamdard Laboratories Ltd., which employ 461 and 174 persons respectively. Both are public limited concerns engaged in the large scale production of Ayurvedic and Unani medicines. Dabur Industries Ltd. established in 1973 in site 4 Industrial area manufactures Ayurvedic medicines. 'Chyvanprash' and Dabur Amla Hair Oil' are the two much popular products of this concern apart from various other Ayurvedic medicines. 'Hamdard Laboratories Ltd.' manufacture Unani medicines most of which e.g. Saduri, Safi, Pachnaul, Taunic Naunihal and Lavan Bhaskar Churan etc. are known for their curative reactions. 'Hamdard Laboratories Ltd.' was set up in 1972 in Meerut Road Industrial Area.

Both these units use a wide variety of raw materials ranging from various types of herbs to spices, dry fruits, oils, sugar and salt etc. Most of the products manufactured here enjoy a nation-wide market and some are even sent to other countries. Both these concerns are functioning well and are likely to expand their capacity in view of large demand of their products in the world of medicines. However establishment of other such units in near future does not seem feasible because this branch depends too much on specialization and only standard and reputed concerns can capture substantial market for their products.

4 *Paper and Board*

Manufacture of paper and board constitutes one of important industrial activities in the city of Ghaziabad. There are 17 registered units in the city which are engaged in the manufacture of paper board and different types of paper products, with a total registered employment of 526 persons representing 1.13% share in the city's total. Amongst the other manufacturing centres of the district, manufacture of paper, board, and paper products is important at Pilkhuwa, Hapur, Modinagar, and Muradnagar where are engaged 59, 64, 55 and 34 persons respectively in this industry at 7 registered factories in all. Out of these 7 registered factories one is located at Pilkhuwa and two each at other three centres. In the following pages, however, our discussion about this industry will mainly concern with its different aspects in the city of Ghaziabad.

Manufacture of paper and board started in the city mainly after 1961, although the famous paper products manufacturing concern of 'Bloom Field Trading Company had been established as early as 1947. First paper and board manufacturing concern viz.'Gopal Paper & Board Mills' was set up in the year 1962 in the Meerut Road industrial area. During succeeding year a number of new factories came up and their number rose to 13 in 1971. The important factories set up in Meerut Road industrial area during this period were M/s. A.K. Board Mills, Bankey Behari Board Mills, and Ganesh Paper Mills.

TABLE 7.3: **Spatial Distribution of Paper & Board Industry at Ghaziabad.**

Name of the Area	No. of Units	No. of regd. employment	Percentage share of the industry in the area
S.E. Industrial Zone	1	35	6.66%
N. Central Zone	6	209	39.73%
C.B.D. Area	-	-	-
Trans-Hindan, Industrial Zone	10	282	53.61%
Total	17	526	100.00%

Apart from Meerut Road Industrial area, another area where are located a number of paper and board mills is Sahibabad and site 4 industrial area. Many of these factories located in this area were established during the decade ending in 1981. Important concerns manufacturing paper and board in this area include M/s. Atlas Board Mills, Bagla Paper Mills, Hindustan Papers, Jagdish Paper & Board Mills, Pragati Paper and Board Mills, Rani Sati Paper Mills, Sanjay Board and Paper Mills, and Munish Paper & Board Mill.

Apart from Meerut Road and Sahibabad industrial areas which respectively contain 6 and 8 paper and board factories, three of the concerns viz. M/s. Climax Trading Co., Siddhumal Paper Conversion Corpn. Pvt. Ltd., and Capital Paper Mills are located in Anand Industrial Estate, Loni Road Industrial Area, and Bulandshahr Road Industrial area respectively.

Manufacture of paper and board at Ghaziabad derived its main inspiration from the growing industrial expansion of the city, a fact which is clearly manifested in the functional structure of the concerns of this industry here. Majority of the concerns here manufacture craft paper, board and wrapping paper used for packing purposes. Almost whole of the craft paper manufactured at Ghaziabad's paper and board mills is consumed by various packaging concerns in the city for the manufacture of corrugated boxes. Some of the board and wrapping paper is also sent to Delhi and Meerut.

Apart from craft paper, board, and wrapping paper, a few of Ghaziabad's concerns e.g. M/s. Capital Paper Mills, and Regal Paper Mills, also manufacture certain special types of paper such as tissue paper, coloured paper and high gloss cast coated paper. Three out of 17 concerns manufacture various types of paper products such as straws, wrappers, paper hankies, board trays, and baking cases. M/s. Siddhumal Paper Conversion Corpn. manufacture flexible paper cartons while 'Bloom Field Trading Co.', and 'Climax Trading Corpn.' manufacture various other types of above mentioned paper products. This branch of industry has thrived mainly on the large urban demand of these items at Delhi and Ghaziabad. However, it employs only 45 persons out of 526 engaged in this industry.

Main raw material used by Ghaziabad's paper and board mills is waste paper which is easily obtained from Delhi by trucks. Straw is also used as raw material by the concerns manufacturing straw board. Other main items required by the industry are various types of chemicals such as caustic soda, sodium sulphate and calcium sulphate which are obtained locally and also from Delhi. In respect of other requirements like power, labour transportation and water etc. industry enjoys the same advantages as those availed by other industries.

All the factories manufacturing paper, board, and various types of paper products at Ghaziabad are of small to medium size, a fact which itself limits very high expectations for the future progress of this industry in the city. None of the factories employs more than or near 100 persons. There are only 5 concerns which employ 40 to 60 persons and remaining 12 units are small factories of only 10 to 40 employees. Manufacture of wrapping paper, and board for packing purposes is conveniently and economically carried out in smaller units and so industry is not handicapped because of the smaller size of the factories. However absence of the manufacture of writing paper is quite pinpointing in the functional structure of the industry in the city, but there is little scope for this branch to develop because of lack of suitable raw materials required for the manufacturing of writing paper. Smaller size of paper and board mills also restricts the manufacture of writing paper which can be economically produced only at large-scale units.

As the functional structure of this industry in the city is closely linked with industrial requirement of the city, it is hoped that manufacture of packing paper and board will make further progress in the city, in view of the growing industrialization at the city. Manufacture of various types of paper products, too, holds good future prospects because of large demand of these items in the urban markets of surrounding areas.

5. *Corrugated Boxes*

Manufacture of corrugated boxes has assumed considerable significance during past 15 years. It now ranks, though last, amongst the 24 important industries in the city with 8 registered units employing 301 persons representing 0.79% share in the total registered employment of the city. This industry is also important at Hapur, Modinagar and Noida. Two of such units are located each at Modinagar and Hapur and one at Noida employing 140 persons in all.

In a growing industrial centre like Ghaziabad development of manufacture of corrugated boxes seems quite natural and relevant. Majority of city's industrial units require corrugated boxes for the final packing of their products. Being a demand-oriented industry, manufacture of corrugated boxes has made significant progress during past fifteen years. Industry was being carried out by small unregistered units even before 1961, but increased demand enhanced the importance of industry resulting in the establishment of a number of comparatively bigger units registered under factories etc.

Apart from the huge demand, this industry also derived its encouragement from the plentiful availability of craft paper here from the various paper and board mills of the city. Near at hand supply of raw material coupled with the immediate disposal of finished products to local industrial units acted as a strong stimulant for the rapid growth of the industry. Apart from the craft paper which represent 75% share in the total cost of production, other things required for the industry are adhesives, stitching wire and inks, which are all required in smaller quantities and are easily obtained from Delhi or locally.

Out of city's 8 registered factories of this industry, only one viz. 'Vikash Packagings' is located at S.En. Industrial zone and remaining 7 units in Trans-Hindan industrial area. Of these 7 units, 'Secure Pack' is the largest factory of the city, manufacturing corrugated boxes. It employs more than 60 persons and supplies to M/s. Hindustan Lever Ltd. and Dabur Industries at Ghaziabad. Other concerns of trans-Hindan area are M/s. Namdhari Gatta Mills, M.S. Packagings, Premier Packagings Products, Packwell Mfg. Co. Pvt. Ltd., Raizada Packing Industries, and Everest Corrugating Industries. More than 90% of manufacture of corrugated boxes is located in trans-Hindan area where is located also a major share of the manufacture of paper and board, which provides raw material to the former. Corrugated boxes manufactured at Ghaziabad not only cater to requirements of local factories but are also sent to Delhi, Meerut and Aligarh. The industry holds a good future in view of the rapid industrialization taking place in the city.

6. *Abrasives*

Abrasives constitute the basic tools of modern industry. All industries do need some sort of abrasive in their manufacturing process and hence manufacture of abrasives assumes a key role in the general process of industrialization at a place.

TABLE 7.4: **Distribution of Corrugated Boxes Industry in Ghaziabad City**

Name of the Area	No. of regd. units	No. of regd. employ.	Percentage share.
1. S.En. Industrial Zone	1	18	5.98%
2. N. Central Industrial Zone	-	-	-
3. C.B.D. Area	-	-	-
4. Trans-Hindan Industrial Zone	7	283	94.02%
Total	8	301	100.00%

At present there are functioning two industrial units in the city which manufacture different varieties of coated and bonded abrasives. The bigger and the older concern viz. M/s. 'John Oakey & Mohan Ltd.' is a public limited establishment employing 192 employees. It is the second biggest concern of its kind in whole of India, the first being M/s. Universal Corborundum Ltd. located at Madras. Originally, this concern functioned at Rawalpindi under the name of 'National Abrasives' which was transferred to Ghaziabad under the proprietorship of 'Dyer Meakins' during the course of partition of the country in 1947. In the year 1961, a new public limited company was formed which took over from 'National Abrasives' and also purchased the plant of 'Hindustan Abrasives' located at Omalur in Salem Distt. of Tamilnadu. The entire plant then was shifted to its present site at Mohan Nagar. As 'Hindustan Abrasives' was set up in collaboration with 'John Oakey and Sons Ltd., London,' this new public Ltd. concern was named as 'John Oakey & Mohan Ltd.' in which Mohans have the largest share and therefore are its managing Directors.

Another units of this industry in the city is 'Elerox Abrasives Pvt. Ltd.', which was established towards the late seventies. It is a smaller concern of 53 persons located at Meerut Road Industrial area. There exists no registered factory of this industry at any other manufacturing centre of the district.

Manufacture of abrasives involves too much of technical complexities and therefore the major factor determining its location is the availability of technical know-how.

This industry uses a number of diverse and specific raw materials which are obtained from wide apart sources in the country as well as from abroad. Nearness of raw materials is completely out of question in the case of this industry because of varied and specific nature of different raw material used for the manufacture of abrasives. Raw materials of this industry can be classed under three heads : (1) Abrasive grains like Silica and garnet grains which are obtained from Rajasthan 'emery grains which are available from Faridabad, and alluminium oxide and silicon carbide which are brought from Porbander in Gujrat, (2) Bonding materials like animal hide glue and bone glue which are obtained from Madras, gelatines which are brought from Jubblepore, and phenolic risins which are available locally (3) Backing surfaces for coated abrasives such as special type of craft paper which is obtained from Punalur in Kerala, Manila paper which is imported from England and Germany and industrial drill cloth which is purchased from Binnys at Madras.

As regards availability of technical know-how, which is the main factor for the success of this industry, Ghaziabad's 'John Oakey and Mohan Ltd.' experienced no such problem, because it was not a new concern, but only succeeded pre-existing concerns of 'National Abrasives' and 'Hindustan Abrasives'.

Various types of coated and bonded abrasives manufactured at Ghaziabad are sent to almost all the states in India and are also exported to countries in Far East. Annual sale value of 'John Oakey & Mohan Ltd.' has shot up from Rs. 5 Lacs in 1961 to Rs. 3 crore in 1981. Not only does this concern hold very good future prospects but industry as a whole also stands good chances of future development because of enormous demand of its products for industry.

7. *Printing presses*

At an industrial and educational centre like Ghaziabad, emergence of printing presses seems to be a most natural phenomenon. It is an industry which is fed mainly by local demand. However, at Ghaziabad, this industry has suffered a considerable setback because of nearness of Delhi. Majority of Ghaziabad's local customers avail printing press services from those in Delhi and this is the reason why this industry has developed only marginally at Ghaziabad. There exist only 7 registered printing presses in the city employing 165 persons in all which represents only .43% share in the total registered employment of the city.

M/s. Delhi Press Samachar Patra Ltd., located in Meerut Road Industrial area is, by far, the largest press of the city with a total strength of 40 persons. Here are printed and published famous magazines like 'Sarita', 'Mukta', 'Caravan' and 'Women's Era'. Other important presses are 'Talpatra Enterprises' and 'Vinapar Mudran' employing 36 and 25 persons respectively. Remaining four presses are smaller units of 10 to 20 persons viz. M/s. 'Lipika Printers Pvt. Ltd.', 'Book Bind Corporation', 'Sahibabad Printers', and 'Law & Management house'. At other manufacturing centres, there are functioning 5 printing presses at Noida, one at Modi Nagar and one at Hapur. All these presses are smaller units of 10 to 20 persons.

8. *Manufacture of Footwear*

Manufacture of footwear employs 157 persons in the city representing .42% share in the total registered employment. There exist five registered units in the city which are engaged in the manufacture of P.V.C. and rubber footwear. Despite a huge demand, footwear industry in the city has not made any significant progress mainly because of competition with other industries in the city, and also with footwear products manufactured at Delhi.

'Swik India Ltd.' is the largest concern manufacturing footwear at Ghaziabad. It employs 65 persons and is located in site 4 Industrial area. Other main concerns are M/s. Jumboo Footwear Pvt. Ltd., Kalinga Udyog, Supreme Plastic Industries, and Foreign Exporters & Manufactures Ltd. Of these, former three are located in Sahibabad Industrial area and the last one at Loni Road in Mohan Nagar. At other manufacturing centres, footwear manufacturing is carried out at Pilkhuwa, at one registered unit employing 27 persons.

9. *Rubber Products*

There are functioning only 3 registered units in the city which are engaged in the manufacture of reclaimed rubber, rubber pipes, rubber sheets and other allied rubber products. Total number of persons employed by these 3 registered factories is 146 which represent .38% share in the total registered employment of the city.

M/s. S.W. Rubber Works located along Meerut Road constitutes the largest factory of the city manufacturing reclaimed rubber and allied rubber products made to order. It employs 100 persons and was established in 1970. Other two concerns are M/s. Mansfield Rubber Works, and Shankar Rubber Industries which employ 28 and 18 persons respectively. Both these concerns manufacture rubber pipes and rubber sheets. 'Mansfield Rubber Works' is also located in Meerut Road Industrial Area and 'Shankar Rubber Industries' in S. En. industrial zone.

Manufacture of rubber products is also important at Jindal Nagar, Noida, Loni and Chapraula where this industry employs 143, 80, 55 and 35 persons respectively. Jindal Nagar which is situated along Hapur Road just near to Ghaziabad has the famous concern of 'Jindal Rubber Industries' which employs 143 persons. At Noida there exist 6 and at Loni 4 registered units engaged in the manufacture of various types of rubber products. One at Chapraula manufactures car matteresses and cushions.

10. *Woollens*

As compared to cotton textile, manufacture of woollens is quite insignificant at Ghaziabad. There exist only two small scale units in the city viz. M/s. Ajmeera Woollen Mills Ltd., and Jai Mates Pvt. Ltd. which manufacture woolen items like blankets and shawls etc. Both these concerns are located in trans-Hindan industrial zone and employ 53 and 35 persons respectively. However, manufacture of woollens constitutes an important industrial activity at Dadri, a small town along G.T. Road in district Ghaziabad. Here are located four registered units employing 244 persons in all, which are engaged in the manufacture of various types of woollen products. It is the only important centre of woollens in district Ghaziabad. There exist no such units at any other manufacturing centre of district.

11. *Cold Storages*

There exist only 3 small registered units of cold storages in the city, employing 35 persons in all. All of these three units are located in S.En. industrial zone which lies nearest to the C.B.D. area. As these cold storages are used for preserving the agricultural farm products specially potatoes, marketing of the products from these cold storages becomes much easier because of the nearness of city core from S.En. industrial zone. M/s. 'Himalaya Cold Storage & Ice Factory' is the oldest unit established in 1948. Other two cold storages are 'Ajanta Cold Storage General Mills' and 'Shri Shankar Ice & Cold Storage General Mills'. Ice for local use is also manufactured at these cold storages.

Amongst other manufacturing centres of the district, cold storages are functioning at Hapur, Modi Nagar and Shimbhauli. Hapur is the most important centre in the district for having the largest number of cold storages. Greater number of cold storages at Hapur owes mainly to the greater significance of the town as an important mandi for agricultural produce. There are functioning 8 registered units of cold storages at Hapur employing over 100 persons in all.

Fig. 22
MISCELLANEOUS INDUSTRIES

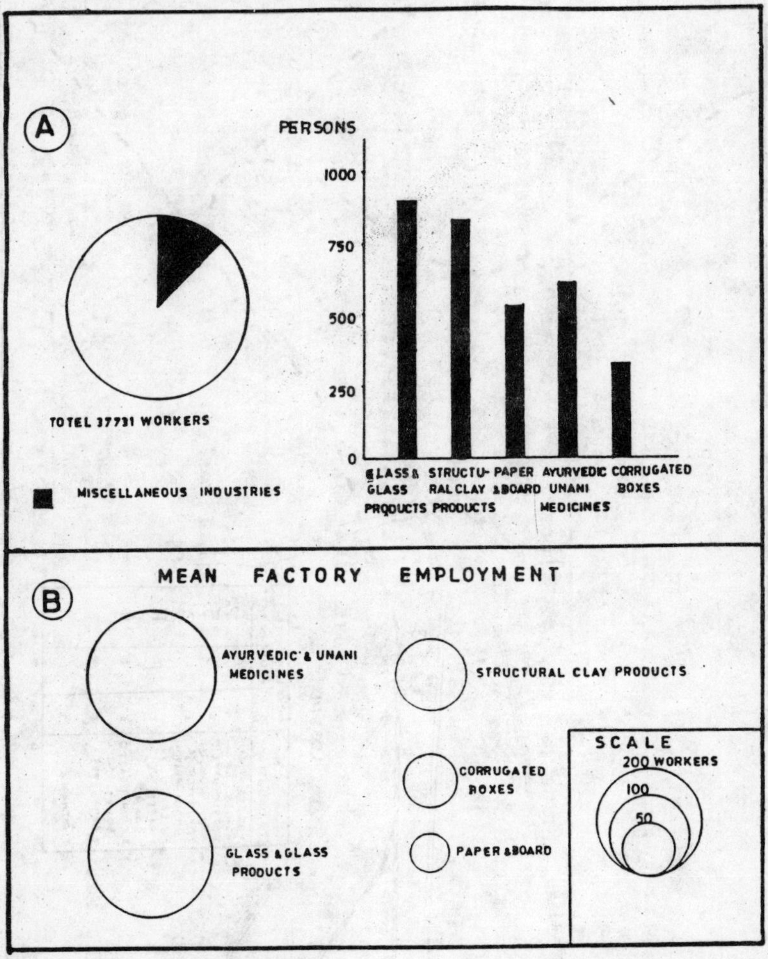

Fig. 23

OTHER MANUFACTURING INDUSTRIES AT GHAZIABAD

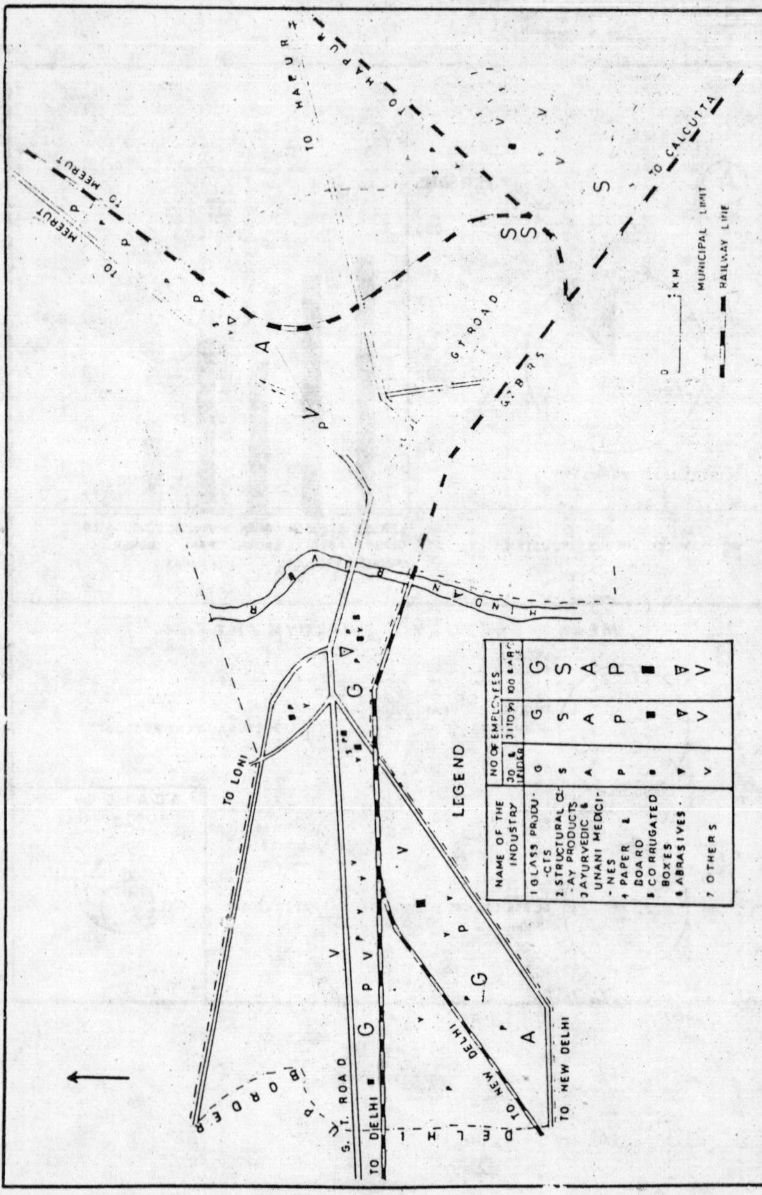

EIGHT

Other Manufacturing Centres of District Ghaziabad

Development of industries constitutes an important part of integrated development programme in a given region. In district Ghaziabad, it is not only Ghaziabad city which has acquired astounding industrial significance in recent past, but other centres of the district have also emerged as industrial nodes which together contribute about 45% share in the total registered employment of the district as against 55% share contributed by Ghaziabad city itself. In view of the substantial share of these centres in the total registered employment of the district, it becomes almost indispensable to attempt a brief reference to the industrial development at these centres, without which we can hardly assimilate the magnitude of industrial activity in the district as a whole.

As illustrated in table No. 8.1 most important of these other manufacturing centres of the district is Modi Nagar which represents about 27% share in the total registered employment of the district, i.e. about half of that represented by Ghaziabad city with 55% share in district's total. Next in importance stands Murad Nagar with about 7% share in the total registered employment of district. Other centres of industrial importance include Noida, Hapur, Shimbhauli, Jindal Nagar, signifying 2.19, 1.50, 2.41 and 1.40% shares respectively in total registered employment of the district.

Industrial centres with less than 1% share in district's total registered employment include Dadri, Dasna, Pilkhuwa, Loni and

Garh. Other minor centres include villages of Kot, Chapraula, Alipur and Chipiana.

TABLE 8.1: **Relative Positions of Other Manufacturing Centres of District Ghaziabad**

Name of the Centre	No. of regd. units.	No. of regd. employment	Percentage share of the centre in the total regd. employment of the distt.
1. Modi Nagar	30	18436	26.75
2. Murad Nagar	7	4965	7.21
3. Shimbhauli	3	1658	2.41
4. Noida	51	1510	2.19
5. Hapur	37	1037	1.50
6. Jindal Nagar P.O. Galland	7	697	1.40
7. Dadri	8	633	.92
8. Dasna	3	526	.76
9. Pilkhuwa	19	498	.72
10. Loni	21	404	.59
11. Garh	3	365	.53
12. Other minor Centres	5	178	.26
Total	194	31177	45.24%

Source : Figures tabulated with the help of list of factories (1981) obtained from Inspector of Factories Office, Ghaziabad

TABLE 8.2: **Functional Structure of Industries at Other Manufacturing Centres of The District**

Name of the Group	No. of regd. units	No. of regd. employment	Percentage share of the group at these centres in the total registered employment of the district.
1. Metal Based industries	62	9600	13.93%
2. Agro-based industries	51	16890	24.51%
3. Chemical & allied industries	19	2591	3.76
4. Other industries	62	2096	3.04%
Total	194	31177	45.24%

Source: Figures tabulated from the list of Factories (1981) obtained from Inspector of factories office, Ghaziabad and field survey.

Functional structure of industries as illustrated in Table no. 8.2. (Fig. 24) reveals the dominant position held by agro-based industries representing about 25% share out of the total of 45% share represented by these other manufacturing centres of the district. In the succeeding pages follows a description of industrial structure at each of these centres separately to have a better understanding of industrial activity in the district as a whole.

1. MODI NAGAR

Modi Nagar, located on Delhi-Meerut highway at a distance of 20 km. from Ghaziabad, is the leading cotton textile centre not only in the district but in whole of Wn. U.P. Accounting for 26.75% share in the total registered employment of the district, it is the second most important industrial centre in the district, first being Ghaziabad representing 54.76% share in district's total

Modi Nagar as a town is much younger than Ghaziabad. The nucleus of the town was laid down in 1933 when late Shri Rai Bahadur Seth Gujarmal Modi established public limited company of 'Modi Industries Ltd.', comprising of 8 industrial units, at the present site which was then simply a small village known as Begumabad, situated on Delhi-Meerut highway. These 8 industrial units of 'Modi Industries Ltd.' manufacture sugar, vanaspati, liquor, soap, paints, electrodes, steel wires, and lantern/torches. 'Modi Steel Ltd.' was another most important unit added to 'Modi Industries Ltd.' Establishment of these industrial units which all belonged to large-scale sector, steadily changed the face of village into a growing industrial centre. In the year 1945 was established famous 'Modi Spinning and Weaving Mills Co. Ltd.' which at present employ 12000 persons, i.e., about 2/3rd of the total industrial employment in the town. Since the establishment of this giant cotton textile unit this town further rose into prominence as an urban centre symbolizing purely a creation of industrial revolution.

Industrial development at Modi Nagar has been fostered neither because of a highly potential situation nor because of extremely favourable Geographical conditions here for industrial growth, but mainly because Modis opted its present site for starting their industrial establishments. The greatest motivating factor behind rapid and vast industrial growth at Modi Nagar was the availability of capital from Modis. Other factors such as vast open tract, availability of power, efficient transport facilities, adequate supply of water, abundant man power, also exerted their influence in sustaining the industrial growth here, but the fact remains that industries have not grown here out of their own, but have been made to grow deliberately.

The functional pattern of industrial growth at Modi Nagar differs a lot from that prevailing at Ghaziabad city. Dominance of agro-based industries is the characteristic feature here in contrast to the superiority of metal-based industries at Ghaziabad. Not only cotton textile, but other agro-based industries such as sugar, hydrogenated oil, soap and liquors etc. also acquire a significant place in the industrial structure of the town. Metal-based and chemical industries obtain 2nd and 3rd place, with manufacture of steel, and synthetic fibres as amongst the dominant industrial activities at the town.

Apart from different functional pattern of industrial structure, another distinguishing feature of industrial development at Modi Nagar is the relative preponderance of larger units in contrast to majority of small scale units at Ghaziabad. 10 out of city's 30 registered industrial units are large scale concerns which together represent more than 90% share in the total registered employment of the town.

Another significant feature of industrial growth at Modi Nagar is the dominance of Modis in all walks of industrial life of the town. Modis are the Managing Directors of all bigger concerns which together represent more than 90% share in the total registered employment of the town. It is in marked contrast to the situation prevailing at Ghaziabad where Mohans who are the largest employer in the city represent only about 10% share in the total registered employment at the city. Modis have pervaded not only in industrial, but also in social, cultural and political aspects of life of the town. However, our main concern being industry below is given a brief outline of important industries at the town in a Geographical perspective.

1. *Cotton Textile Industry*– is the biggest industry accounting for 2/3 of the total registered employment at the town. Out of 18436 employees, 12000 work in famous 'Modi Spinning & Weaving Mills Co. Ltd.', which is the biggest cotton textile concern in Wn. U.P. Cotton for this mills is obtained from 'Abohar' in Punjab and also from Maharashtra. This big industrial unit is divided into 5 sub units. 2 of these units function as yarn mills, 1 as rayon and silk mill and one as thread mill manufacturing 'Modi' threads for sewing purposes and the biggest unit is that of 'Modi Cloth Mills' where are manufactured cotton, terylene and other blended fabrics for suiting, shirting, dress material and sarees. Modi Prints are famous for their fine finish and fast colours. Poplins, long cloth and towels, made by 'Modis' are also known for their superior quality.

TABLE 8.3: **Functional Pattern of Industries at Modi Nagar**

Name of the industry	No. of regd. units	No. of regd. employment	Percentage share of the industry in total regd. employment of the district.
1. Cotton Textile	3	12031	17.46
2. Sugar Mill	1	915	1.33
3. Hydrogenerated Oil	1	441	.64
4. Soap	1	166	.24
5. Distillery	1	95	.14
6. Paints & Varnish	1	182	.26
7. Synthetic fibre	1	1600	2.32
8. Gases	1	92	.13
9. Paper, Board and packaging paper products	5	170	.25
10. Steel ingots & billets	2	1970	2.86
11. Other metal-based Industries	7	614	.89
12. Miscellaneous Industries	5	160	.23
Total	30	18436	26.75%

Source : Ibid, Table no. 8.2

2. *Manufacture of Steel*: is the second most important industry at the town. The two units of 'Modi Steel Ltd.' employ 1970 persons, representing more than 10% share in total registered employment at the town. 'Modi Steel Ltd.' unit No. 1 is the bigger concern with 1646 persons. Both these units manufacture

steel ingots and billets from the scrap which is obtained from Delhi and other nearby urban centres. 'Modi Steel Ltd.' unit no. 1 constitutes the biggest mini steel mill of Wn. U.P.

3. *Other Metal-Based Industries–* Apart from steel other metal based industries of the city include manufacture of electrodes, locks, lanterns and torches, tools, auto parts, general hardware and utensils. Amongst 7 units belonging to these varied branches, three viz. M/s. Modi Arc Electrodes Corpn., Globe Engineers, and Modi Hurricane lantern Factory are larger concerns employing 196, 138 and 270 persons respectively. These three concerns manufacture electrodes, klik quality padlocks, and lanterns respectively. Of the remaining four units which are smaller factories of 10 to 35 persons, one each is engaged in the production of tools, general hardware, cups, medals and shields etc., and utensils.

4. *Synthetic Fibre–* is the third biggest industry of the city after cotton textile and steel. The famous 'Modipon Ltd.' employing 1600 persons is the only concern of this industry in the city. It manufactures nylon 6 filament yarn and polyester yarn.

5. *Sugar–* Manufacture of the sugar is the fourth most important industry represented by 'Modi Sugar Mills' employing 915 persons, which is the second biggest sugar factory of the district, the first being one located at Shimbhauli with 1523 persons.

6. *Hydrogenated Oil–* is the fifth biggest industry of the city represented by single large scale concern of "Modi Vanaspati Manufacturing Corpn.' employing 441 persons. It manufactures famous 'Ruchi' Vanaspati. Formerly it used to manufacture 'Kotogem' brand of vanaspati.

7. *Paint & Varnish–* 'Modi Paints & Varnish Company' employing 182 persons, manufactures paints, varnish, lacquers & thinner etc.

8. *Paper board and packaging paper Products*: There are 5 registered units in the city engaged in the production of craft paper, board and packaging paper products. All these units are smaller

concerns, important amongst which are 'Reliance Packaging Industries' and 'Nav Bharat Paper Products'.

9. *Soap*– The single registered unit of this industry is the large scale concern of 'Modi Soap Works' which manufactures washing soap for household purposes.

10. *Liquor*– Liquors are manufactured at 'Modi Distillery' employing 95 persons.

11. *Gases*– 'Modi Gas Ltd.' produces various types of industrial gases.

12. *Miscellaneous Industries* : There are 5 registered units in the city engaged in the miscellaneous industries like rope making, stationery items, repair work of tubewells, cold storage and enamelling japaning and electroplating of metal products.

While concluding it is to be stressed that Modi Nagar may experience further industrial expansion under the auspices of Modis, but because of present policy of decentralization aimed at by the Government, no more licences are being given to establish new industrial units in the city. Modis are at present, investing for their newer concerns at Modipuram which stands along Roorkee Road at a short distance from Meerut.

NOIDA

Noida, the acronym for 'New Okhla Industrial Development Authority' established by the Government of Uttar Pradesh under the U.P. Industrial Area Development Act 1976 ranks 5th amongst the industrial centres of the district with 2.19% share in the total registered employment. These figures, however, give only a glimpse of the vast and varied industrial activity taking place at this small-scale industrial paradise, located on the left banks of Jumna facing Okhla on the other side of the river. The existing Master Plan of Noida envisages development of 3218 hectares to accommodate 4000 small industrial units and a sprawling township of over 5 lakhs in the first phase.[1] To promptly realize these goals, 3000 developed plots and 1000 built-up shades have already been allotted in the township to small entrepreneurs, out of which 700 units have already gone into production giving employment to about 5000 persons in all. However majority of these units are functioning as small unregistered units not covered under Factories Act for the reason of employing less than 10 persons. Total number of registered units at Noida stood at 51 in the year 1981, employing 1510 persons in all, which represents only a quarter of actual number employed by industries here. In our present study, so far, we have based all observations on the figures of employment pertaining to registered units only, but the same approach can not hold good in the case of Noida where vast complex of small-scale enterprises has been developed on such a large scale that it has become a unique industrial endeavour of its kind in whole of U.P. Noida has been designed and developed with particular emphasis on improving the competitive strength of the small-scale sector and to enable small entrepreneurs, particularly from weaker sections of society, to set up their own industries under the self-employment scheme.

Salient Features of Noida Industrial Township

In close proximity to Delhi, Noida township covers, on the banks of River Jamuna, a vast area of 3218 hectares encompassing 37 villages from Dadri Tahsil of District Ghaziabad. It stands at a distance of 12 kilometers from Connaught Place and 8 km. from Nizamuddin Bridge (fig. 25). It is approachable from Delhi by four roads which are now being constructed for all weather heavy load traffic. Fifth link to Delhi will be provided by the bridge cum-barrage on Jumna at Okhla which is under construction these days. After its completion Noida township will be only about 4 to 6 km. from the residential areas of south Delhi. The town-ship is also connected to Ghaziabad by a regional level road. Plans are also under way to link the township with the National Highway 24 bye-pass road near Ghaziabad. All parts of the town are well connected by bus service of Delhi Transport Corporation. It is also connected with Bulandshahr by a regular bus service of the U.P. State Roadways. The whole scheme of establishing a huge industrial, commercial and residential township owes its genesis to dynamic and progressive ex-Chief Minister of U.P. Shri Narayan Dutt Tiwari who wanted to tap every possible source to give Uttar Pradesh a new image in industrial field.

Apart from efficient transport facilities and its close links with Delhi, other attractions for starting industry at Noida, include various types of benefits provided by state Govt. on account of its previously belonging to industrially backward area of district Bulandshahr. These benefits include concessional finance power subsidy, rebate in income tax for 10 years from the start of production, and interest free loans. Bestowing of such benefits acquires special significance in view of the fact that no such benefits are available at various industrial areas of Delhi such as Mayapuri, Trinagar and Wazirpur etc. which are located almost at the same distance from Connaught place as is Noida. Uninterrupted power supply is additional boon to the small entrepreneur at Noida. It is supposed to be an oasis in respect of power supply. No scheduled power cuts were reinforced at Noida during the current power crisis at Delhi. Another great facility for entrepreneurs at Noida is the easy availability of raw materials and building construction materials through the office of Directorate of Industries set up specially by the state Govt. in this complex. The regional office of U.P.F.C. and the office of U.P. Industrial Consultancy Organisation are also located at Noida which help the entrepreneurs in getting the loans sanctioned and in preparing the project for raw entrepreneurs respectively. In addition to the above facilities for starting the industry at Noida, efforts are afoot to get Railway siding for quick and prompt movement of raw materials and finished products.

Apart from providing excellent facilities for setting up industry here, Noida also offers many other advantages which are prerequisites for clean and wholesome living of entrepreneurs and industrial workers. The whole township is designed to develop into a self-contained unit catering to the residential, commercial, recreational, educational and social requirements of population which is expected to be about 5 lakhs by 1992.

Functional Structure of Industries at Noida

Industrial structure at Noida covers a wide array of items like ready-made garments, textile printing, machinery and their parts, electronics and electrical goods, food products, rubber products, packaging items, tin containers, chemicals, and many others. Cotton textile with garment manufacturing, and textile printing as its major activities, constitutes the leading industry of township with over 40% share in the total registered employment at the complex. Important garment manufacturing units at Noida include M/s. Associated India Exporters, The Handicraft and Handloom Export Corpn. of India, Monarch Exports, Libbubas Private Ltd., Singh Export Corpn., and Ram Narayan Anil Kumar which employ 95, 84, 92, 98, 53 and 29 persons respectively. All relatively bigger factories at Noida belong to garment manufacturing branch of the cotton textile industry. Here are produced export quality garments which are sent to the countries in Africa, Middle East and Far East. Textile printing is another important branch of cotton textile industry but it characterizes mostly smaller units, which are unregistered under Factories Act.

Second most important industry amongst registered units is the manufacture of various types of engineering goods such as industrial machines of lathe, press and cranes, wire drawings, wire rods, and tractor parts etc.. Important concerns of engineering goods include M/s. Precision Drilling Equipments Pvt. Ltd., Tanco Steel & Engineers, Prestige Engineers Pvt. Ltd., and Tuff Tool International.

TABLE 8.4: **Functional Pattern of Industries at Noida**

Name of the Industry	No. of Regd. units	No. of regd. employment
1. Cotton textile including garments	13	619
2. Engineering goods other than electrical	10	225
3. Electronics & Electrical goods	8	150
4. Food Products	3	124
5. Rubber Products	4	120
6. Packaging Items	3	67
7. Printing Press	2	25
8. Tin Containers	2	60
9. Other miscellaneous industries	6	110
Total	51	1510

*Employment figures tabulated from list of Factories (1981) obtained from Inspector of Factories Office, Ghaziabad. Other information collected by field survey.

Manufacture of electronics and electrical goods such as computers, calculators, gas lighters, T.V. games, electronic panels, voltage stabilizers, starters, electric bulbs and P.V.C. cables is the third important industry at Noida Industrial township. M/s. Hindustan Computers, Mansfield Cables, Rajiv Electronics, Rajvansh Electricals, and Lozi Tronics are the important registered concerns of electronics and electrical goods at Noida. Important food products concerns at Noida include M/s. Super Foods Pvt. Ltd., and Vikash Traders, which manufacture biscuits and other bakery products. Another unit of this industry is 'Dharam Pal Satya Pal Pvt. Ltd.' which manufactures 'Zafrani Zarda' and 'Kiwam'. Manufacture of rubber products is also important at Noida with Noida Rubber Mills, Sovereign Rubber Products, and Philips Brakiers Rubber Corporation as its important concerns at the complex. M/s. Shilpi Sales, & Plas Packaging manufacture corrugated boxes and polythene bags for packaging purposes. Important printing presses at Noida are M/s. Dhumimal Printers, and Multiplex Corporation and important tin container manufacturing units are 'Keshav Metal Works,' and 'Tin Containers Pvt. Ltd.' Other miscellaneous industries at Noida include manufacture of soaps, paints and lubricants, plastic products, mixed fertilizers, and chemicals, etc. For strength and sustenance of small scale units at Noida and for boosting up the pace of industrial development here, the proposal to allow setting up of medium-sized industrial units in the complex is under consideration of the state Government. The medium-sized units, if they come up, will provide supporting structure to the ancillary units and also accelerate the pace of industrial development at the complex. Noida scheme also aims at accommodating those industrial units of Delhi, which are functioning in nonconforming areas of the capital.

Noida scheme, which was launched in 1976, is still passing through its infancy years. Undertaking a project of the scale and nature like that of Noida is really a herculean task likely to be confronted with many odds in its execution. Fortunately a good beginning has been made and the first phase of Noida Master Plan which envisages establishment of 4000 small industrial units together with social infrastructure facilities is underway in all its earnest with more than 600 industrial units already having gone into production by 1982. Ultimate targets set for Noida industrial township, however, are highly ambitious. According to Mr. N.S. Chaudhary, chairman of New Okhla Industrial Development Authority, the township will eventually accommodate 10000 small industrial units of different types, giving employment to 80,000 industrial workers. Annual turnover by these units is estimated to be of the value of Rs. 814 crores. There is every hope that these goals will be achieved by the end of this century and Noida will be poised to become a unique township of its kind in whole of India.

3. HAPUR

Hapur, situated at a distance of 35 km. from Ghaziabad on Delhi-Moradabad highway, is the biggest trading centre of the agricultural produce in the district. However, it also contributes considerably in the industrial activity representing 1.5% share in the total registered employment of the district. Apart from abundant agricultural raw materials, Hapur is well placed in respect of other requirements of the industry also, such as efficient transport facilities, adequate supply of power, plentiful labour, and nearness to markets etc. Despite fulfilling all industrial requirements, the town signifies only a moderate amount of industrial development. Relative insignificance of industrial activity at the town has been also caused, to some extent, by the overwhelming significance of Hapur as an important commercial centre. Commercial importance of the town can be best adjudged by the high reputation of 'Hapur Chamber of Commerce' in the country. Another factor accounting for relatively lesser degree of industrial development at the town is the lack of initiative and indifference on the part of civic authorities and Govt. bodies in this direction.

Functional Structure of Industries at Hapur

There are functioning 37 registered units at the town with total registered employment of 1035 persons. More than 50% share of total registered employment at the town is engaged in metal-based industries such as machinery and their parts, general hardware and utensils. Out of total of 510 persons employed by these industries 284 are working in the Sewing Machine manufacturing factory of the town which constitutes the biggest concern of the Hapur. Two smaller units at the town are manufacturing sewing machine parts. Apart from sewing machines, other important machinery manufacturing units of the town are M/s. Standard Workshop, and Hind Engineering Company, which manufacture oil engines and other light agricultural machinery. M/s. Hari & Sons Weaving Machines and 'Jasbir Engineering Works' manufacture weaving machines, and cutting and slothing machines respectively. Other metal-based industrial units of the town manufacture general hardware and utensils.

Next important industry at Hapur is manufacture of sugar with 4 registered units employing 177 persons in all. Biggest unit of this branch is M/s. Jagdish Sugar Works, employing 110 persons. Other units namely, M/s. Hapur Sugar Works, Dhani Ram Sharma &Sons, & Rajbir Singh Cane Crushers are smaller factories of 15 to 35 persons.

TABLE 8.5: **Functional Pattern of Industries at Hapur.**

Name of the Industry	No. of regd. units	No. of regd. employment
1. Metal-based Industries	13	510
2. Sugar	4	177
3. Chemical & Allied industries	6	116
4. Packaging & paper Products	4	102
5. Cold Storages	8	101
6. Other Miscellaneous Industries	2	31
Total	37	1037

Chemical group of industries acquires 3rd place in the functional structure of industries at Hapur, representing more than 10% share in the total registered employment of the town. There exist 3 industrial units of plastic products, one of pharmaceuticals, one of glue and gelatine and one of bone mills. Except M/s. Uppar India Bone Mills which employs 41 persons, all the other units of chemical-based industries are smaller factories of 10 to 20 persons.

Packaging and paper products, and Cold Storages, are the other two important branches of industrial structure at Hapur, each representing about 10% share in the total registered employment of the town. Important packaging and paper products manufacturing units at Hapur include M/s. Sundeep Cones, Seth Nagarmal Jai Narayan Modi, Sunder Cones & Tubes Works, and Sunil Packaging Corpn.

Importance of Hapur as an important trading centre of agricultural produce is clearly manifested in the largest number of cold storages here amongst all industrial centres of the district. Apart from the 8 cold storages operating in the town, Hapur also possesses Asia's most modern and biggest foodgrain storage centre known as Sylo-cum-Elevator which can preserve thousands of tons of foodgrain by safe and scientific methods. This famous establishment of town which employs 26 persons, is managed by Food Corporation of India. Other units of miscellaneous industries at Hapur belong to printing presses and manufacture of decorative materials.

While concluding it is again to be stressed that Hapur holds very good future prospects for the development of agro-based industries, which unfortunately, represent a very meagre share in the present industrial structure of the town. These industries can be reasonably klicked off, if only developed sites with infrastructure facilities are made available to entrepreneurs.

4. PILKHUWA

Pilkhuwa symbolizes an industrial node that has risen into prominence for its handloom and powerloom cotton textile carried out mainly as household industry by traditionally skilled labour. It is a township of about 30000, located along Hapur Road at a distance of 22 km. from Ghaziabad. It is a famous centre for weaving, printing and finishing of textile items like blanket covers, shawls, bedsheets, table clothes, lungies and many other types of wearing apparels. Every year textile products worth Rs. 15 crores are produced at this town and are sent to different part of Wn. U.P., Delhi, Haryana, and Punjab. A small proportion of textile production is also sent to Asian and African countries. Pilkhuwa is specially known for its exotic printing on Khadi and other varieties of cotton cloth.

There are functioning 15 registered units at Pilkhuwa manufacturing different types of textile goods with a total registered employment of 331 persons, which represents more than 65% share in the total registered employment at this town. However number of small unregistered units of textiles is far greater than the registered ones and it is because of this reason that relative position of Pilkhuwa as illustrated by its .72% share in the total registered employment of the district does not give a true idea of the importance of this town as a major cottage cotton textile centre. Roughly about 1000 persons are engaged in the manufacture of cotton textile at Pilkhuwa. It constitutes the major household industry of the town characterising the traditional skill of the local people in this specific branch of manufacturing.

Amongst the registered textile units M/s. Maharaj Textiles employing 46 persons is the biggest factory. Other important units include M/s. Agarwal Textiles, Ratan Textile Industries, Nirmal Textile Industries, and Mohan Textiles which employ 32, 29, 25 and 21 persons respectively. All the other registered textile units are smaller factories of 10 to 20 persons.

Apart from cotton textile units, 4 registered units at the town belong to other industries such as alluminium goods, paper board and surgical goods. The biggest factory of the town viz. M/s. Century Metals Ltd.' employing 81 persons manufactures alluminium milk cans. Another bigger unit is 'Swatantra Bharat Paper Mills' which employs 59 persons. It manufactures paper and mill board. Other two units are M/s. Anand Industries, and United India Surgical Works which manufacture chappals, and bandages for surgical use respectively.

Apart from cotton textile industry, other main cottage industry at Pilkhuwa is the manufacture of cycle seats which is the main occupation of low caste people at this town. Every day about 20 to 30 gross of cycle seats are manufactured which are sent to Delhi, Lucknow, Saharanpur, Roorkee, Aligarh and Hathras. Another important cottage industry is manufacture of wooden moulds used for textile printing.

Pilkhuwa signifies an industrial centre which has mainly thrived on cottage industries. It sets an example as to how significant role can the cottage industry play in the economic life of an urban centre.

5. MURADNAGAR

Murad Nagar, though a small town, stands as 3rd most important industrial centre of the district with 7.21% share in the total registered employment of the district. Industrial significance of this small town owes mainly to the establishment of Govt. Ordnance Factory here which employs 4685 persons out of total of 4965, engaged in the registered units at the town. Apart from the Ordnance Factory which manufactures different types of defence equipments, another defence establishment at the town is 'Detachment Air Armament Inspection Wing' which employs 53 persons. Thus defence items represent more than 95% share in the total registered employment of the town.

In the private sector, the only large scale concern of the town is 'Radhu Industries' employing 166 persons. It manufactures much popular 'Radhu' tyres and tubes for cycles and rickshaw. All the other units are smaller factories of 10 to 20 persons, two of which viz. M/s. Nav Bharat Paper Mills, and Raghu Paper & Board Mills manufacture paper and mill board. Other two units viz. M/s. Ethichemical Pvt. Ltd., and Gopal Ispat manufacture chemicals and iron rods respectively.

6. JINDAL NAGAR

Jindal Nagar is the 7th most important industrial centre with 1.4% share in the total registered employment of the district. It is an industrial node which has developed at village Galland along Hapur road between Dasna and Pilkhuwa. There is no town in the census named as Jindal Nagar. But the village Galland is now popularly known as Jindal Nagar because of major share of industrial establishments here is owned by Jindals, who are amongst the leading industrial magnets of the country.

Major industrial activity at Jindal Nagar consists of the manufacture of G.I. pipes and tubes which accounts for 78.08% share in the total registered employment at this centre. Four out of 7 registered units here are engaged in this branch of manufacturing only. Three of these units viz. M/s. Ajanta Tubes Ltd., Jindal Pipes Pvt. Ltd. and Hindustan Pipe Udyog constitute bigger units employing 472, 141, and 124 persons respectively. Jindals are a trusted name for black and galvanized M. S. pipes and tubes.

Another important industry of this centre is the manufacture of conveying belts which represents 14.8% share in the total registered employment.'Jindal Rubber Industries Pvt. Ltd.' employing 143 persons is the reputed concern for conveying belts. Other two units at this centre are M/s. Ghaziabad Iron & Steel Company, and National Wire Industries employing 24 and 21 persons. These units manufacture iron bars and steel wires respectively.

7. DADRI

Dadri, a tahsil town situated on G.T. Road and a station along Delhi-Kanpur rail-route, at a distance of 17 km. from Ghaziabad, is the 8th most important industrial centre representing .92% share in the total registered employment of the district. There are functioning 8 registered units at this town employing 633 persons in all.

Metal-based, woollens, and leather industries are the important constituents of the functional structure at Dadri, representing 50.40, 39.34 and 10.26% share in the total registered employment of the town. 2 of the 8 registered units viz. M/s. Fibre Tech Engineers and Mnufactures, and Ram Kishan Spat employing 273 and 46 persons belong to metal-based group of industries. Registered industrial units of woollens at the town include M/s. Kalindi Woollen Mills Pvt. Ltd., Rajiv Woollen Mills Pvt Ltd., Coronation Spins (India) Pvt. Ltd. and Krishan Woollen Pvt. Ltd. Two registered units at the town viz. M/s. Leathero Leather Pt. Ltd., and Elegant Leather are engaged in tanning and finishing of industrial leathers. These units employ 30 and 35 persons respectively.

Situation of Dadri on National highway, at only 30 kms from Delhi offers good opportunities for industrial development. In the near future, however, the chances of any major breakthrough in the field of industry at this town are quite out of sight because of rapid growth of industries at Noida which lying in its close vicinity, has become the main focus of industrial expansion at the suburbs of Delhi.

8. DASNA

Like village Galland which has grown into an industrial node, now popularly known as Jindal Nagar, Dasna is also a village located along Hapur Road. It is also a station of Delhi Moradabad railway line at a distance of just 11 km. from Ghaziabad. It has acquired industrial significance because of the establishment here of the famous D.C.M. concern of M/s. Hindan River Mills which employs 494 persons out of the total registered employment of 526 at this centre. With .76% share in the total registered employment Dasna ranks 9th amongst the industrial centres of the district.'Hindan River Mills' at Dasna is one of the important textile concerns of Nn. India which manufactures superfine polyester cotton cloth for suitings, shirtings, dress materials and sarees.

Other two registered units at Dasna are M/s. K.B. Ceramics & Refractories, and Prem Metal Products employing 18 and 14 persons. The former manufactures ceramic items and furnace bricks, and the latter alluminium utensils.

9. SHIMBHAOLI

Shimbhaoli, located along Delhi-Moradabad route between Hapur and Garh, ranks 4th amongst the industrial centres of the district in terms of total registered employment. Largest sugar factory of the district is located at Shimbhaoli. It is mainly a sugar mill town where 1523 persons out of the total of 1658 at this centre are working at M/s. Shimbhaoli Sugar Mills Ltd. Sugarcane for this mill is obtained from nearby villages. Other two registered units at this centre are M/s. Shimbhaoli Industries Ltd., and Shimbhaoli Cold Storage & Ice Factory, employing 124 and 11 persons respectively. M/s. Shimbhaoli Industries Ltd. manufactures biscuits and other cereal products.

All the three registered units at this centre derive their raw materials from agricultural produce. Shimbhaoli's industrial structure clearly emphasizes the relevance of agro-based units being located in producing areas.

10. **LONI**

A town of antiquity and at the same time carrying glimpses of modern industrial activity, Loni stands as a potential industrial centre of the district, situated on Shahdara-Baghpat route at a distance of just 16 km. from Delhi. However, at present, Loni exhibits only a very limited amount of industrial development with only .59% share in the total registered employment of the district. Notwithstanding its nearness to Delhi, it has not been able to make substantial strides in industrial field. Major factors hampering the growth of industries at this place are unfavourable site conditions and inefficient transport facilities. Loni was included in the regulated area of Ghaziabad Master Plan. However, because the land was low-lying and having high salinity, it could not be possible for authorities to execute the development work in this area as per Master Plan's provisions. Very little has been accomplished in the direction of improvement of civic amenities at this town. With the efforts of U.P.S.I.D.C. industrial estate have been set up in Arya Nagar and Roop Nagar and rural area of Loni, where apart from developed sites, other facilities such as interest free loan, power subsidy and technical assistance are also provided to small entrepreneurs. There are at present functioning more than 100 small industrial units employing a total of 800 persons. The number of units registered under Factories Act, however, was only 21 in 1981 with the total registered employment of 404 persons in all.

Functional structure of industries at Loni acquires a distinctive character with manufacture of rubber products as the leading industry followed by metal-based, chemical-based and readymade-garments in terms of registered employment. M/s. 'Naresh Udyog' which is the biggest unit at the town with 75 persons manufactures tyres and tubes for cycles and rickshaw. Another important unit of this branch is M/s. 'Brickley Engineering Works Pvt. Ltd.' which employs 45 persons. Other important units of rubber products are M/s. National Rubber Works, and Amar Rubber Chemicals (India) Pvt. Ltd. which manufacture rubber sheets, and rubber mattresses and cushions respectively.

Registered units of metal-based industries at Loni manufacture auto parts, G.I. pipe fittings, structurals, machinery parts, re-rolled products and tin-containers. M/s. Auto Light Industries, and Auto and General Industries manufacture steering wheels and other auto parts. M/s. J.K. Enterprises, and Keco Industries manufacture re-rolled products and structurals respectively. Bobbins for textile machinery and G.I. pipes fittings are manufactured at M/s. P.C. Girdhari Lal Jain, and Prakash Udyog respectively. M/s. Silver Toe Manufacturing Corpn. of India is the important factory manufacturing tin-containers at Loni.

Chemical-based industrial units at the town acquire 3rd place in the industrial structure in terms of registered employment. Basic heavy in-organic chemicals are manufactured at M/s. Haryana Laboratories, and J.K. Jogsaran Singh and Brothers. Other two units of chemical-based industries viz. M/s. Jaipal Udyog, and 'Industrial Chemicals' manufacture pesticides and rubber chemicals respectively.

TABLE 8.6: **Functional Pattern of Industries at Loni***

Name of the Industry	No. of regd. Units	No. of regd. employment.
1. Rubber Products	6	152
2. Metal-Based Industries	7	120
3. Chemical-based Industries	4	59
4. Ready-made Garments	2	43
5. Others	2	30

* *Source* : Ibid, Table No. 8.2.

Manufacture of ready-made garments is also an important industry at Loni. Although registered units of this branch are only 2, but small unregistered units manufacturing ready-made garments number more than 15 at Loni. This industry is sustained mainly by the large metropolitan markets for its products.

Loni, because of its nearness to Delhi stands good chances for future industrial expansion, if site conditions are improved and town is provided with an efficient network of transport and communication facilities. Danger of recurring floods has considerably lessened as a result of shifting of Jamuna farther away from the town. Development of civic amenities at the town also requires special attention to make Loni an attractive location for entrepreneurs. At present, because of its relative nearness to Delhi and availability of backward area incentive, Noida offers the optimum industrial location but in the long run Loni may also rise to prominence in the field of industrial activity if civic bodies and Govt. make sincere efforts to this end.

11. GARH

Garh, the most important religious centre of the district, situated on the banks of Ganga, also contributes a small share in the industrial activity of the district with 3 registered units employing 365 persons in all. Amongst the 12 industrial centres of the district, it ranks only last but glass industry at Garh holds considerable significance, since after the transfer of M/s. Narendra Glass Works here which was previously located at Mohan Nagar in Ghaziabad. It is a large scale concern of 241 persons manufacturing bottles for pharmaceuticals, liquors and wine. Here are manufactured all sizes and shapes of bottles in white, green and amber colour. This concern belongs to Mohan Group of Industries and is the biggest concern of the town. Other two industrial units at Garh employing 78 and 48 persons belong to sugar industry. These are M/s. M.K. Industries , and Agarwal Sugar Works, respectively. Sugarcane for these units is obtained from nearby villages. Garh holds good future prospects for further expansion of sugar industry.

12. OTHER MINOR CENTRES

There are also found some scattered registered units located in the rural areas of the district. There were functioning 5 such industrial units in the district with a total strength of 178 employees in 1981. Biggest of these is M/s. Sumita Conductors employing 87 persons, located at village Chapraula in Dadri tahsil. It manufactures A.C.S.R. and A.A.C. conductors. Another important scattered industrial units is M/s. Sahni Malviya Automobiles Industries Pvt. Ltd. employing 35 persons located at village Kot of Dadri tahsil. Here are manufactured rubber mattresses and cushions for automobiles. Two of these units which are small cane-crusher factories of 21 and 15 persons are located at Alipur in tahsil Garh. One small unit manufacturing iron bars is located at Chipyana in tahsil Dadri.

Industrial centres are located in all the four tahsils of the district. However, degree of industrial development in different tahsils varies a lot. 7 out of 12 industrial centres of the district are located in Ghaziabad tahsil itself which represents more than 90% share in the total registered employment of the district. Ghaziabad, Modi Nagar, Murad Nagar, Loni, Pilkhuwa, Dasna and Jindal Nagar are the industrial centres falling in Ghaziabad tahsil. Next in importance is Dadri tahsil with two industrial centres of Noida and Dadri. Garh rank 3rd with Simbhaoli and Garh as the two industrial centres. Hapur is the least industrialized of all the four tahsils with only one industrial centre of Hapur. Distribution of industrial units lacks an integrated pattern but as compared to many other districts of Uttar Pradesh, process of industrialization in different parts of the district envisages far greater coherence and harmony. Pace of industrial development in relatively less industrialized areas of the district can be reasonably triggered off only if Govt. and local bodies make concerted efforts in this direction.

REFERENCE

1. Hindustan Times dated July 28, 1982.

Fig. 24

OTHER MANUFACTURING CENTRES OF DISTT GHAZIABAD: INDUSTRIAL STRUCTURE

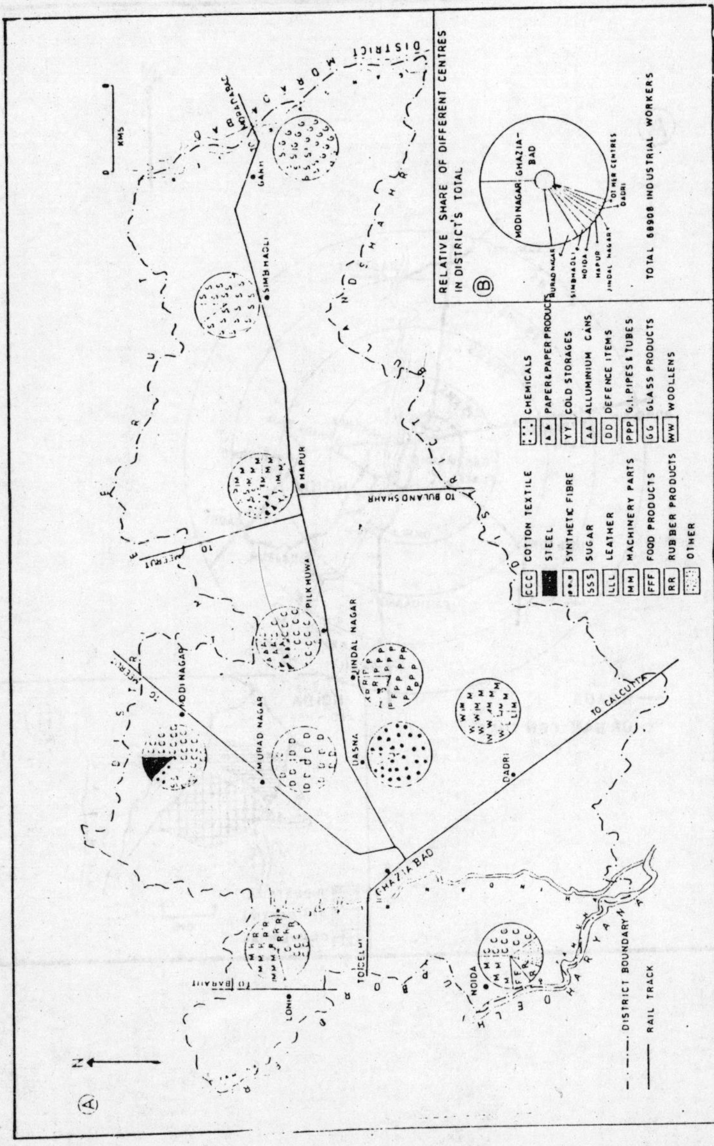

Fig. 25
NOIDA

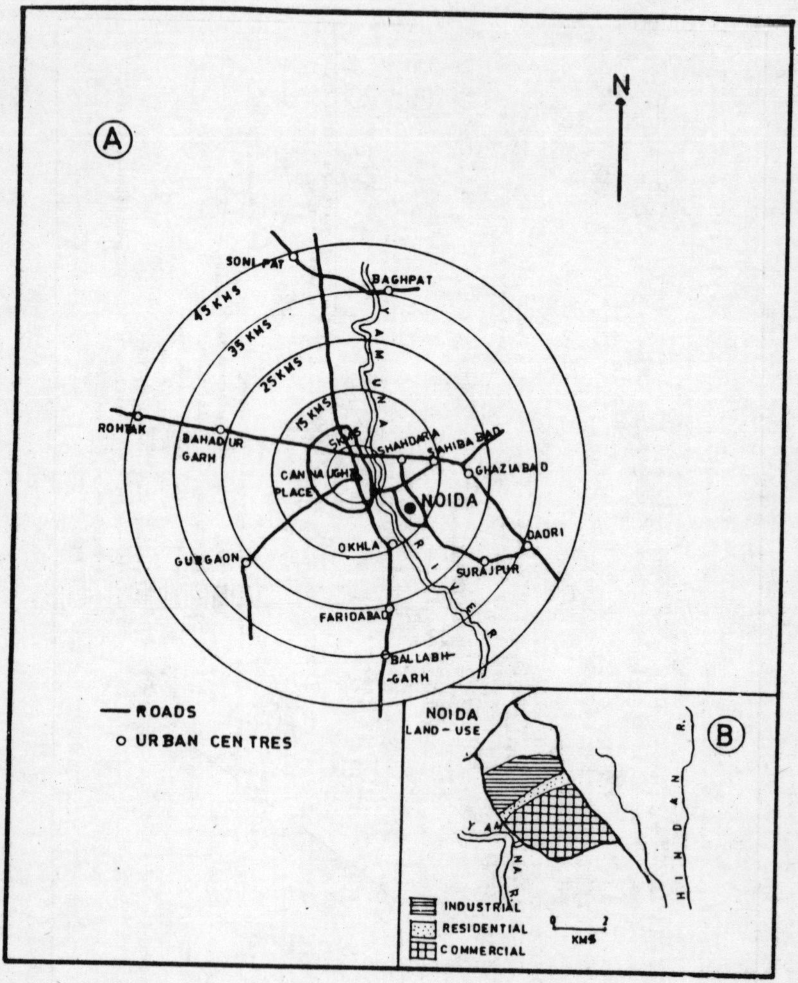
A
N
SONI PAT
BAGHPAT
45 KMS
35 KMS
25 KMS
15 KMS
ROHTAK
BAHADUR
GARH
SHAHDARA
SAHIBABAD
GHAZIABAD
CANNAUGHT
PLACE
NOIDA
DADRI
OKHLA
GURGAON
SURAJPUR
FARIDABAD
BALLABH
-GARH
YAMUNA
RIVER
ROADS
URBAN CENTRES
NOIDA
LAND - USE
B
HINDAN R.
INDUSTRIAL
RESIDENTIAL
COMMERCIAL
KMS

NINE

Some Problems of Industrial Development at Ghaziabad

Ghaziabad offers optimum conditions for industrial growth, yet not each and every industrial enterprise, pre-existing or newly established one, can be guaranteed of a fair amount of success for ever. Every year 3 to 5 factories close down for ever and an even larger number dwindle even before the commencement of manufacturing operations. Closures of the factories can be, to some extent, attributed to the process of selective growth amongst industries but it is not always so. Often the factories run into trouble for the lack of executive and managerial ability on the part of entrepreneur or the company. Geographical and economic background of the area is generally conducive to industrial progress, but much depends on entrepreneur's administrative ability, his marketing know-how, his capacity for policy formation and decision making, and above all his far-sightedness. Howsoever favourable the Geographical and economic conditions of an area may be, ultimately it is mainly the human aspects pertaining to managerial capacity and adoption of technological innovations, which make a factory a productive reality. Poor management and the ignorance of latest technological developments in the field of industry concerned may lead to disastrous consequences. During last two years quite a number of important factories at Ghaziabad have closed down because of these and various other reasons. The biggest factory which closed down only recently is M/s. Poysha Industrial Corporation, a tin container manufacturing concern of 850 employees. Other factories which were closed for ever during last two years include M/s. Gadodia and Sons, Narwar Engineering Company, Regal Papers Ltd. Durga Enterprises, Bharat Tin Udyog, Shakti Electronics Pvt. Ltd., Electronics & Computer India, & Electric Switch Gears Pvt. Ltd.

Incidence of factory closures at Ghaziabad clearly indicates that it is not all smooth-sailing in respect of city's industrial life. There do exist some persistent problems apart from those concerning managerial aspects, which can be broadly classed into two sub-groups: (A) Problems faced by the industry in general (B) Problems arising out of the process of rapid industrialization in the city and which are faced by the urban industrial population. Below we shall discuss each of these problems separately.

TABLE 9.1: **Labour Unrest Situation at Major Industrial Centres of U.P. 1982.**[1]

Name of the centre	No. of strikes & Lock-Outs.	No. of employees affected	Total wage loss in Lakh Rs.	Total Prod. loss in Lakh Rs.
1. Kanpur	46	19227	63.80	288.80
2. Ghaziabad	44	29868	30.94	247.65
3. Agra	36	30720	165.60	494.30
4. Lucknow	23	14115	60.90	341.40
5. Bareilly	15	2974	14.78	286.20
6. Varanasi	13	1436	78.60	246.30
7. Allahabad	12	6125	14.20	97.80
8. Gorakhpur	10	5126	13.90	145.40
9. Meerut	7	1153	2.38	18.70
10. Dehradun	7	830	6.65	176.22
11. Haldwani	10	2123	.51	18.90

(A) Problems faced by the industry in general

(1) *Labour Unrest*: The biggest problem threatening the industrial life at Ghaziabad at present, is the growing incidence of strikes and lock-outs, resulting from labour unrest provoked by a variety of reasons such as demand for reinstatement of the employees suspended or dismissed by the management, demand for wage hike, protest against non-payment of bonus or matters pertaining to overtime issues. The problem of labour unrest is further accentuated by the rivalry amongst the leaders of various trade-unions operating within the same factory. There are only a handful of factories in the

city, such as those belonging to Mohan Meakin group and a few others, which are free from the influence of trade-union activities. At most of the other factories, trade unions play an active role in matters pertaining to labour disputes and the situation more often worsens instead of being reconciled. Ghaziabad at present stands close to Kanpur in terms of total number of strikes and lock-outs (Table No. 9.1), although industrially, it is far much younger and relatively much less industrialized than the latter.

TABLE 9.2: **Increase in the Incidence of Strikes & Lockouts at Ghaziabad** 2

Years	Number of strikes & Lock-outs	No. of employees affected	Total wage loss in lakhs Rs.	Total Prod. loss in lakh Rs.
1981	38	6638	16.13	134.40
1982	44	20868	30.94	247.65

Source 1 & 2: Annual Report 1982 published by labour Commissioner, U.P., kanpur.

Trade-union activities in the city are aggravating the situation, instead of playing a positive and constructive role. As is evident from the table No. 9.2, there has been recorded a considerable increase, during the last two years (1981-82) in the total number of strikes and lock-outs, employees affected, and the total loss of the wages and production caused by labour unrest. The most powerful trade union operating in the city at present is CITU (Centre of Indian Trade Union) which is backed by CPIM and is patronized by about 15 thousand factory workers at city's various industrial units. Other important trade unions which have won the support of factory workers at Ghaziabad are A.I.T.U.C. (All India Trade Union Centre), backed by CPI, B.M.S. (Bhartiya Majdoor Sangh)backed by Jansangh, H.M.S. (Hind Majdoor Sabha) backed by Janta Party and INTUC (Indian National Trade Union Congress) backed by the ruling party of Congress I.

As Segal states, labour costs often form a significant proportion of total production costs and are of considerable locational importance to many industries.[1] Unfavourable labour attitudes increases the proportion of labour cost substantially in the total cost of production creating an adverse effect on the industrial economy of a place. However until 1975, labour situation at Ghaziabad was far much better than at present. During the earlier phases of industrial

TABLE 9.3: **Incidences of Strikes and Lock-outs at Ghaziabad's Factories***

1981 Name of the Factory	Days of strikes & Lock-out periods	1982 Name of Factory	Days of Strike & Lock-out Periods.
1. Usha Mill Associates Pvt. Ltd.	130	1. Aknos Paper Mills	107
2. Premier Packagings	41	2. Naswar Engineering Co.	197
3. Dowells & Company	101	3. Jagannath Dalip Singh	20
4. Shakti Auto Valves Engg. Co. Pvt. Ltd.	108	4. Some Plumbering Fixtures Ltd.	129
5. Swadeshi Polytex Ltd.	57	5. Delhi Press Samachar Patra Pvt. Ltd.	54
6. Hindustan Monarch Pvt. Ltd.	75	6. Scientific Instruments Co. Pvt. Ltd.	70
7. Sri Ram Pistons & Rings Limited	218	7. Shakti Auto Valves & Engg. Co. Pvt. Ltd.	30
8. Metal Board Containers Pvt. Ltd.	64	8. U.P. Ceramics & Potteries Ltd.	29
9. S.W. Rubber Works	112	9. Jain Processors & Engineers.	30
10. Tin manufacturing Co. of India	30	10. S.W. Rubber Works Pvt. Ltd.	45
11. National Genaral Industries	43	11. Pravin Chemicals	62
12. Aknos Paper Mills	73	12. Heatly & Gresham India Ltd.	93
13. Naswar Engineering Co.	73	13. United Wheels Pvt. Ltd.	19
14. Leatherite Industries Pvt. Ltd.	53	14. Peerless Foundry	30
15. Jagannath & Dalip Singh	69	15. Dewrance Mcneill & Company	21
		16. Mcneill & Magor Ltd.	21
		17. Federal Chemical Works	10

**Source*: Based on information obtained from Deputy Labour Commissioner Office, Ghaziabad.

development of fiftees and sixtees, there was little or no labour problem in the city. Favourable labour attitude was also one of the important factors which inspired many a reputed concerns to establish their factories at Ghaziabad. Many of the West Bengal firms, where labour situation was deteriorated to the worst, have also opted for Ghaziabad for relocating their factories. Some of the important West bengal concerns, relocated at Ghaziabad include M/s. B.K. Plastics Pvt. Ltd., Bengal Plastics Pvt. Ltd., Shekhar Tubes Pvt. Ltd., and Paharpur Cooling Towers. Important factories relocated here from Punjab in the wake of country's partition include M/s. Shree Guru Nanak Engineering Company, Punjab Oil Expeller Co., Lyallpur Engineering Co. & Sachdeva Steel Rolling Mills.

However the earlier advantage of favourable labour attitude started disappearing towards the late sixtees and since after 1970 labour unrest began to mount gradually. Rapid industrial growth during last two decades gave a big boost to trade union activities with the result that the strikes and lock-outs became the regular feature in the industrial life of the city. Reluctance of employers to understand and realize the genuine difficulties of employees and their tendency to flout various labour laws, are also equally strong causes for growing labour unrest in the city. As shown in table No. 9.3 many a big factories of the city have undergone prolonged periods of strikes during last 2 years resulting in a huge loss of industrial production. In a healthy industrialized society both the employer and employees should benefit from the gains of industrialization and it is here that trade unions can play a positive role by helping in reconciling the matters peacefully. What is required is not the condemnation or suppression of trade-union activities but a thorough review of the situation so that trade unions may stand for the good of the factory workers, instead of creating chaos and unrest.

(2) *Labour Housing*

Provision of housing accommodation for rapidly growing industrial population at Ghaziabad poses a real problem which must be tackled effectively to ensure a check on the haphazard growth of unhealthy dwellings in and around the city. The number of slums has arisen alarmingly during recent years and not infrequently these slum dwellers work as casual labour force at the various industrial units of the city. However, provision of adequate housing facilities for industrial workers can do little in remedying this problem but it will certainly lesser its intensity in view of the substantial number of slum dwellers working in the factories.

At Ghaziabad only about 15% of the total 37731 industrial workers at 452 registered units have been able to avail of the housing accommodation provided by either G.D.A. or State Labour Housing Department. Construction of cheap-type quarters by G.D.A. for low income group has helped much in easing out the acute shortage of labour housing in the city. These quarters, though not specifically meant for industrial workers, accommodate quite a large number of industrial workers who cannot afford to pay exhorbitant rents of private houses. There exist 1500 cheap type quarters at Raj Nagar, 2500 quarters at Vivekanand Nagar and 1200 quarters at Vijai Nagar.[2] More than 60% of these quarters are occupied by persons working in the factories. G.D.A. allots these quarters on rental basis. Some of these quarters have also been sold out by G.D.A. to the persons belonging to low income group. G.D.A. received huge sums of loans from HUDCO (Housing and Urban Development Corporation), a Govt. of India Enterprise, for financing these housing projects.

Apart from G.D.A., State Labour Housing Department has also made a significant headway in this direction by constructing a labour colony of 792 houses near Naya Ghaziabad Railway Station, wherein several of Ghaziabad's important factories such as M/s Jain Tube Company, Hind Cycle Ltd., and Tata Oil Mills Co. etc. have been allotted quarters to accommodate some of their employees.[3] Construction work of another set of 690 labour houses near the old labour colony has already been completed by State Labour Housing Department and very shortly these too will be allotted to the various factories for providing housing accommodation to their workers.[4] After allotment of these new quarters State Labour Housing Department will fulfil about 4% housing requirements of the total employees at the registered industrial units of the city. It has also constructed 1652 labour quarters at Modi Nagar, the second biggest industrial centre in the district after Ghaziabad.

Housing accommodation for factory workers has also been provided by several employers, many of whom have constructed 5 to 15 quarters within factory premises for their technical staff, whose services can be required at any odd hour of the day. The biggest residential complex has been developed by Bharat Electronics Ltd. which provides houses to more than 50% of its employees.

At Ghaziabad, still about 80% industrial workers live in dwellings which provide the barest minimum shelter. Govt., local bodies and the factory owners must give the highest priority to this issue, in order to channelize the city's industrial growth in a right and healthy direction.

(3) *Difficulties in procuring the raw materials*

In the wake of city's industrial field survey, it was found that more than 75% employers complained about not getting the timely arrival of raw materials for a variety of reasons such as short supply of raw material at the source, damage caused to products enroute, disruption of transport services at some point due to floods or storms, and so on. Long distances of raw materials sources do create some problems, although city is served with an excellent system of road and rail transport services. Delay in the supply of raw materials often causes interruptions in the manufacturing operations and resultantly manufacturers have to suffer considerable financial losses. Interruptions in the manufacturing operation also create some technical problems in certain industries, which makes the problem even worse.

As far as Govt. role is concerned, it has provided all sorts of help to manufacturers for procuring the raw materials. U.P.S.I.C. makes arrangements for the supply of iron, alloys, non-ferrous metals and chemicals to the manufacturers through its depot located at Ghaziabad. For other types of raw materials, district Industries Officer or Area Development Officer forward the applications to Directorate of Industries, Kanpur for sanctioning the required quota. PICUP (Pradeshiya Industrial Investment Corporation, Uttar Pradesh) helps the large-scale industrial units in getting their raw materials. State Govt. has also exempted sales tax for three years on raw materials used in the manufacture of 34 specified items in the case of newly established factories. Many of these items constitute amongst the important industries of Ghaziabad such as oil engines, oil expellers, pumps and compressors, electronic items, switch gears and electric motors, cycles and cycle parts, refractories, ceramics and potteries, and scientific instruments.

There are no grievances, as far as the facilities provided by the Govt. are concerned. However, manufacturers still often fail to arrange the timely arrival of the raw materials, mainly, because of red-tapism involving a long procedure of formalities to be completed, before the final delivery is made. Corrupt practices in the concerned offices make the matter even more difficult. The problem of timely procurement of raw materials can be considerably eased if the procedure for obtaining the raw materials through UPSIC and PICUP, and Directorate of Industries is simplified and if officers and staff in concerned offices make sincere efforts to help the manufacturers in this respect.

(4) *Erratic Supply of Electricity*

Electricity failure is the most common phenomenon in the city of Ghaziabad. So frequent are the breaks in the supply of electricity that one cannot rely on its continuance for a sufficiently long duration, however, important the work it may be. It can deceive any moment and hence some alternative arrangement is a must for all users of electricity, be it industry, domestic consumers or any other type of activity.

At Ghaziabad majority of factories obtain motive power from electricity. Frequent failure of electricity disrupt the smooth functioning of manufacturing process. Worst sufferers are the many hundereds of smaller units which cannot afford to have their own generators, notwithstanding the offer of the advantage of capital and interest subsidy scheme initiated by the State Govt., since 1.2.73 for the purchase of diesel/turbo generating sets. Under this scheme capital subsidy is payable to the extent of 50% to small units and 25% to other units. UPFC acts as agent of the State Govt. for the disbursement of this subsidy which has benefitted quite a large number of small and medium sized industrial units in the city. Since the inception of the scheme, repurcussions of the problem of electricity failures on the industry have been alleviated to some extent but nevertheless many hundreds of small units in the city still depend fully on the local supply of electricity and eventually face difficult time in the event of electricity going off, all of a sudden, for hours together.

Until a couple of years ago, industries had to put up with drastic load shedding by Electricity Department. Power cuts compelled the employers to resort to labour lay off, which in turn created various other types of problems. However for the last two years, no power cuts have been imposed by the electricity department and this has naturally resulted in considerable improvement in the electricity supply conditions in the city. Incidence of electricity failure has also gone down considerably for the last one year. Now-a-days often there is no electricity failure for days-together. Electricity failures in the city are caused largely due to in-efficiency of staff in electricity department. If necessary steps are taken to maintain the level of efficiency amongst the staff, there is no doubt about the problem being solved fully, as there is already no deficit problem in respect of the availability of electricity. Absence of power-cuts for the last two years bears a clear proof of the bountiful situation in respect of adequate supply of electricity in the city.

(5) *Higher rate of Sales Tax*:

Sales Tax rates imposed by U.P. Govt. are relatively higher than those in many other states. This certainly lends a disadvantage to the manufacturers as the market price of their products increases appreciably and they have to struggle hard in competing with the corresponding manufacturers in other states where the sales tax rates are relatively lower. Despite some reliefs given by State Govt. to the manufacturers in this respect such as exemption of sales tax on the raw materials used in the manufacture of 34 specified items, many of which constitute amongst the important industries of the city and conversion of sales tax into long term interest free loan given to manufacturers by PICUP (Pradeshiya Industrial Investment Corporation U.P), equivalent to the sum to be paid as sales tax by the manufacturers for three years on the finished products, the problem of higher rates of sales tax poses a real difficulty to the manufacturers. State Govt. must consider the matter to revise the sales tax rates to bring them at par with those in other states.

B. Problems arising out of the process of rapid industrialization in the city and which are faced by the Urban-industrial population.

(6) *Social Pollution*:

Growing industrialization is also one of the factors causing degeneration in the city's social life, as manifested by a noticeable increase in the incidence of dacoities, thefts, murders, pick-pocketing, and other anti-social activities like liquor addiction and gambling etc. Prosperous agriculture combined with a flourishing industry has resulted in the accumulation of relatively greater wealth with the people, while the ethical, social and educational standard of the people has not risen to a proportionately higher level. Anti-social activities find their origin not only due to relatively greater wealth but also due to poverty conditions arising our as a result or frequent practice of labour lay off at city's various industrial establishments for some reason or the other.

Greater part of city's working population comprises of industrial labour force who largely represent low-income group people. Social standard of this class of city's population is much below the level of healthy industrialized societies. Moderate incomes, lack of proper educational,recreational and medical facilities, improper execution of social security schemes of E.S.I.C. and Provident Fund, are the main impediments in the way of raising the social standard of city's industrial population. Social security schemes must be expanded further and implemented more briskly and sincerely. Employers must also endeavour to give more benefits to their employees in order to improve their social standard.

(7) *Problem of Air Pollution*:

Air pollution is caused by a variety of factors such as vehicular exhaust, cooking fire, heaps of domestic garbage, stagnant pools of water etc. but in and around an industrial urban centre such as it is the case with Ghaziabad, 'the greatest single factor causing air pollution is the fume emitted by chimneys of the factories, which contains substantial quantities of sulphur dioxide, dust particles and other impurities. A case study of Bombay in this respect reveals a higher correlation coefficient of 0.70 between incidence of respiratory diseases and levels of air pollution in different areas of the city.[5] Similar results were obtained by a study of air pollution at Kanpur.[6] It is mainly because of the adverse effects of air pollution on human health, that the study of air pollution level assumes significance in the context of industrial cities. The spectacular industrial growth at Ghaziabad during last few decades has resulted in a considerable increase in the level of air pollution in the city. Though no quantitative studies have so far been taken to measure the exact degree of air pollution, but the overall effect of air pollution as felt by the city's inhabitants is so marked and real, that we cannot afford to dismiss it as no cause for alarm. Many of the city's important industries such as primary metal products, chemicals, synthetic fibre, structural clay products, glass products, G.I. Pipes, and breweries emit huge quantities of fume into the air through chimneys. The level of air pollution is much more accentuated because of the location of major commercial and residential areas in the downwind direction from the major industrial areas at the city. 60% of city's industrial strength lies to the west of city proper across river Hindan, 18% to the east and 18% to the north. For most of the time during the year, the city is in the grip of either easterly or westerly wind with the result that level of air pollution within the city proper rises considerably, causing harmful effects on the health of urban population. Obviously, the factor of wind direction was given little or no consideration at all by the planning authorities while formulating the lay-out of city's residential, commercial and industrial areas. This is a serious mistake which should not be repeated while planning future urban industrial development of the city. Enforcement of threshold limit values of pollutants for future industrial establishments will also help much in controlling the level of air pollution within reasonable limits.

To mitigate the harmful effects of air pollution on the health of factory workers, the employers must make necessary arrangements for providing adequate bathing and washing facilities specially in the factories which use too much of chemicals in their manufacturing process. Provision of health check-up facilities and proper ventilation inside the factory are also important measure in the direction. In the noisy section of factories, workers should be provided earplugs and halmets to lessen the harmful effects of noise on their hearing capacity and brain.

(8) *Problem of Water Pollution*:

Problem of water pollution at Ghaziabad is much less acute as compared to that of air pollution. The low level of water-pollution owes much to the underground sources of drinking water over larger part of the city. All newly developed residential colonies and industrial areas of the city make use of underground water obtained through tube-wells, except for a small part of the old city area where water is obtained from River Hindan, which, of course, is much polluted because of uncontrolled discharge of domestic sewage and industrial effluents into the river. Industrial liquid waste of cyanides, sulphides, phosphoric acids and various other harmful substances poured out by city's synthetic fibre, breweries, paper board, and chemical industries, ultimately finds its way into the river, along with domestic sewage, and it certainly increases the level of river water pollution to alarming proportions. The real danger of river water pollution is faced by the rural folk living in the bordering villages along lower reaches of River Hindan. Greater incidence of jaundice, cholera, gastroentritis and fluorosis in these villages is largely due to the use of polluted river water. Despite the problem of water pollution being not so acute in the city area, city authorities must insist on the prior treatment of sewage and industrial liquid waste before being disposed off into the river, to protect the rural health from diseases caused by water pollution.

(9) *Deterioration of Natural Environment*:

Growing industrialization at Ghaziabad has resulted in the considerable damage done to the natural environment in the near-by villages, where there have been noticed marked climatic and vegetational modifications, caused mainly by excessive heat produced by the furnaces of the city's factories. Forests and trees are gradually disappearing. Excessive heat of the furnaces at near by factories also creates an adverse effect on the standing crops in the farms. In an interview with rural folk at the villages of Pasaunda,

Raispur and Gookhna, which lie close to major industrial areas of the city, it was revealed that agricultural productivity in these villages has registered a downward trend during the last two decades because of the lowering down of the quality of the soil. The fertility of the soil has gone down, partly because of the drop-outs of the atmospheric impurities emitted by chimneys on the ground area and partly because of the chemical changes produced by the dumps of solid waste at city's various industrial units. No doubt the solid waste of various machinery manufacturing units in the city which accrues in the form of scrap, is used by the various small steel making units in the city, but solid waste of other industries, which is largely not usable, does create chemical reactions in the nearby soils, which in turn affect its fertility. Somewhat similar findings were obtained in a study carried out to ascertain the adverse effects of industrial pollution on agriculture, economy and health hygiene at Guldhar, Garhi and Darhagal Villages.[7]

Thus it is quite obvious, that we cannot stop altogether, the damage done to the adjacent farmlands by the process of industrialization, but every care should be taken by the authorities to lessen its effects to the minimal, because in India we can hope of economic betterment of the people only if agriculture and industry go hand in hand in promoting the general welfare of the masses.

REFERENCES

1. Segal, M. (1960) 'Wages in the Metropolis: Their influence on the location of Industries in the NEW YORK Region.' Cambridge, Mass: Harvard University Press.
2. Based on information obtained from the office of Ghaziabad Development Authority.
3. Based on information obtained from the office of Deputy Labour Commissioner, Ghaziabad.
4. Based on information obtained from the office of Deputy Labour Commissioner, Ghaziabad.
5. Bladen Wilford A. & Karan P.P. (Kentucky University, Lexington, U.S.A.) 'Air pollution and Health in Bombay'. National Geographer, Vol. XVII (No.1, June 1982) p. 1-4.
6. Kumra V.K., 'Environmental Pollution and Human Health: A Geographical Study of Kanpur City. The National Geographical Journal of India, Vol. 26, Parts 1 & 2 March-June 1980, Special issue on 'Environmental Perception and Problems' 24th T.G.C. Tokyo, 1980. pp. 60-69.
7. Singh, B.B. Verma, R.K. & Mathur, A.K. 'Environmental Management'. Proceedings of the National Symposium on Environmental Management, Allahabad (July 23-25, 1982) pp. 208-220.

Fig. 26

RELATIVE POSITIONS OF INDUSTRIAL AREAS AND RESIDENTIAL COLONIES AT GHAZIABAD

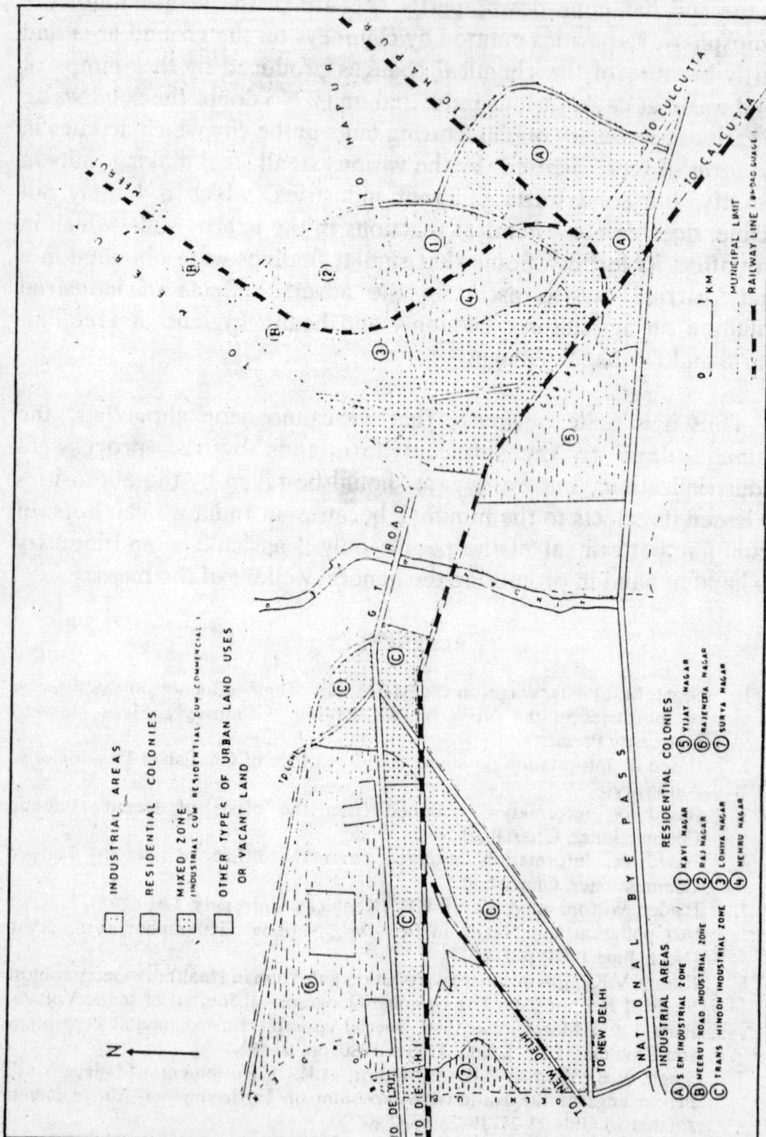

TEN

Theoretical and Conceptual Aspects of the Industrial Location at Ghaziabad

1. *Classical Location Theories of Weber & Losch*:

Classical location theory of Weber which has been improved and modified by Hoover, and D.M. Smith, holds no significance whatsoever with reference to Ghaziabad's industrial location.[1] Weberian theory held considerable significance for describing industrial location during earlier part of the present century but in the modern times when composition of industrial structure has changed in favour of light and high value-added industries, it has lost much of its value. Least cost theory of Weber accords prime importance to the factor of transportations costs. Other two factors which he took into consideration for indentifying minimum cost points are labour costs and agglomeration economies. He used isodapanes for identifying minimum cost location. According to him, optimum industrial location was one where transportation costs were at their minimal or the one where savings in labour costs and agglomeration economies exceeded the additional costs incurred on transportation. In modern times, however, importance of transportation costs as the major locational influence is diminishing fast because of extremely efficient use of raw materials, use of substitutes and by-products, improvement in the quality or purity of raw materials, and improved transport technology of the present age. In the light and high value-added industries, transportation costs account for only .7 to 1.8% of the total cost of production. Moreover, there is not found much spatial variability of transportation costs within the industrial heartland, although in the hinter-land and peripheral regions, transportation costs rise steeply as pointed out by Lindberg and Tornquist with reference to paper and garment industries of Sweden respectively.[2]

In the present phase of manufacturing, spatial variability of labour costs which is the second most important factor in Weber's least cost theory, is also much less marked at the regional level, firstly because of introduction of minimum wage legislation and secondly because of remarkable increase in the occupational and residential mobility of industrial workers these days. There is enough empirical evidence supporting this fact. Studies conducted by Scully, Easterlin and Chernick clearly indicate about this increasing modern trend towards reduction of regional wage inequalities.[3] Variations at regional level are further minimized when we view the labour costs in relation to labour productivity. Low wage level at a place may signify higher labour costs for want of efficiency and motivation on the part of workers. As Borts has pointed out, generally there is found a positive correlation between wage level and labour productivity and as such factor of labour costs works just the reverse of that postulated by Weber.[4] It is mainly on these grounds that Weber's theory has been criticized by Beckman, Greenhut, and Isard.[5] It is not relevant to the contemporary conditions in industrial world. It is particularly so in the context of Ghaziabad firstly because of city's characteristic industrial structure with more than 40% share representing the manufacture of high value-added products of machinery and their parts, and secondly because of late development of manufacturing here as the first important factory of Ghaziabad viz. M/s. Amrit Banaspati & Co. Ltd. was started here in 1940 only.

Losch's market area theory also does not seem relevant in the case of majority of modern industrial activities.[6] It has been criticised by Isard firstly for its assumption of a uniform demand surface which is most unrealistic and secondly for its concept of discrete market areas which is not feasible because of their frequent overlapping with each other.[7] Demand of industrial goods seldom characterizes an uniform pattern because of uneven distribution of population and also because of variations in the socio-economic level of the various groups of population in case the region denotes a more or less uniform distribution of population. Spatial concentration of demand is further accentuated because majority of industrial goods are sold either to other manufacturers or to wholesalers who are even more concentrated than the final consumers. In case of Ghaziabad's industrial location, major part of demand is concentrated in Delhi metropolitan area despite the fact that the region as a whole signifies a densely populated area with a fairly good level of socio-economic standard.

Another major criticism of Losch's theory relates to its concept of discrete market areas which is practically impossible. Market areas of two or more industrial locations frequently overlap with each other. Moreover, in the modern times, majority of industrial goods characterize a world-wide market. At Ghaziabad too, quite, a number of finished products manufactured here such as Oil engines, electronic items, various types of industrial machinery, furnishing handloom & power-loom fabrics, G.I. pipes and tubes etc. enter international market. It is mainly on these grounds that Losch's market area theory is rejected for explaining the present day industrial location. No doubt Ghaziabad's manufacturing exhibits a remarkable orientation towards market, but industrial location here can hardly be explained in the light of assumptions made by Losch.

2. *Behavioural or Adaptive - adoptive Approach*:

In view of the diminishing utility of traditional location theories of Weber and Losch, it became pertinent to evolve an alternative approach which could explain the existing industrial location, giving full consideration to changing economic conditions of the present-day world. It was at this juncture that behavioural or adaptive- adoptive approach advocated by Alichian, Tiebout and several others seemed to be quite realistic and relevant for understanding the strategy of industrial location at a newly developed industrial centre like Ghaziabad.[8] In practice, individual entrepreneur gives no thought whatsoever to the abstract spatial economic theories, while making decision about the location of his firm. He is neither rational nor perfectly well-informed about the prospective locations. Generally he prefers an established centre of industry in order to avail of the various economic benefits accruing at such a place and also to avoid the element of risk and uncertainty involved at some newer location. However, human behaviour is most unpredictable. He can also choose a place with little or no industry at all. Sure and steady profits are generally the common goal of all manufacturers but sometimes non-economic factors may be equally important in matters pertaining to decisions of industrial location. Not infrequently location decisions are made on purely sentimental grounds and thus any theory which overlooks the human factor can hardly be suitable for explaining all types of industrial location at regional level.

All manufacturing firms operate in a changing economic environment to which they adapt themselves from time to time in their own specific ways. An industry as a whole must adapt itself to its economic and social environments, partly by means of birth and death of the firms and partly by modifications in the behaviour of existing firms. Apart from minor adjustments related to price and demand, major adaptations of a firm to its changing economic conditions may result in the relocation or expansion of the existing plant, modernization programmes, or setting up of a branch unit at some newer location.

While often it is the firm which adapts itself to its economic and social environment, but not infrequently economic and social conditions of a place may also adopt a firm located just per chance, making it a big success. At Ghaziabad the pioneer industry of oil engines and agricultural implements was started here as a result of relocation of some factories from Punjab in Pakistan in the wake of partition. Economic environment of the region, however, favoured the rapid growth of this industry, because there existed an ever increasing demand of oil engines and agricultural implements in the prosperous and progressive agricultural region of Wn. Uttar Pradesh. Behavioural approach emphasizes both adaption and adoption and therefore it is aptly referred to as adaptive-adoptive approach, which gained much popularity during 1950's and 1960's for explaining different types of industrial location in the industrial world. Pred, Leblanc and Gilmour have explained the locational dynamics of manufacturing in particular study areas on the basis of this adaptive-adoptive approach.[9] Behavioural studies of a number of individual firms can be incorporated to evolve a generalized aggregate pattern of adaptive-adoptive strategy of firms over a particular area. In the present study of Ghaziabad's industrial landscape, which has been accomplished with the help of a sample industrial field survey, technique adopted has been somewhat similar to the concept of behavioural or adaptive-adoptive approach but as no quantitative basis was given to this aspect, the present study does not strictly fall within the purview of the same.

3. *Norcliffe's Contemporary Location Theory*:

Lastly a mention of contemporary location theory of Norcliffe is also worthwhile, without which our discussions on theoretical considerations will hardly be complete.[10] Norcliffe's industrial location theory which was presented in the year 1970, seeks to provide a framework of locational influences. It is much more relevant to contemporary conditions and is flexible enough to accommodate changes in locational patterns through time and space. Norcliffe gives due consideration to non-economic factors as well because least cost location may not be a feasible location in most of the cases. In his theory he has used the term 'locational influences' in place of cost factors. He has mentioned three major locational influences which are (1) infrastructure availability, (2) Internal and external economic and (3) Contact fields.

Ghaziabad's industrial locations can be aptly described in the light of framework provided by Norcliffe's contemporary location theory. Although industrial beginnings were made here on account of concerted efforts made by Punjabi entrepreneurs during early post-Independence years, but the tempo of industrial activity picked up only ever since there was made provision of infrastructure facilities by U.P.S.I.D.C. and Ghaziabad Improvement Trust which allotted fully developed plots to entrepreneurs at reasonable rates. Availability of infra-structure facilities assumes special significance in the case of small and medium sized concerns which for financial reasons can not afford to provide various services at the site such as water supply, waste disposal facilities, electricity, and access to rail and road links. It is mainly because of much heavier capital outlay required for developing new sites that major part of industrial expansion takes place in the form of extension of the existing plant rather than opening new ones. Provision of developed sites & various other types of infra-structure facilities at Ghaziabad seems even more significant in view of its close proximity to Delhi. By locating his factory at Ghaziabad, the entrepreneur avails the double advantage of various urbanization economics of the metropolis and at the same time being at an established centre of industry where mass clustering of industrial units has led to the development of many agglomerative economies which are so vital for sustaining the industrial growth at a place.

Norcliffe names another major locational influence as internal and external economies. Internal economies are those associated with large scale production such as adoption of specialized techniques, maximum utilization of the capacity of the plant, and bulk purchasing and selling of raw materials and finished products. Industrial development at Ghaziabad clearly emphasizes the significance of various internal economies with 2/3 rd of its total registered employment represented by large-scale concerns. External economies are those which result from the concentration of industries over a place. As already mentioned, these economies too play a significant role in fostering the industrial growth at Ghaziabad.

Norcliffe mentions linkage and contact fields as the third major locational influence. Ghaziabad's industrial structure owes much to the factor of inter-industry and intra-industry linkages. By contact fields Norcliffe implies personal or face to face contacts between manufacturers and the customers which are so vital for providing impulses for innovations and improvements, in the case of various machinery manufacturing branches of industry at Ghaziabad because of nearness of the vast size of metropolitan market. Thus Ghaziabad's industrial location can be best explained in the framework of locational influences provided by Norcliffe's contemporary location theory. Availability of infra-structure facilities resulted in a mass clustering of industrial units, within a very short span of time, which in turn, led to the development of various external economies and linkage patterns. Close proximity to Delhi bestowed the advantage of contact fields and together these three locational influences befittingly explain the process of rapid industrial development at Ghaziabad during post-Independence period.

REFERENCES

1. Weber, A. (1929), 'Thoery of the Location of Industries', Translated by C.J. Friedrich, University of Chicago.
Hoover, E.M. (1971), 'An Introduction to Regional Economics', New York, Alfred A.Knopf.
Smith, D.M. (1966). A Theoretical Framework for Geographical Studies of Industrial Location, 'Economic Geography', 42. 95-113.
2. Lindberg, O. (1953) An Economic Geographical Study of the localization of the Swedish Paper Industry, 'Geografiska Annaler'. 35, 28-40.
Tornquist, G. (1962) 'Transport costs as a location Factor for Manufacturing industry'. Lund Studies in Geography, Series C., General & Mathematical Geography 2.
3. Scully, G.W. (1971) The North South Manufacturing Wage Differential, 'Journal of Regional Science'. 11, 235-252.
Easterlin, R.A. (1958), Income Differentials among States 1880-1950, 'Papers & Proceedings, Regional Science Association, 4, 22-59.
Chernick, S.E. (1966), 'Interregional Disparities in Income', Economic Council of Canada: Staff Studies No. 14, Ottawar: Queen's Printer.
4. Borts, G.H. (1960) The Equalization of Returns and Regional Economic Growth, 'American Economic Review', 50, 319-347.
5. Beckmann, M. (1968) 'Location Theory'. New York: Random House.
Greenhut, H.L. (1956), 'Plant Location in Theory & Practices' Chapel Hill: University of North Carolina Press.
Isard W. (1956) 'Location and Space Economy', Cambridge, Mass: M.I.T. Press.
6. Losch, A. (1954) 'The Economics of Location' Translated by W.H. Woglom & W.F. Stopler, New York: Wiley.
7. Isard, W. (1956), 'Location & Space Economy', Fig. 52, p. 272, Cambridge Mass: M.I.T. Press.
8. Alchian. A.A. (1950) Uncertainty, Evolution and Economic Theory, 'Journal of Political Economy', 58, 211-221.
Tiebout, C.M. (1967) Location Theory, Empirical Evidence and Economic Evolution, Paper & Proceedings, Regional Science Association, 3, 74-86.
9. Pred A.R. (1966) 'The Spatial Dynamics of United States Urban-industrial Growth 1800-1914', Cambridge Mass: M.I.T. Press.
Leblanc, R.G. (1969) 'Location of Manufacturing in New England in the 19th Century'. Dartmouth: Centre for the study of Social Change.
Gilmour J.M. (1972), Spatial Evolution of Manufacturing: Sn. Ontario 1851-1861 Toronto, University of Toronto, Department of Geography.
10. Norcliffe, G.B. (1970) 'A Theory of Manufacturing Places', An Essay in 'Locational Dynamics of Manufacturing Activity' edited by Lyndhurst Collins & David F. Walker.

ELEVEN

Conclusions

(A) SALIENT FEATURES OF INDUSTRIALIZATION AT GHAZIABAD

Industrial growth is a curious phenomenon resulting from the balanced operation of a combination of physical, historical, political, social and economic factors. Obviously the various determinants of industry occur in varying proportions at a place and they interact with each other and with industry with even greater variations. Thus the resultant picture of industrial growth at a place acquires a distinctive character of its own, reflecting the specific pattern of interaction amongst the various factors involved.

The pattern of industrialization which has evolved at Ghaziabad clearly reflects the impact of various physical, economic, political and social factors working here since the inception of industrial activity a little over 40 years ago. After making a study of the whole gamut of industrial activity in its various geographical aspects, we certainly notice certain characteristic features associated with city's industrialization, which can be enumerated as under:

1. *Marked Preponderance of Private Sector*

Though Govt. activity has played a key role in promoting the industrial activity in the city, major part of industrial structure at Ghaziabad characteristically consists of private sector enterprises with public sector representing only 10% share in the total registered employment of the city. The real strength of the private sector was obtained through Govt. bodies and Corporations but the role of Govt. as an entrepreneur has been very meagre. There exist only 3 public sector industrial undertakings in the city viz. M/s Bharat Electronics Ltd., Central Electronics Ltd. and Hind Cycles Ltd. which employ 2850, 750 and 324 persons respectively. Public sector undertakings, no doubt, render a valuable service by accelerating the industrial growth and by upholding the cause of social justice, but at a place like Ghaziabad with so many inherent advantages for industry, lack of public sector enterprises never acted as a dampening effect on the general process of industrialization in the city. Private sector has done well in respect of both small and large industrial concerns. Amongst the 449 private sector registered units in 1981, 52 concerns were functioning as public Ltd. companies, 125 as private Ltd. companies and remaining 272 factories were operating as proprietorship or partnership concerns. Biggest proprietorship concern of the city is the famous M/s Modern Industries, which employs 636 persons. Biggest five Public Ltd. concerns of the city include M/s Mohan Meakin Breweries Ltd., Jain Tube Company Ltd., Shri Ram Pistons & Rings Ltd., Ajanta Textile Ltd. and Poysha Industrial Corporation Ltd. which respectively employ 1452, 1178, 935, 920 and 850 persons. Biggest private Ltd. concerns of the city are Indure Pvt. Ltd., Jayna Time Industries Pvt. Ltd., Mascot India Tools & Forgings Pvt. Ltd. and Bramic Suri Pvt. Ltd. which employ 441, 461, 326 and 275 persons respectively. Thus private sector enterprises represent all the sizes in the industrial structure of Ghaziabad, but the biggest industrial establishment of the city viz. Bharat Electronics Ltd. employing 2850 persons belongs to Public Sector.

2. *Large-Scale and Small-scale Industries Complementary to Each Other*

Industrial structure at Ghaziabad serves a good example of coherence and coordination between large and small or medium-sized industrial establishments. Large scale firms, account for 2/3rd of the total registered employment of the city, although they numbered only 79 out of the city's total 452 registered units in 1981. Remaining 1/3rd of the registered employment is represented by small or medium-sized industrial units. However, there exist over

1500 unregistered small scale units in the city which are not covered under Factories Act for the reason of employing less than 10 persons. Thus overall strength of smaller units is no less significant than that of large scale firms. Small or medium-sized industrial units make a considerable contribution to the total industrial output in the city. Being labour intensive and capital saving, these small and medium-sized industrial units continue to render a valuable service to the industrial activity in the city. It is only through small industrial units that uneducated and unskilled labour force receives the preliminary training which is of great help in inducing the development of basic industrial skills required in large scale enterprises.

Predominance of large scale over small scale amongst the registered industrial units in the city can be reasonably attributed to the vast market potential offered by the proximity to capital metropolis of Delhi. No doubt, large scale enterprises obtain substantial economies by operating the machinery to their maximum capacity, by adopting improved techniques of production and by bulk purchasing and selling of the material, but these economies prove futile, if there is not available vast size of the market which can absorb the increased output. Thus growth of large scale concerns in respect of cotton textile, oil mills and soap, tin products, structural clay products, and various types of machinery at Ghaziabad owes largely to the vast size of market which is at once of local, national and even of international character in some cases.

Relevance of large scale production is also determined, to a great extent, by the type and nature of industry concerned. There exist a number of such important industries at Ghaziabad, wherein the necessity of large-scale production is not as much motivated by the vast size of the market, as by certain other considerations peculiar to the industry concerned. Preponderance of large-scale production in respect of breweries, cigarettes, and ayurvedic and unani medicines, at Ghaziabad is governed by the factor of reputation of the firm which counts a lot in the sale of these products. Large scale concerns of synthetic fibre, glass products and hydrogenated oil have been guided by the huge investment in the plant and equipment required by these industries.

While making a study of scale of production in respect of

Ghaziabad's industries, a reference, to city's oil engine and agricultural implements industry which is the pioneer and leading industry of Ghaziabad proper, invokes special interest in view of its characteristically small-scale character despite involving the manufacture of intricate machinery. There exist 70 registered and 300 unregistered industrial units in the city manufacturing oil engines and agricultural implements or their parts. 3/4th of these registered units function as small-scale units and are located at Ghaziabad proper. However, the industry suffers no disadvantage because of smaller size of the units and continues to make rapid strides since its very beginning. In this case it is mainly the close geographical association of the factories of this industry, which has given strength and vigour to this industry. Lack of large scale concerns in this industry has been more than offset by the geographical proximity of small scale catering to the specific needs of this industry.

Industrial structure at Ghaziabad signifies a complete absence of large scale concerns in respect of chemicals and gases, paper and paper products and corrugated boxes. These are the industries where small or medium-sized industrial units are economically more viable than the large enterprises. Thus large, medium and small, all sizes of concerns assume special significance in fostering the cause of industrial development in the city.

3. *Key Role by Govt. Bodies and Corporations*

The original advantages of the industrial location at Ghaziabad have been, to a great deal, augmented by the role played by various Govt. offices, corporations and banks located at Ghaziabad e.g. Area Development Office, U.P.State Industrial Development Corporation, U.P. Financial Corporation, U.P.Small Industries Corporation, Industrial Development Bank of India, and other Govt. and Commercial Banks. These Govt. bodies generally work in coordination, rendering valuable service in fostering the industrial development in the city. They promote and accelerate the industrial growth of the city by providing infra-structure facilities and financial assistance, by helping in the procurement of the raw materials, machinery, coal, and oil, by giving technical assistance and consultancy services in the industry concerned, and also in several other ways covering all aspects of the industrial activity. Apart from these direct influences,

Govt. also supports the cause of industrial growth in the city indirectly by developing various services in the area such as adequate water and power supply, efficient transport facilities, sewage facilities and housing for industrial workers and other sections of the society, thus adding to the attractiveness of the city for industrial location. Other indirect influences include the structure of local taxation, and normal laws relating to minimum wages, working hours, minimum ages of the male and female labour, and sanitation and health requirements etc. However, in the context of Ghaziabad, it is mainly the direct assistance in various forms which assume much greater significance in giving a phillip to the industrial activity in the city. We cannot underrate the service done by Govt. bodies in exhorting the industrial growth of the city, but one must be cautioned not to overstress it, because Govt. efforts bear fruits only when a location already possesses certain inherent advantages for industry.

4. *Sound Technical Background*

Manufacture of agricultural, transport, electrical and various other types of industrial machinery accounts for more than 40% share in the total registered employment of the city. Ghaziabad enjoys a high reputation for many of its machinery products such as oil engines, oil expellers, boilers, electronics, auto-parts, cranes, surface grinders, watches and clocks, ash-handling plants, and automatic controls etc. Most of these items manufactured here, not only find a nation-wide market, but are also exported to countries of Middle East, Africa and Far East.

Development of machinery manufacturing branches of metal-based industries in the city owes largely to the availability of technical know-how of high order not only from indigenous sources, but also from abroad in many cases by seeking technical collaboration with foreign firms. Apart from the manufacture of various types of intricate and sophisticated machinery, other industries involving technical delicacies, in the city include manufacture of coated and bonded abrasives, breweries, cigarettes, synthetic fibres, and glass. These industries have grown and flourished in the city mainly because of the sound technical background of the city as a whole.

Fortunately, technical know-how was not scarce in the city even during the earlier phase of industrial development. Real spurt in the industrial growth of the city was acquired towards the end of forties when there were transferred here some of the important concerns from Punjab in the wake of country's partition in 1947. M/s Shri Guru Nanak Engineering Company, and Punjab Oil Expellers Pvt. Ltd. which are the two leading concerns of Oil engines and agricultural implements industries in the city, were previously located at Layalpur and Lahore. Other factories which were transferred here from Punjab include M/s Sachdeva Steel Rolling Mills, Layalpur Engineering Company, and National Abrasives Pvt. Ltd. Plant and equipment of these factories were only relocated here, and so there arose no problem of any technical nature whatsoever, in the successful functioning of these concerns in the city.

Technical background in the city has been also strengthened, to a great extent, by seeking technical collaboration with foreign firms by a number of important concerns. To quote a few examples, M/s Indure Pvt. Ltd. functions in technical collaboration with 'Allen-Sherman Hoff Company' of U.S.A., Rathi Alloys & Steels Ltd. with 'TOR-ISTEG Steel Corporation' of Luxembourg, Electric Construction and Equipment Company, with 'Toshiba' of Japan and with 'Schinders' of Switzerland and 'John Oakey and Mohan Ltd.' with 'John Oakey & Sons Ltd.' of London. Apart from technical collaborations there were also established a number of foreign firms in the city such as 'Danfoss India Ltd.', 'International Tobacco Company Ltd.' & "Indo-Bulgar Food'. At present however only 40% shares of these firms are owned by foreign companies and 60% shares by Indian Management.

Another factor which sustains & fosters the technical aspects of city's industry is the presence of a number of industrial research and industrial training institutes in Delhi. Vitality and vigour of city's industries owe much to these institutions.

5. *Evidence of General Economies of Concentration*

During the past 40 years of city's industrial history, there has been witnessed not only springing up of a wide range of newer industries but also marked clustering of metal consuming industrial units, which now represent more than 60% share in the total registered employment of the city. Obviously concentration of metal-based and other industries in the city has further enhanced the industrial potentialities of the location. Initially it was a nodal situation and availability of infra-structure facilities which acted as the strongest stimulant for encouraging the city's industrial growth, but now it is mainly the existence of an active industry which exhorts more and more entrepreneurs to start industry here so that they can avail of the several general economies which have developed as a natural sequence to the expansion of city's industrial node. Some of the important general economies of industrial concentration in the city include adequate and flexible labour supply with wide range of industrial skills, adaptability of means of transportation to the specific needs of the various industries, readily available maintenance and repair services for industrial plants, publication of industrial journals, orientation of technical institutions to the specific needs of the local industries, expansion of insurance and banking facilities, easy availability of capital through banks & other Govt. financial bodies, development of facilities for testing the quality of finished products, & the provision of technical consultancy services through various private and Govt. bodies. Social advantages of housing, recreation and education also add to attraction of industrial location at Ghaziabad. Combined effect, of all the above mentioned general economies of concentration, creates such a strong impact on the location decisions that other factors are relegated into considerable background. Economies of concentration are so real and substantial that these can more than offset the absence of some of the important requisites of the industry concerned.

Apart from the general concentration of various types of industries, physical proximity of the industrial units belonging to the same industry provides even greater economies. At Ghaziabad 17 out of 24 important industries of the city possess more than 70% of their registered employment in one single industrial area, a fact that clearly indicates the significance of economies gained through the physical proximity of factories of the same industry. These factories achieve considerable economies by contracting out the different phases of the manufacturing process, or different parts of the final product to other factories which specialize in the concerned activities. Physical proximity facilitates the movements of goods from one factory to the another. The factories which undertake contract jobs, generally adopt specialized techniques and thus overhead costs are considerably reduced both for the seller and the buyer. Development of congenial social relationships between such units and the local dealers in the product, facilitates the task of marketing the finished goods to a great extent. These dealers keep in tough with the specialized areas where the product is manufactured and then it becomes quite easy for them to arrange the sale of the finished products. Thus Ghaziabad's rapid industrial progress owes much to the clustering of linked industrial units in different industrial areas.

The process of industrialization at Ghaziabad is still in full swing and at the same time it is much far behind the stage when the economies of concentration begin to be exceeded by diseconomies of concentration such as competition amongst industrial units, intensified labour union activities, high cost of land and living, congestion in respect of transportation services, water supply and power supply, and other nuisances associated with industrial growth. Labour unions are, no doubt, getting increasingly powerful to press for their demands regarding higher wages and other facilities, but on the whole they have not created too much of an adverse influence on the city's industrial fortunes. General economies of concentration at Ghaziabad are so genuine, that some minor problems like labour unrest & handicap of distant raw materials do not seem to make any substantial impact on the location decisions.

6. *Linkage - A Vital Factor*

Apart from the general tendency towards concentration, industrial distributions at Ghaziabad also exhibit a marked grouping, in space, of inter-related industries, a phenomenon which is called linkage in the terminology of industrial Geography. Industries feed upon each other by virtue of linkage. Finished products of one industry are utilized as materials by others. Sometimes a single raw material undergoes a series of industrial processes before being converted into a final product and often each of these constitutes a separate industry. Such type of linkage is called "vertical linkage'. 'Horizontal linkage' implies manufacture of different parts and accessories of one single product at separate industrial units before being assembled at some bigger establishment for turning out the final product. 'Diagonal linkage' includes those industrial units which provide services or produce items which are required by several other industries. 'Technological linkage' includes those industries wherein finished product of one single industry is used as raw material by several others.

Industrial structure at Ghaziabad can hardly be explained without making any reference to the operation of the factor of linkages amongst several important industries of the city. Linkage has played a vital role in giving impetus to the growth of several new industries e.g. manufacture of tin containers, glass bottles, craft paper, and primary metal products, which were started in the city mainly to cater to the needs of hydrogenated oil, breweries and drugs and medicines, corrugated boxes, and machinery manufacturing industrial units of the city respectively. Other important industries which owe their growth to the factor of linkage include synthetic fibre, and chemicals which meet the requirements of cotton textile,and paper, glass, and soap industries. General process of industrialization in the city encouraged the establishment of refractories and the manufacture of coated and bonded abrasives.

Industrial structure of the city furnishes the examples of all the four types of linkages mentioned earlier. Industries related to the manufacture of wrought iron from pig iron, primary metal products from wrought iron, and machinery or their parts from primary metal products present the example of vertical linkage. Horizontal linkage exists between the various casting and forging industrial units,and machinery manufacturing units because latter often get various parts and accessories of the machinery, manufactured at several of the former. Diagonal linkage is exemplified by the industries engaged in the manufacture of nuts and bolts, nails, ball bearings, tools, gauges, jigs and fixtures etc. because these are the items which are used by a large variety of industries. Manufacture of steel wire at Ghaziabad signifies technological linkage as it is used as raw material by several other industries of the city such as manufacture of nails, screws, chains and cables etc.

Thus it is clear from the foregoing accounts that geographical association of inter-related industries has played a vital role in stimulating the tempo of industrial activity in the city. There are substantial economies to be gained by such association such as cheap and easy movements of goods, and personal contacts between the the buying and selling firms which make the matters easy for both. Linkage is not an original but rather an acquired advantage of an industrial location which evolves only after a certain level of industrialization has been achieved. It is thus quite natural that industrial development at Ghaziabad during earlier phases shows little or no relevance to the factor of linkages. However, industrial growth during sixtees and seventees derived much of its strength from the geographical proximity of inter-related industries.

7. *Market-Orientation*

Major factor determining industrial locations at Ghaziabad is one related to nearness of market. In modern times only market location is considered as the most normal industrial location, and Ghaziabad testifies this criteria to the maximum possible extent. Proximity to Delhi at once provides a local, regional and national market for a wide variety of finished products ranging from consumer goods items to highly sophisticated machinery. The vast size of the market exerts a profound influence on the scale and nature of industrial structure in the city. Some of Ghaziabad's important industries such as breweries & glass products etc. qualify for market location because of fragility of their finished products while in the case of industries engaged in the manufacture of agricultural, transport, electrical and various other types of machinery which represent more than 40% share in the total registered employment of the city, market location provides the advantage of personal contacts with the customer which gives impulses for improvements and innovations. Market location also assumes significance in view of the after sale service required by these various types of machinery.

Vast size of the market also bestowes advantages to the various consumer goods industries of the city such as cotton textile, plastic products, general hardware, utensils, hydrogenated oil, cigarettes, oils and soap, allopathic, unani and ayurvedic medicines etc. There are still other industries which benefit from market location in respect of supply of their raw materials such as manufacture of steel, and craft paper, from scrap, and waste paper, respectively. All these industries constitute amongst the 24 important industries of the city.

Market location also assumes significance in the case of those industries which supply their finished products to the other industries of the city. To this category may be added manufacture of glass bottles, tin containers, craft paper and steel the products of which are respectively consumed by city's breweries, hydrogenated oil, corrugated boxes, and machinery manufacturing units.

Although Delhi metropolitan market has remained the most dominant influence in promoting the industrial activity at Ghaziabad, the size of local urban market has also helped significantly in fostering the industrial development of the city.

8. *Significant Proportion of Immigrant Labour force*

Influx of population from rural areas is a common feature associated with a growing industrial town. More and more people pour into the city in order to avail themselves of better employment opportunities and improved educational, health and recreational facilities. Ghaziabad, too, is no exception with 40% of its industrial labour force belonging to areas falling outside the district's limits. It is important to note that 12% out of the total 40% immigrant labour, originally belonged to Pakistan and majority of these hailed from urban areas, who naturally had greater sense of wisdom and far-sightedness, a fact which made a considerable impact on the subsequent industrial growth in the city.

Another characteristic feature of immigration at Ghaziabad lies in the fact that it was not the growth of industries which attracted the population to the city but instead it was the influx of immigrants from Pakistan which inspired and boosted the industrial development here. The foundations of city's industrial edifice were laid down by these Punjabi entrepreneurs who came and settled here in the wake of country's partition in 1947. Majority of the Punjabi immigrants hold skilled or semi-skilled jobs in the factories and quite a large number of these own their own factories.

About 60% of the total labour force is obtained from sources within the district. Adoption of improved means of agriculture has made available substantial number of persons in the rural areas of the district to be employed by industries. Majority of these local industrial labour force serve as unskilled labour, but because of comparatively better socio-economic conditions of the area in general, they easily adopt the specific skills required by the particular industries. As the tempo of industrialization is still in full swing, it is hoped that more and more people will be pouring in here from other districts of U.P. and also from other states of India.

9. *Insignificant Female Participation in Industrial Labour Force*

Male and female labour always occur more or less in a joint supply, but the proportion of female participation in the industrial labour force varies a lot from place to place depending upon the prevailing socio-economic conditions. Ghaziabad, the fastest growing industrial town of U.P. exhibits a very low female participation share of a little more than 2% only in the total registered employment of the city. Female labour work only at a handful of concerns e.g. M/s Jayana Time Industries Pvt. Ltd., Dass Hitachi Pvt. Ltd., Piya Pharmaceuticals, Emson and Company, and Bharat Electronics Ltd. The number of female labour at these concerns varies from 5 to 25%. Predominance of male labour is an apparent feature at all industrial establishments at Ghaziabad.

Insignificant female participation in the Industrial labour force at Ghaziabad clearly reflects the impact of prevailing social attitudes towards ladies going out for work in factories. Working at factories is considered as a sort of social stigma for ladies in the middle class society. Ghaziabad's industrial structure with more than 60% share consisting of metal-consuming industrial units hardly provides much scope for unskilled female labour. Jobs requiring simple industrial skills and those related with office work, however, can be efficiently carried out by ladies belonging to middle class families but the social environment at medium sized urban centres like Ghaziabad is not much liberal in this respect. Another reason for lesser quantum of female employment in the factories is the reluctance of factory owners to employ female labour for the reason of their taking long maternity leave which disrupts the smooth functioning of manufacturing operations. Another reason for their not preferring female labour concerns with the development of various types of other nuisances resulting from the co-working of males and females inside the factory premises.

However, these are only the temporary phases associated with the specific stages of industrial development at a place. As and when industrial nucleus acquires further dimensions, female labour is apt to come forward to avail of the economic advantages provided by the growing number of factories in the city.

10. *Availability of both Rail and Road Transport for the Movement of Industrial Goods*

At Ghaziabad both rail and road transport play an equally important role in fostering the industrial activity of the city. In respect of assemblying the various ferrous and non-ferrous metals, rail transport assumes greater importance. Thus raw material requirements for metal-consuming industrial units, which represent more than 60% share in the total registered employment of the city, are met largely via railways. Rail transport is more desirable for bringing metals firstly because all metals are brought from long distances, and secondly because railway freight charges are comparatively cheaper for crude unfinished products like metals. Apart from metals, coal and oil are also brought by rail. Raw materials for agro-based, chemicals and other industries, which together represent only 1/3rd of the total strength, are however, brought mainly by road transport. Even long distances hauls are carried by trucks e.g. tobacco for the manufacture of cigarettes at M/s. International Tobacco Co. Ltd. and apple pulp for Gold Coin apple juice at M/s. F.D.M. Food Products Breweries Ltd. are brought from Guntur and Kashmir respectively, via road transport. But the overall position of road transport in respect of assemblying the raw materials is relatively weaker than that of rail transport which accounts for 2/3rd share in the movement of unfinished goods.

Role of road transport, however, assumes much greater significance in respect of movement of finished products. Because of its greater operational flexibility, sending of finished products via trucks implies on-the-spot delivery of goods, and lesser time taken in the transit. Another advantage of using road transport for finished products is the greater scope for careful handling which is of prime significance in respect of items like intricate machinery, liquor bottles, medicines, chemicals, and so on.

Thus both road and rail transport assume distinctive role in the movement of goods for industries. Each of the two modes is valuable in its own way. Both provide regular and efficient services for sustaining the industrial development in the city.

11. *Industrial Structure at Ghaziabad Moving East Towards the Stage of Maturation*

There is ample evidence of city's industrial structure acquiring the stage of maturation notwithstanding the fact that industrial development started here quite late only about a little more than 40 years ago. The stage of maturation is best adjudged by the proportionate share of industries which turn out finished or unfinished products for other manufacturers. At Ghaziabad because of development of intra-industry and inter-industry linkages, industries belonging to this category have gained far greater significance as compared to those which produce consumer goods items. At a place where primary manufacturing, i.e. industries engaged in the processing of domestic natural products, are not much significant such as it is the case with Ghaziabad, the first industries to grow, after the inception of growth process, are those belonging to consumer goods group. Other two groups of industries i.e. producer goods and unfinished producer goods industries, develop at successively later stages because these require relatively greater skill, experience and specialization. These industries grow only after the threshold of consumer goods industries has been fully touched upon. If the geographical and economic conditions of a place are not much conducive to industrial growth, industrial structure never moves beyond the consumer goods level. Majority of Ghaziabad's major industries such as electronics and electricals, transport equipments and their parts, different types of industrial machinery, and oil engines and agricultural implements, produce goods which are mostly not directly used by consumers but more often pass through some other manufacturers before being converted into final products to be sold out to the consumers. The pioneer industry of Ghaziabad proper, i.e. oil engines and agricultural implements, however, produce goods for a special class of producers i.e. farmers.

Apart from machinery manufacturing branches which represent more than 40% share in the total registered employment of the city, other metal-based industries of Ghaziabad which produce finished or unfinished goods for producers include primary metal products, tools and gauges, moulds and dies, and jigs and fixtures etc., and tin products. Other important industries of Ghaziabad which produce goods for other industries include synthetic fibre, glass bottles, and paper and board, the products of which are used by cotton textile, wines and medicines, and corrugated boxes industries respectively. Chemicals and gases and refractories are the industries which meet the requirements of quite a wide range of industries.

Growth of finished and unfinished producer goods industries at Ghaziabad has been caused as a result of cumulative process of industrial growth resulting in the disproportionately larger share of industries here in whole of the district. Other manufacturing centres of the district which together represent only about 45% share in the total registered employment of the district, are far behind the stage of maturation. There is little hope in the near future for these centres to move beyond the level of consumer goods industries, because spatial concentration of industries at Ghaziabad creates an adverse effect on the extensive development of industrial activity at these centres. Even at Modinagar, which is the second biggest industrial centre in the district and which had its industrial beginning earlier than Ghaziabad, industrial structure has moved only a little beyond the consumer goods level.

Relative share of manufacturing at Ghaziabad in respect of the district's total will increase further because of the maturation of industrial structure here. Economic benefits derived from the subdivision of labour and intra-industry and inter-industry linkages,will continue to attract more and more industrial units in the city and the industrial structure may get further enriched with even larger proportion of finished and unfinished producer goods industries.

(B) SUGGESTIONS FOR FUTURE INDUSTRIAL DEVELOPMENT AND PLANNING

Suggestions for alleviating the various specific problems e.g. labour unrest, labour housing, difficulties in procuring the raw materials, erratic supply of electricity, higher rates of sales tax, air, water and social pollution, and deterioration of natural environment, have already been given in Chapter IX while discussing the problems. Following are the suggestions regarding certain general aspects of future industrial development and planning for the district as a whole and at Ghaziabad.

1. *Relevance of Co-ordination between Industry and Agriculture*

Agriculturally prosperous and progressive district of Ghaziabad offers a good example of the benefits brought about by an ever increasing degree of co-ordination between industry and agriculture. The pioneer industry of Ghaziabad proper i.e. manufacture of oil engines and agricultural implements has rendered a good service in boosting up the agricultural economy of the area. Increasing use of machinery by the farmers in the villages has substantially raised the agricultural output in the district making it a surplus area in this respect. Rapid industrialization in the city has helped the agriculture of the region also by creating a huge demand of agricultural products for the growing urban-industrial population. But still there remains much which the industry can do to assist the farmers in their agricultural operations. Establishment of a fertilizer plant in the district can go a long way in further solidifying the agricultural base of the area. Another industry which can help the agriculture is the manufacture of pesticides and insecticides which are so much in demand for a successful agriculture. However, at present, manufacture of pesticides and insecticides ranks only nominal in the industrial structure of Ghaziabad and there is a persistent need to develop this industry in order to meet the requirements of the farmers in the villages.

Agriculture of the area has also contributed a lot in fostering the industrial growth of the city. The prominence of oil engines and agricultural implements industry at Ghaziabad proper owes largely to the huge demand of these items in the villages made possible by the flourishing agriculture of the region. Agriculture of the area has helped the cause of industrialization at Ghaziabad and other manufacturing centres of the district by ensuring regular and adequate food supplies for growing urban-industrial population. Adoption of modern implements has substantially cut down the number of persons required for cultivating per unit of land and thus the surplus man-power is made available to be absorbed in manufacturing.

Regular and adequate supply of labour-force from the villages serves as a definite advantage for promoting the industrial development at the city and other manufacturing centres of the district.

Another way in which the rural economy can help the industry is by way of investing the extra wealth of the rural rich for the development of manufacturing in the villages. However, this is no easy task because there is no such previous tradition in our villages neither there are such institutions in the rural areas which can guide and offer technical assistance to the rural rich for starting the industrial enterprises. Our Govt. should explore the possibilities in this direction. The investment of savings of the rural rich in resource-based manufacturing at the village level will certainly bring a radical change in the general standard of the living of rural masses by increasing their purchasing power which in turn will increase the demand for industrial goods, exhorting the cumulative process of industrial growth in the area as a whole.

Thus it is essential that the planning bodies realize the significance of co-ordination between industry and agriculture for accelerating the process of economic growth in the district. A micro criteria for industrial planning is the most unrealistic in the modern times of close integration amongst all productive activities. The problem of future industrial planning cannot and should not be isolated from the general framework of other economic activities. The Geographer is concerned not merely with the location of the industry but rather with the location of a combination of inter-related productive activities. In our district, as the agriculture constitutes the most dominant economic activity of the region, there must be established a link between the industrial planning agencies and those for agriculture at some common forum. Integration of the results of various research projects in the fields of industry and agriculture is also essential for making the programme a real success. Obviously all this is possible only if our Govt. makes concerted and serious efforts in this direction. No doubt, enough work is being done under the new industrial policy to promote cottage and small industries in the villages and towns with less than 50,000 population. The list of industries exclusively reserved for small, tiny and cottage sector includes more than 500 items. Small and village entrepreneurs are provided all the services and support required for starting the industry in hinterland areas under the single roof of District Industries Centre located at Ghaziabad. Khadi and Village industries Commission is also making steady efforts to promote manufacturing at the village level. But there do occur certain persistent problems such as those related to the marketing of the products, regular and adequate supply of raw materials and power, villagers' ignorance and lack of motivation, transport bottlenecks and so on. If we sincerely wish to accelerate the process of economic growth in the region, these will have to be tackled effectively. Better standards of living for the masses can come about only if industry and agriculture march hand in hand together. Single-handedly it will take a long time for the industry to change the face of the region to any appreciable extent.

2. *Industrial Development at Ghaziabad in the Context of National Capital Region (N.C.R)*:

At the district level, industrial planning for Ghaziabad can trigger off the process of economic growth simply by establishing a rapport with the agriculture which is the dominant economic activity of the area. However, industrial planning for Ghaziabad city, must conform to the general framework of schemes envisaged for National Capital Region which covers an area of 30,300 Sq. Kms. from the adjoining states of U.P., Haryana and Rajasthan, with an estimated population of 14 million and estimated cost of Rs. 200/- crore at 1977 price level. The main objective of N.C.R. plan concerns with an orderly growth of the entire area by securing decentralization of industry and other activities to other small urban centres in the region. The Master Plan for urban and industrial development at Ghaziabad was formulated only as per provisions laid down in the general scheme of N.C.R.

Firstly because of its being nearest to the National Capital amongst all the ring towns, and secondly because of availability of industrial infra-structure coupled with a highly nodal situation, Ghaziabad has emerged as the most important suburban industrial location outside Delhi metropolis area during post-Independence period with only Faridabad as its match to certain extent. Nearness to Delhi has served as the most dominant influence in matters pertaining to industry, yet somehow Ghaziabad has managed to retain its own urban and industrial identity. Heavy clustering of industries has led to the development of agglomerative economies enhancing the industrial prospects of the city even further. However to ensure an integrated development of National Capital Region, it is necessary to watch that extra-ordinary growth of industries at one centre does not create an unfavourable impact on the industrial development at other urban centres in the region. The principle of circular and cumulative process of industrial growth is obviously at work in the context of Ghaziabad and if it is not properly channelized, it may accentuate the regional imbalances in the National Capital Region, causing a threat to the broad objective of integrated development.

Ghaziabad is still in the prime of its youth in respect of its industrial evolution, although industrial structure here has moved fast towards the stage of maturation as denoted by increasingly larger share of industries producing finished or unfinished goods for the producers. The factor of Geographical inertia which implies continuance of an industry despite the original advantage for the same having been disappeared, does not seem at work in the context of Ghaziabad's industrial structure. Original advantages for the start of industrial activity in the city were those related to its nodal situation and the vast size of near-at-hand market of Delhi metropolitan area and these hold as good even in the present context. There is no question of any decay or decline in the importance of these factors and therefore the factor of Geographical inertia is quite out of question with reference to Ghaziabad's industries at least in the foreseeable future.

With a short industrial history of only 40 years or so, Ghaziabad is also far behind the stage when diseconomies of concentration begin to appear. So far there is no cause for alarm for future industrial development and therefore industrial expansion should be allowed to continue for some more years specially in the case of machinery manufacturing branches which require a good deal of experience and specialization and therefore are not likely to be developed at other centres signifying the initial stage of industrial development. With the exception of Faridabad the future industrial development at other urban centres of National Capital Region will largely reflect a resource-based pattern with the preponderance of agro-based and consumer goods industries. Growth of chemicals and allied industries at Ghaziabad will also create a favourable impact on the general process of industrialization in the region. Under the new industrial policy, Ghaziabad for the reason of having a population of less than 5 lakh, will continue to get licences for the new industrial units for some more years to come. But ultimately when its population reaches the level of 5 lakh, it will have to be subjected to Governments stringent measures for decentralization of industries to smaller towns.

In authoress's opinion, regional imbalances in the National Capital Region should be reduced not so much by imposing curbs on industrial expansion at a rapidly growing centre like Ghaziabad but rather by promoting industrial growth at industrially less developed urban centres and at new centres as and where required. However a co-ordination amongst the schemes of industrial development at various centres is an important pre-requisite in order to ensure an integrated development of the entire area. Uptil now the programmes of N.C.R. have moved only little beyond the take-off stage but these have to be implemented in right earnest in order to avert the chaos of uncontrolled growth of population and industry in the capital metropolis. By accommodating a vast magnitude of industrial development, Ghaziabad has already done a commendable task to achieve this end. In future too it will play a major role in relieving the pressure of population and industry in Delhi metropolitan area.

3. *Future Prospects of Industrialization at Ghaziabad*:

Very existence of a vast magnitude of industrial activity at Ghaziabad, is a fair guarantee for a continued period of industrial growth in the years to come. With the industrial structure moving fast towards the stage of maturation, the relative share of finished and unfinished producer goods industries will increase further. Of these, however, machinery manufacturing branches hold the brightest future because these are the industries involving highly technical and intricate manufacturing operations which can be successfully carried out only at an established centre of industry such as Ghaziabad which signifies considerable experience and specialization in this respect.

Electronics and electricals which enjoy the dominant position in respect of employment figures, are likely to make even greater strides in future because of the establishment of U.P. Electronic Corporation Ltd. (UPEC) which offers wide ranging help to entrepreneurs in the electronics field. Apart from acting as a management, industrial, financial and technical consultants to entrepreneurs setting up electronic units in the state, UPEC also undertakes identification and promotion of new projects. Availability of latest technical know-how and innovations in the field from the research centres of Delhi is another great advantage which is so vital for the progress of this industry.

Oil engines and agricultural implements, which is the pioneer industry of Ghaziabad proper will grow further because of the ever increasing demand of these products in the region. Manufacture of transport and various types of industrial machinery will expand on account of high reputation of the city for many of these products. G.I. Pipes, primary metal products, and tools and gauges, also hold good future prospects due to specialized nature of these products.

In view of the proximity of Mathura Oil Refinery, development of petro-chemical industries at Ghaziabad holds a good future, although at present, chemical-based industries represent only about 7% share in the total registered employment of the city. Large demand of fertilizer in the agriculturally prosperous region of Wn. Uttar Pradesh well justifies the localization of a fertilizer plant at some suitable location in the area. Amongst the existing chemical-based industries of the city, drugs and medicines, synthetic fibre, chemicals and gases, and plastic and foam products may progress well in the coming years in view of the growing demand of these products in the area.

Agro-based industries, though holding an important place in the present industrial structure of the city with 17.6% share in the total registered employment, have been experiencing a sort of stagnation in the recent past. Although existing agro-based industrial units which are mostly large-scale enterprises are doing well but no new units have come up for the last 8 or 10 years. Ghaziabad is known for its breweries, hydrogenated oil, cigarettes, and handloom and powerloom furnishing fabrics, but future of these industries here is not so bright because of stiff competition with machinery manufacturing branches. Establishment of a dairy plant, however, can be a big success in view of the rapidly growing urban industrial population.

However, at other manufacturing centres of the district, agro-based industries have a good scope for future expansion. Agro-based units such as handloom and power-loom textiles, sugar mills, dal and flour mills, and oil and soap works etc. can be of great help in boosting up the industrial economy of these relatively less developed industrial centres. At some of these centres such as Hapur, Noida, Dadri and Loni, machinery manufacturing branches of the industry, represent significant relative share in the total registered employment of the town, but in absolute terms they rank almost negligible in terms of districts total. There is no justification, also, in encouraging those industries at these centres, because machinery products manufactured here can hardly match the quality and standard of those produced at Ghaziabad, Moreover, agro-based industries, being simple in nature, can be more easily developed at these centres which are still in the initial stage of industrial development. Apart from agro-based units, consumer goods industries like plastic products, utensils, general hardware and packaging items can also progress well at these centres. Modi Nagar which is the second biggest industrial centre of the district, with more than 20,000 industrial workers, offers a good example of the usefulness of consumer goods industries in strengthening the industrial base of a centre. Relative insignificance of consumer goods industries at Ghaziabad is also a strong ground for supporting the case of these industries at other manufacturing centres of the district.

Besides, there is every likelihood that extraordinary growth of industries at Ghaziabad may create an unfavourable impact on the process of industrial development at other urban centres of the district. Thus with the exception of Noida which enjoys certain specific advantages, all the other manufacturing centres of the district hold only moderate prospects for future industrial growth. Even at Modinagar, they are not encouraging further industrial expansion but instead, are establishing majority of their new industrial enterprises at Modipuram, which lies along Roorkee Road at a short distance from Meerut.

At Ghaziabad, the circular and cumulative process of industrial growth is already at work and it would continue so in future too. Due to multiplier effects of industrialization and also due to development of agglomerative economies, more and more factories are being added every year. Besides, fear of uncertainty at newer locations is also a strong reason for encouraging the growth of an established centre of industry such as it is the case with Ghaziabad. Within the present municipal limits, major part of future industrial development would take place in Trans-Hindan industrial Zone which is sufficiently large and which exerts greatest pull because of being nearest to the Capital metropolis. At Ghaziabad proper, future industrial growth would take place near the suburbs because factories in S.En. and N.E. Central industrial zones have already come upto the last point where the municipal limits end on Bulandshahr Road and Meerut Road highways respectively.

While talking about the future industrial prospects at Ghaziabad, it is important to note that it is no easy matter to predict the exact nature and pace of industrial development because of the variable nature of the factors like Govt. policy at centre and local level, labour attitudes, nature of demand, and the manufacturers' outlook towards the prospective location. Govt. policy may be either positive or negative or indifferent towards the future industrial development and as such it would make the biggest impact on the future prospects of industry in the city. Besides, increasing level of education may develop an apathy towards manual work amongst the general public thus, posing a threat to an adequate supply of required labour-force. There may also occur significant changes in the demand pattern forcing relevant changes in the industrial structure. Manufacturers' outlook towards optimum location may also change in course of time. Developments in political situations may also influence manufacturers' choice of location to a certain extent. Stiffer laws against pollution would also create a definite impact on the spatial and functional aspects of future industrial growth. Thus the aggregate pattern of future industrial activity at Ghaziabad would evolve only in conformity with the changing economic, social, and political situations prevailing in and around the area.

Fig. 27
SIZE DOMINANCY OF IMPORTANT INDUSTRIES AT GHAZIABAD

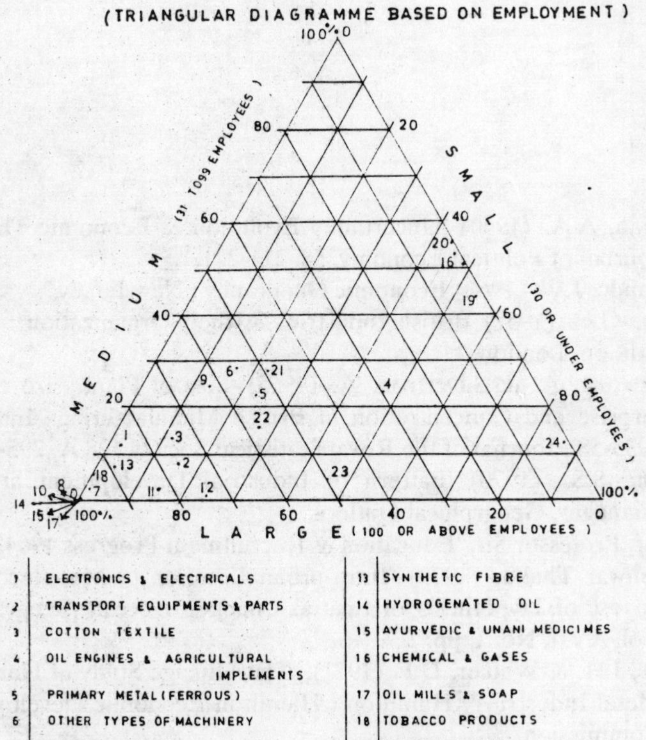

1	ELECTRONICS & ELECTRICALS	13	SYNTHETIC FIBRE
2	TRANSPORT EQUIPMENTS & PARTS	14	HYDROGENATED OIL
3	COTTON TEXTILE	15	AYURVEDIC & UNANI MEDICIMES
4	OIL ENGINES & AGRICULTURAL IMPLEMENTS	16	CHEMICAL & GASES
5	PRIMARY METAL (FERROUS)	17	OIL MILLS & SOAP
6	OTHER TYPES OF MACHINERY	18	TOBACCO PRODUCTS
7	G I PIPES & TUBES	19	PAPER & BOARD
8,	BREWERIES	20	PLASTIC & FOAM
9	TIN PRODUCTS	21	DRUGS & MEDICINES
10	GLASS & GLASS PRODUCTS	22	GENERAL HARDWARE
11	TOOLS & GAUGES ETC.	23	UTENSILS
12	STRUCTURAL CLAY PRODUCTS	24	CORRUGATED BOXES

Bibliography

Alchian, A.A. (1950) 'Uncertainty Evolution & Economic Theory', Journal of Political Economy, 58, 211-221.

Alexande, J.W. (1963) Economic Geography : New Jersey.

Allen, G.C. (1952) British Industries & their Organization : Third Edition, London.

Armstrong, A. & Silvertron, A. (1965) 'Size of Plant, size of Enterprise and Concentration in British Manufacturing Industry, 1935-58', Journal of the Royal Statistical Society 128 A. 295-420.

Azam, S.S. (1970) 'Pattern of Industrial Development at Dalmianagar, Geogrphical Outlook.

Baker, Professor Sir, 'Education & Recruitment Progress 1964.'

Baleshwar Thakur (1979) "Intra-urban Location of Manufacturing: A test of Hypothesis of Spatial Change, Deccan Geographer, Vol. XVII, No. 1, pp. 1-7.

Bater, J.H. & Walker, D.F. (1971), 'The Linkage Study of Hamilton Metal Industries', Hamilton : Hamilton Economic Development Commission.

Beckmann, M. (1955) ' The Economics of Location', Kyklos, 8. 416-421.

Beckmann, M. (1968) 'Location Theory' New York: Random House.

Bengston, N.A. and Van Royen, W. (1957) Fundamentals of Economic Geography: London.

Bhasin, M.G. (1969) 'Aerial Distribution of Manufacturing in Maharashtra, India'. The Geographical Outlook.

Burgess, E.W. (1925): 'The Growth of the city: An Introduction to a Research Project', in R.E. Park & E.W. Burgess, editors (1925);

'The City', 47 (Chicago).

Chaudhary, M.R. (1970), 'Indian Industries: Development & Location–A Economic Geographic Appraisal'. Fourth Edition Calcutta.

Chaudhary, M.R. (1970): 'The Industrial Profile of Orissa– An Economic Geographic Evaluation'. Calcutta.

Chaudhary, M.R. (1971): 'The Industrial land-scape of W. Bengal': Calcutta.

Chernick, S.E. (1966) 'Interregional Disparities in Income' Economic Council of Canada: Staff Studies No. 14: Ottawa: Queens Printers.

Chinitz, B. (1960): 'The Effects of Transportation From on Regional Economic Growth', Traffic Quarterly, 14, 129-142.

Clark. C. (1966) 'Industrial Location and Economic Potential' Lloyds Bank Review, 82, 1-17.

Cohen, J. (1964) 'Behaviour in Uncertainty and its social Implications', London: Allen & Unwin.

Collins, L. (1972) 'Industrial Migration in Ontario, Ottawa Statistics Canada.

Dales, J.H. (1962-63) 'Estimates of Canadian Manufacturing Output by Markets (1870-19150)', Papers, Canadian Political Science Association Conference on Statistics 1962-63.

Estall, R.C. & Buchanan, R.O. (1961) 'Industrial Activity and Economic Geography', London.

Estall, R.C. (1966) 'New England--A Study in Industrial Adjustment', London: Bell.

Easterlin, R.A. (1958) 'Income Differentials Amongst States (1880-1950)', Papers & Proceedings: Regional Science Association, 4: 22-59.

Friedman, M. (1953) 'Essays in Positive Economics' Chicago: University of Chicago Press.

Friedman, J. (1966) 'Regional Development Policy : A Case Study of Venezuela', Cambridge, Mass: M.I.T. Press.

Fryer, D.W. (1965) 'World Economic Development' New York.

Fuchs, V.R. (1962) 'Changes in the location of Manufacturing in the United States since 1929' New Haven: Yale University Press.

Garwood, J.D. (1953) 'An Analysis of Post-war Industrial Migration to Utah and Colorado', Economic Geography, 29.

Gibson, J.R. (1958) 'Effluent Disposal and Industrial Geography' Geography. 43.

Gilewska, S. (1964) 'Changes in Geographical Environment brought about by Industrialization and Urbanization' Paper published in 'Problems of Applied Geography' II Warsaw.

Gilmour, J.M. (1960) "The Joint Anarchy of Confidentiality and Definitional Change". Canadian Geographer, 10, 40-48.

Gilmour, J.M. (1972) 'Spatial Evolution of Manufacturing: Sn. Ontario (1851-1891)', University of Toronto, Deptt. of Geography; Research Publication No. 10.

Greenhut, M.L. (1956) 'Plant Location in Theory & Practice', Chapel Hill: University of North Carolina Press.

Greenhut, M.L. and Colberg, M.R. (1962) 'Factors in the Location of Florida Industry'. Tallahasee, Florida: Florida State University.

Gupta, A. (1971) 'Silk Industry of Varanasi', Indian Geographical Journal 46 (1 & 2).

Gupta, R.C. (1970) 'Industrial land-scape of Ghaziabad'. Geographical Knowledge, 2.

Gupta, R.C. (1971) 'Industrial Ghaziabad–A Great Node of Transportation', Geographical Knowledge 3.

Guthrie, J.A. (1954) 'Economics of Scale & Regional Development' Papers & Proceedings, Regional Science Association, 1, 121-131.

Hagget, P. (1965) 'Locational Analysis in Human Geography', London Arnold.

Hall, P.C. (1962) 'The Industries of London since 1861'. London Hutchinson.

Harris, C.D. and Ullman, E.L. (1945) 'The Nature of Cities', Ann. Am. Acad. Pol. Sci.

Harris, C.D. (1954) 'Market as a factor in the Localization of Industry in the U.S.', Annals. Association of American Geographers, 64, 315-348.

Highsmith, R.M. (1961) 'Case Studies in World Economy', Englewood Cliffs, New Jersey.

Hiner, O.S. (1961) 'Industrial Development on South Humberside' Geography (Nov.).

Hirschman, A.O. (1958) 'The Strategy of Economic Development' New Haven: Yale University Press.

Hoover, E.M. (1948) 'The Location of Economic Activity', London.

Hoover, E.M. & Vernon, R. (1959), 'Anatomy of Metropolis', Cambridge, Mass: Harward University Press.

Hoover, E.M. (1968) 'Trends in Location and Location Theory',

Centre for Regional Economic Studies, University of Pittsburg, Occasional Paper No. 6.

Hoover, E.M. (1971) 'An Introduction to Regional Economics' New York, Alfred. A. Knopf.

Hoyt, H. (1939), 'The Structure of Growth of Residential Neighbourhoods in American Cities', Washington.

Hurley, N.P. (1959), 'The Authomobile Industry: A Study in Location', Land Economics (Feb.).

Isard, W. (1956) 'Location & Space Economy'. New York.

Isard, W. and Schooler, E.W. (1959) 'Industrial Complex Analysis: Agglomerative Economics & Regional Development', Journal of Regional Science 1, 19-33.

Jarret, H.R. (1969), 'A Geography of Manufacturing', London.

Karyannavar, M.F. (1971) 'Industries of Bhadrawati Town', Deccan Geographer 9. (1).

Kayastha, S.L. and Singh, M.P. (1979) 'A spatial Analysis of Manufacturing in Uttar Pradesh', Geographical Review of India, Vol. 41, No. 2. 93-104.

Keeble, D.E. (1972) 'Industrial Decentralization and the Metropolis: The North West London Case'. Trans. Inst. Brit. Geographers 54, 1-54.

Kerr, D.P. and Spelt, J. (1958) 'Manufacturing in suburban Toronto', The Canadian Geographer, 12, 11-19.

Kerr, D. (1959) 'The Geography of Canadian Iron & Steel Industry', Economic Geography.

Knewles, L.C.A. (1944) 'Industrial and Commercial Revolutions in Great Britain during 19th Century', London.

Leblance, R.G. (1969) 'Location of Manufacturing in New England in the 19th Century', Dartmonth: Centre for the Study of Social Change.

Lifeber, L. (1958) 'Location in Space' Amsterdam: North Holland Publishing Company.

Lindberg, O.(1953) 'An Economic Geographical Study of the Localization of Swedish Paper Industry', Geografiska Annales, 35, 28-40.

Linge, G.J.R. (1960) 'The Concentration and Dispersion of Manufacturing in Newzealand'. Economic Geography, 36, 326-343.

Linge, G.J.R. (1963) 'The Diffusion of Manufacturing in Auckland, New Zealand', Economic Geography 39, 23-39.

Llyod, P.F. and Dicken P. (1972)'Location in Space: A Theoretical Approach to Economic Geography', New York: Harper & Row.

Loewenstein, L.K. (1963) 'The Location of Urban Land-uses', Land Economics, 39, 406-20.

Losch, A. (1954) 'The Economics of Location', Translated by W.H. Woglom and W.F. Stolper, New York: Wiley.

Mandal, B. (1971), 'Manufacturing Regions of North Bihar: National Geographical Journal of India, 17 (4).

Marcova, C. (1969) "Location of Industrial Plants in India built with Czechoslovak Assistance'. Journal of the Institute of Economic Geography of india.

Martin, J.E. (1957) 'Location Factors in the Lorraine Iron & Steel Industry'. Trans. Inst. Brtt. Geog. 23.

Masser, I.F. (1964) 'Changing Pattern of African Employment in Sn. Rhodesia', pub;lished in 'Geographers and the Tropics' (Liverpool Essays) London.

Maxwell, J.W. (1965) 'The Functional Structure of Canadian Cities'. Geographical Bulletin, 7, 79-104.

Miller, A.A. (1956) 'The Use and Misuse of Climatic Resources'. Advances of Science, 13.

Miller, E.W. (1962) 'A Geography of Manufacturing'. Englewood Cliffs: New Jersey.

Morrison, J.L., Scripter, M. W. and Smith, R.H.T. (1968), 'Basic Measures of Manufacturing in the United States', Economic Geography 44, 296-311.

Mountjoy, A.B. (1963) 'Industrialization and Under-developed Countries', London.

Mukharjee, M. (1970) 'The Aspects of Recent Industrialization in Chota Nagpur', National Geographical Journal of India, 16 (2).

Myrdal, G. (1963) 'Economic Theory and Under-developed Regions', London: Methuen.

Nakayama, S. (1970) 'Asansol-Durgapur Industrial Complex', Journal of the Institute of Economic Geography of India 1(1).

Neutze, G.M. (1963) 'The External Diseconomics of Growth in Traffic', Economic Record, 39, 332-345.

Norcliffe, C.B. (1970) 'A Theory of Manufacturing Places'. An Essay in 'Locational Dynamics of Manufacturing Activity edited by Lyndhurst Collins and David. F. Walker.

Nourse, H.O. (1968) 'Regional Economics'. New York : Mcgraw-

Hill.

Nurkse, R. (1955) 'Problems of Capital Formation in under-developed countries', Oxford.

Pandey, P. (1969) 'Industrial Land-scape of Greater Ranchi', Geographical Outlook, 6.

Patni, R.L. (1968) 'A New Method for measuring Locational Changes in a Manufacturing Industry', Economic Geography, 44, 210-217.

Pounds. N.J.C. (1959) 'The Geography of Iron & Steel', London.

Prasad, A. (1970), 'Industries of Chota Nagpur', Geographical Outlook 1.

Pred, A.R. (1964) 'The Intra-metropolitan Location of Manufacturing'. Ann. Assoc. Am. Geog. 54, 165-80.

Pred. A.R. (1965) 'The Concentration of High value-added Manufacturing', Economic Geography, 41, 108-132.

Pred, A.R. (1965) 'Industrialization : Initial Advantage and American Metropolitan Growth'. Geographical Review, 55, 158-185.

Pred, A.D. (1966) 'The Spatial Dynamics of U.S. Urban-Industrial Growth, 1800-1914', Cambridge : M.I.T. Press.

Pred, A.R. (1967) 'Behaviour & Location', Part I, Lund. C.W.K. Gleerup.

Pollen, M.J. (1964) 'Transportation Costs and the Disappearance of Space in the Theory of the Firm', Yorkshire Bulletin, 16, 3-14.

Quintans, E.F. (1964) spain : 'A Society in full Development', Progress 50, 1964.

Rawstrom, E.M. (1958) 'Three Principles of Industrial Location'. Transactions and Papers : Institute of British Geographers 27, 135-142.

Rawstrom, E.M. & Coates, B.E. (1966) 'Opportunity and Affluence', Geography, Jan.

Raddaway, W.B. (1965-66), External Capital and self-Help in Developing Countries', Progress, 286.

Reddy, K.V. (1970) 'Industrial Growth and Fluctuations in Telenghana–1956-67'. Geographical Viewpoint I, (2).

Richter, C.E. (1969), 'The Impact of Industrial Linkages on Geographic Associations', Journal of Regional Science 9, 19-28.

Robson, R. (1957) 'The Cotton Industry in Britain', London.

Rodgers, A. (1962), 'Industrial Inertion, A Major Factor in the Location of Iron & Steel Industry of the U.S.A.', Geographical

Review.

Rosenbluth, G. (1957) 'Concentration in Canadian Manufacturing Industries'. Princeton: National Bureau of Economic Research, General Series No. 61.

Rostow, W.W. (1961) 'The Stages of Economic Growth, Cambridge.

Scargill, D.I. (1963) 'Factors Affecting the Location of Industry: The Example of Halifax', Geography, 48.

Scully, G.W. (1969) 'Human Capital & Productivity in U.S. Manufacturing', Western Economic Journal, 8, 334-340.

Scully, G.W. (1971) 'The North-South Manufacturing Wage Differential'. Journal of Regional Science, 11, 235-252.

Segal, M. (1960) 'Wages in the Metropolis: Their Influence on the Location of Industries in New York Region', Cambridge, Mass: Harvard University Press.

Singh, R.P. (1969) 'Evolution of Industrial Land-scape', Geographical Outlook 6.

Sinha, B.N. (1972) 'Industrial Geography of India,' Culcutta.

Sinha, R.P. (1971) 'Copper Industry in India', Geographical Outlook 8.

Smith, D.M. (1966) 'A Theoretical Framework for Geographical Studies of Industrial Location', Economic Geography 42, 95-113.

Smith, D.M. (1971) 'Industrial Location: An Economic Geographical Analysis', New York: Wiley.

Smith, W. (1952) Geography and the Location of Industry', Liverpool.

Smith, W. (1955) 'The Location of Industry' Trans. Inst. Brit. Geographers.

Stafford, H.A. (1966) 'Population as a Determinate of Industrial Type', East Lakes Geographer, 2, 71-79.

Stamp, L.D. & Beaver, S.H. (1963) 'The British Isles'. Fifth edition, London.

Steed, G.P.F. (1971) 'Plant Adaptation, Firm Environments and Location Analysis', Professional Geographers, 23, 324-28.

Tewari, C.B. (1969) 'Sugar Industry in En. U.P.–A Plea for Redistribution'. Deccan Geographer 1 (1).

Tiebout, C.M. (1967) 'Location Theory', Empirical Evidence & Economic Evolution', Papers & Proceedings, Regional Science Association, 3, 74-86.

Tornquist, G. (1969) 'Flows of Information & Location of Economic

Activity'. Lund. Studies in Geography, Series B, Human Geography, 30.

Ullman, E.L. (1954) 'Amenities as a factor in Regional Growth', Geographical Review, 44, 119-132.

Weber, A. (1958) 'The Theory of the Location of Industries' Translated by Friendrich C.J. Chicago.

Weber, M.J. (1972) 'Impact of Uncertainty on Location', Cambridge Mass: M.I.T. Press.

White, C. Langdon, (1957) 'Water–A Neglected Factor in the Geographical Literature of Iron & Steel', Geographical Review, 47.

Wilson, A. (1966) 'The Impact of Climate on Industrial Growth', Tueson, Asizona, in Sewell, W.R.D. (ed.) 'Human Dimensions in Weather Modifictions'. University of Chicago, Department of Geography, Research Paper No. 105.

Zelinsky, W. (1962) 'Has American Industry been Decentralizing? The Evidence for the 1939-54 Period', Economic Geography, 38, 251-69.

Index